Written Texts and the Rise of Literat(

From the sixth through the fourth centuries B.C.E., the landmark developments of Greek culture and the critical works of Greek thought and literature were accompanied by an explosive growth in the use of written texts. By the close of the classical period, a new culture of literacy and textuality had come into existence alongside the traditional practices of live oral discourse. New avenues for human activity and creativity arose in this period. The very creation of the "classical" and the perennial use of Greece by later European civilizations as a source of knowledge and inspiration would not have taken place without the textual innovations of the classical period. This book considers how writing, reading, and disseminating texts led to new ways of thinking and new forms of expression and behavior. The individual chapters cover a range of phenomena, including poetry, science, religion, philosophy, history, law, and learning.

Harvey Yunis is professor of classics at Rice University. He has been a Humboldt fellow and a fellow of the Center of Hellenic Studies in Washington, D.C. He is the author of *Demosthenes: On the Crown* and serves as the editor of *Rhetorica*.

Written Texts and the Rise of Literate Culture in Ancient Greece

Edited by

HARVEY YUNIS

Rice University

CAMBRIDGE
UNIVERSITY PRESS

CAMBRIDGE UNIVERSITY PRESS
Cambridge, New York, Melbourne, Madrid, Cape Town, Singapore, São Paulo

Cambridge University Press
The Edinburgh Building, Cambridge CB2 8RU, UK

Published in the United States of America by Cambridge University Press, New York

www.cambridge.org
Information on this title: www.cambridge.org/9780521809306

First published 2003
This digitally printed version 2007

A catalogue record for this publication is available from the British Library

Library of Congress Cataloguing in Publication data
Written texts and the rise of literate culture in ancient Greece / edited by Harvey Yunis.
p.   cm.
Includes bibliographical references and index.
ISBN 0-521-80930-4
1. Greek literature – History and criticism.   2. Written communication – Greece – History.
3. Language and culture – Greece – History.   4. Greek language – Written Greek.
5. Literacy – Greece – History.   6. Greece – Civilization.   7. Transmission of texts.
I. Yunis, Harvey.

PA3009 .W75   2002

880.9´001 – dc21   2002071492

ISBN 978-0-521-80930-6 hardback
ISBN 978-0-521-03915-4 paperback

Contents

Contents

Preface

Behind this volume lies not one, but two, conferences. The first gathering took place at Rice University in Houston, Texas, in April 2000 under the title "Written Text and Transformations of Thought and Expression in Classical Greece." The papers and discussions were lively and interesting so far beyond the norm that we were compelled to consider publication. Beyond revising the individual papers, we wanted a volume that would strike the reader as a seamless, integrated, multifaceted inquiry into the subject. To that end, an extensive series of collaborative steps was planned, culminating in a second gathering, also at Rice University, in November 2001. At the second gathering, no new papers were delivered; our efforts were devoted entirely to mutual criticism and to fashioning one book out of ten papers. For their hard work and devotion to the project, I am hugely indebted to my fellow participants. Anything worthwhile in the final product should be attributed ultimately to the critical and collaborative efforts of the group. In place of acknowledgments to the rest of the group placed at the end of each chapter, the contributors asked to record here their general acknowledgment of detailed criticism, advice, and comments received from the other participants.

The roster of those who contributed to this volume extends beyond the contributors. At the conference in April 2000, Dirk Obbink and Hilary Mackie also delivered papers, but it was not possible to publish

Preface

them in this volume. That first conference was further enlivened by the presence and comments of Johan Schloemann, Christian Brockmann, and John Marincola, who were invited specifically to add to the discussions. The April 2000 conference was made possible by generous support from Rice University's School of Humanities and Center for the Study of Cultures. Colleen Morimoto, the center's assistant director, was invaluable in bringing things together smoothly.

Following the April 2000 conference, I received an enlightening and generous introduction to writing and ancient India at the hands of Johannes Bronkhorst, professor of Indology at the University of Lausanne. Professor Bronkhorst's explorations of writing and literacy in ancient India will see the light elsewhere. Beatrice Rehl welcomed the project for Cambridge University Press and shepherded it through the acquisition process. At a crucial moment, a conference grant from the Gladys Krieble Delmas Foundation made it possible for the participants to reconvene at Rice in November 2001; the participants and I express our gratitude to the foundation. The project continued to enjoy the support of Rice's Center for the Study of Cultures. Sandra Gilbert, the center's current assistant director, helped bring about a reunion as smooth as the initial gathering. Finally, a special word of gratitude, from both me and the contributors, to our fellow participant Dirk Obbink, for his criticism and suggestions at the November 2001 meeting. Though no chapter in the volume bears his name, he has left an imprint on the volume as a whole.

Harvey Yunis
Houston, Texas

Contributors

DAVID COHEN teaches in the Departments of Rhetoric and Classics at the University of California, Berkeley. His research focuses on Athenian social and legal history.

LESLEY DEAN-JONES is associate professor of ancient Greek literature at the University of Texas, Austin. A specialist in ancient medicine, she is the author of *Women's Bodies in Classical Greek Science* (Oxford University Press).

ANDREW FORD is professor of classics at Princeton University. He has written on numerous aspects of oral and literate approaches to Greek poetry. His most recent book is *The Origins of Criticism: Literary Culture and Poetic Theory in Classical Greece* (Princeton University Press).

MICHAEL GAGARIN is James R. Dougherty, Jr., Centennial Professor of Classics at the University of Texas, Austin. In addition to writing on Greek law, he is currently editing a series of new translations of the Attic orators.

ALBERT HENRICHS is Eliot Professor of Greek Literature at Harvard University. He has written extensively on Greek literature, religion, and myth. Major areas of research include the Greek god Dionysos and his modern reception, the representation of ritual in literature and art, the religious self-awareness of the Greeks, and the history of classical scholarship since 1800.

RICHARD HUNTER is Regius Professor of Greek at the University of Cambridge and a fellow of Trinity College. He has written extensively on postclassical Greek literature. His most recent books are *Theocritus, Encomium of Ptolemy* (University of California Press) and (with Marco Fantuzzi) *Muse e modelli. La poesia ellenistica da Alessandro Magno ad Augusto* (Laterza).

CHARLES H. KAHN is professor of philosophy at the University of Pennsylvania. He has written numerous books and articles on the pre-Socratics, Plato, and Aristotle. He is the author most recently of *Pythagoras and the Pythagoreans* (Hackett).

GEOFFREY LLOYD is emeritus professor of ancient philosophy and science at the University of Cambridge. He has written extensively on Greek science and is currently engaged in comparative studies of Greek and Chinese philosophy. His most recent book is *The Way and the Word*, a collaboration with the sinologist Nathan Sivin.

ROSALIND THOMAS is professor of Greek history at Royal Holloway, University of London. She has written on literacy, written records, and orality in the Greek world. Her most recent book is *Herodotus in Context: Ethnography, Science and the Art of Persuasion* (Cambridge University Press).

HARVEY YUNIS is professor of classics at Rice University. He has written extensively on political and rhetorical theory in classical Athens. His most recent book is an edition of Demosthenes, *On the Crown* (Cambridge University Press).

Introduction: Why Written Texts?

Harvey Yunis

While the Homeric poems continued to be the dominant works of literature, it would scarcely be an exaggeration to say that during the four generations which extended from the mid-fifth century to the death of Aristotle in 322 the minds of men were to a considerable extent remade by contemporary books.[1]

This book considers a number of intellectual and social practices of ancient Greece: religion, law, medicine, science, philosophy, and several kinds of literature. In each case, we ask how the practice in question was affected by the introduction and use of written texts. Now, the relation between human activities and the tools employed in those activities is generally worth reflecting on, as the startling pace of modern technology cannot but remind us. Yet the case of written texts is compelling for reasons of its own. While the practices under consideration may not require writing for them simply to be carried out, they do require language as a vehicle for communicating intentions and meanings. So much is clear from Greece and elsewhere. Yet it is a fundamental fact of human history that, as a way of recording and transmitting language, writing established itself, over time and much of the world, as an indispensable feature of the practices under consideration. The current set of essays inquires into the conditions

---

[1] W. V. Harris 1989: 84.

and consequences of the establishment of written texts within these cultural practices in ancient Greece.

Further, Greece, as so often, forms a special case by virtue of the significance and influence of its cultural achievements. The landmark developments in ancient Greek society and the critical works of Greek thought and literature were accompanied by a growth in the use of written texts. There is nothing self-evident about this development as a whole or about particular features of it within this or that discipline or cultural practice. (Such questions are reserved for the individual essays.) Yet permanent, decisive changes resulted. Alongside traditional modes of oral discourse, which maintained their centrality long after the introduction of writing, a new culture of literacy and textuality had come into existence by the end of the classical period (ca. 320 B.C.E.). This is evident in the documentary record of virtually all disciplines. This turn to written texts was one step in a more extensive process of textualization that continued in succeeding generations and in some sense continues today.[2] Yet this turn made it possible for the historical, scientific, and literary achievements of classical Greece to be preserved and passed on. The very creation of the "classical" and the perennial use of Greece by later European civilizations as a source of knowledge and inspiration would not have taken place without the textual innovations of the classical period.[3]

The background to this study has two parts. First, there is the situation in ancient Greece itself. Then there is the modern study of orality, literacy, and cultural development in ancient Greece and elsewhere. A brief word about these topics is followed by a glimpse at the subject matter of the book.

ORALITY, WRITING, AND LITERACY IN ANCIENT GREECE

This book focuses on developments over roughly three hundred years, from religious and legal inscriptions and technical treatises from the middle of the sixth century B.C.E. through a variety of written phenomena of the fifth and fourth centuries to the mathematician Euclid

[2] Assmann, Assmann, and Hardmeier 1983; O'Donnell 1998; Jahandarie 1999: 199–261.

[3] Even where the rise of literacy took a rather different course from that in Greece, it often prepared the way for the emergence of canonical texts that acted as a source of knowledge and inspiration as in Greece and Europe.

and the poet Theocritus of the third century. Extending just before and after the traditional demarcations of Greece's classical age (ca. 480–320 B.C.E.), this period is marked by a combination of change and constancy. While basic modes of oral communication persisted, rudimentary written texts led rapidly to sophisticated ones. The information presented here gives a sense of how orality, literacy, and writing developed in Greece before and during the period under scrutiny.[4]

In the Mycenaean palaces of the Late Bronze Age (ca. 1400–1100), there existed a system of Greek writing known today as Linear B, a syllabic script used by a few specialists just for keeping records.[5] Linear B died as the palaces were destroyed, and from that time through the Dark Ages (ca. 1100–750) no evidence of writing in Greece is preserved. Yet toward the end of the Dark Ages, writing, and therefore literacy, was burgeoning. The earliest material remains show that from the middle of the eighth century several versions of the Greek alphabet, varying slightly according to locale, began to be used for mundane purposes such as dedications, epitaphs, and graffiti on cups and bowls.[6] These scripts were adapted to represent the sounds of Greek from a script of the Semitic language spoken and written in Phoenicia on the eastern Mediterranean shore. For lack of hard evidence, it is impossible to say when and where the Greek alphabet was created. It may have occurred in Cyprus, where Greeks and Phoenicians came into contact. It probably occurred just before the earliest surviving remains, though it is not impossible that the Greek alphabet was invented earlier in the Dark Ages and used on perishable materials.[7]

Alphabetic writing emerged in Greece (so far as we can tell) at virtually the same time that the *Iliad* and *Odyssey* reached completion. Some have seen a connection between the two events,[8] but nothing in the creation of the Homeric poems requires writing. The *Iliad* and *Odyssey*

---

4 See R. Thomas 1989 on classical Athens, R. Thomas 1992 on ancient Greece generally.
5 Chadwick 1970, 1989 on Linear B; Palaima 1987 on Mycenaean literacy.
6 Jeffery 1990.
7 An earlier date is unlikely because there is no apparent reason why the alphabet would have been used at first only on perishable materials and then on durable ones only in the middle of the eighth century. See Woodard 1997 on the creation of the Greek alphabet.
8 Powell 1991.

are the products of a tradition of oral poetry that stretches back, in some form, to the Mycenaean world. Their composition and reception were shaped without writing by the demands of performance before live audiences.[9] It is not writing, but the oral Homeric poems that are the true representatives of the early archaic period. During the eighth and seventh centuries, writing was exceptional, finding few uses at first and spreading slowly. Beyond inscribed dedications and artifacts, writing was used by some Greek poets of the seventh century in the composition and preservation of their texts, which nevertheless were presented to the public strictly in performance. Greek life and society were indeed developing, but they did so, as they had previously, primarily without writing, relying on oral communication.[10] Writing's heyday in Greece lay in the future.

Oral discourse flourished because of the public, collective activities of Greek communities. Through the sixth century all poetry – choral, lyric, rhapsodic, cultic – was performed in public settings or private symposiastic ones.[11] Most of what was known or thought about the past was received through oral traditions relating to the community, to noble families, or to cults.[12] Worship was largely communal. Military musters defined the citizen body. Ideas and knowledge were transmitted mainly face-to-face. In the fifth century, the arenas and practices of oral communication were maintained and expanded. In Athens, theaters were built as places for mass communication, especially for the new kinds of civic performance poetry, tragic and comic drama. Athens' democracy created outdoor forums where citizens gathered in large groups to decide policy and conduct trials. In addition to rhapsodes and other performers of poetry, sophists and other itinerant intellectuals gave public performances of their skills in prose.[13]

Yet the sixth century saw the first great expansion of writing into the public realm, as manifested by names on coins, stone inscriptions

---

[9] Recent overviews of the orality of the Homeric poems may be found in Foley 1997, Edwards 1997. For the view that writing played a role in the transmission of the poems after the eighth century, see Janko 1990. For the view that oral transmission continued long after the eighth century, see Nagy 1996.

[10] W. V. Harris 1989: 45–64.

[11] Gentili 1988; Edmunds and Wallace 1997.

[12] Finley 1965; R. Thomas 1989; von Ungern-Sternberg and Reinau 1988: 153–233.

[13] Goldhill and Osborne 1999 on performance culture in classical Athens.

of laws, and writing on vases.[14] It was the middle to late sixth century that saw the expansion of writing as a medium for prose expression by the earliest scientists and thinkers. Prose texts about the past (not yet history) were first written at the end of the sixth century. In Athens, the flow of public documents concerning politics, administration, and finance begins with a trickle in the late sixth century, grows in the fifth, and rises to a flood in the fourth. Likewise, the distribution and use of writing for a myriad of purposes grew significantly in the fifth century and dramatically in the fourth.[15] An inventory would include the following among a much longer list of written phenomena in late fourth-century Athens: inscriptions on stone or other durable media of laws, decrees, honors, memorials, and other kinds of messages issued by both collectives of the citizen body and private individuals; archives on papyrus containing political, legal, financial, and cultic documents extending beyond Athens itself to the overseas empire;[16] collections of literary documents, constituting the first libraries in Greece; technical treatises on such subjects as medicine, theater, architecture, siege-craft, rhetoric, and music; texts used for elementary schooling and more advanced education; public and personal letters; public and personal contracts of various kinds; new kinds of written artistic literature, distinguished by posterity as belonging to genres such as philosophy, history, and rhetoric, though at the time such distinctions of genre were either unknown or inchoate. Books, in the form of papyrus rolls[17] and containing the kinds of texts just mentioned, were written and read, reproduced and deposited in archives, bought, sold, and copied by individuals, stolen, cited, and misrepresented.[18] Mixing of the media occurred in various permutations: books were read in private and aloud to groups;[19] speeches delivered in public were circulated in written form; plays, composed for public performance, were read privately by students of literature; written documents were integrated into oral performances and speeches.

---

[14] W. V. Harris 1989: 50–56. Svenbro 1993 offers an "anthropology" of reading in the late archaic period.

[15] W. V. Harris 1989; 65–115; R. Thomas 1989.

[16] Sickinger 1999 on Athens' public archives.

[17] Turner 1952; Blanck 1992 on ancient books.

[18] Johne 1991, Knox 1985 on the book culture and book trade in Athens.

[19] S. Usener 1994.

Each written document necessarily presumes a writer and at least one reader, though it may presume many readers. The entire picture indicates that literacy was spreading as writing found new and popular uses, but it is another matter entirely to infer from this picture the extent and quality of the literacy of the population at large. Only Athens offers even a modicum of evidence. Complete illiteracy must have been common in the early fifth century, much less so in the late fourth. Yet even then, large segments of the populace had little reason and no means to become literate beyond the ability to read and write names.[20] The traditional forms of oral communication sufficed for most of their needs, kept them in touch with communal and familial affairs, and enabled them to participate in the sacred and profane rituals of life. Outside of Athens, literacy would likely have been even less common, but in fourth-century Athens, illiterate or barely literate citizens daily encountered written texts that expressed state and divine power.

One can identify in fourth-century Athens at least two types of fully literate individuals. Functionaries of both citizen and slave status used written texts in their daily activities as scribes, archivists, record keepers, teachers, and accountants. Then there were those, predominantly if not entirely from the elite social and economic class, who became literate not merely in the sense that they could decode written messages and turn them into speech. Rather, these individuals used written texts daily for political, legal, financial, and personal affairs. Some among this group owned and used books. Also among this group were those who composed, read, and studied written texts for the sake of politics, art, science, and philosophy. These elites moved easily between the traditional orality of the society at large and the new culture of written texts that they were creating and learning to manipulate.[21]

It is impossible to assign numbers to the groups just described. Each kind and level of literacy is a matter of being schooled in particular linguistic and cognitive practices, ranging, for example, from scratching a name on a potsherd to consulting the text of a law in an archive to formal reasoning conducted in writing. In considering literacy, one must simultaneously consider the practices for which the literacy at issue is

---

[20] W. V. Harris 1989: 114.   [21] T. J. Morgan 1999.

used.[22] We are also stuck with the paradox that our access to ancient Greek orality, from Homer onward, is inevitably through ancient Greek written texts.

CONTEMPLATING ORALITY AND LITERACY IN ANCIENT GREECE AND BEYOND

Homer's overriding importance and the groundbreaking work on oral poetry by Milman Parry and Albert Lord brought orality and performance to the forefront of classical studies in the middle of the twentieth century.[23] At first, work concentrated on revealing further strands of orality in the archaic period, where orality's dominance was conspicuous. Over time, the oral and performative aspects of much of Greek and Roman literature and of Greek and Roman culture generally, extending into late antiquity, have been extensively discussed.[24] Parry and Lord, however, spawned an industry of research into oral and literate discourse that sprawls well beyond the classics into all periods of human history and all corners of human society. Orality and literacy are nearly ubiquitous. They are studied and contested not only by students of literature, but also by historians, historians of science, psychologists, linguists, sociologists, and anthropologists. No overview of the breadth, achievements, and problems of this huge, diverse body of work is possible here.[25] As a prelude to this book, a few points are pertinent.

Orality and literacy spurred interest because it was expected that these concepts, properly identified and understood, would have great explanatory power. After all, oral and written discourse are basic, distinct forms of human communication. As forms of language, they reflect the workings of the mind. The passage from orality to literacy belongs to both the education of the individual and the development of societies. High levels of literacy are typical of advanced civilizations; high levels of nonliteracy or illiteracy are typical of technologically primitive

---

[22] R. Thomas 1989 on Athens; Olson 1994: 20–44 generally.

[23] Parry 1971 (containing papers published from 1928–1935); Lord 1960, 2000.

[24] Most recently Worthington 1996; Mackay 1999; Watson 2001. Small 1997 is a study of orality, literacy, and cognitive processes in Greco-Roman antiquity.

[25] Jahandrie 1999 presents an overview. See also Foley 1985.

societies. Greece, the romantic cradle of Western civilization, offered a pristine narrative of the original paradigm shift that unleashed vast intellectual and cultural development.[26] Further, the concept of mentalities, popular in European sociology, supplied the orality–literacy dichotomy with a model for explaining cultural development.[27] As always, there was much to explain.

Several scholars have proposed the transition from orality to literacy as the cause of particular cultural developments in ancient Greece, such as the discovery of logic, the rise of law and democracy, the rise of tyranny, and the invention of drama.[28] Eric Havelock proposed the most comprehensive and influential argument of this type. At first, Havelock argued that at the end of the fifth century and the beginning of the fourth there occurred a shift from the inherited oral culture, represented by Homer and typified by memory, to a new literate culture, represented by Plato and typified by abstract thinking.[29] Later, Havelock argued that this shift really began when the Greeks invented the first true phonetic alphabet, which was not merely an adaptation of Phoenician script, but something entirely new.[30] The Greek alphabet, which represents sounds abstractly, itself promoted abstract thinking on the part of those who used it. It enabled the inherited oral culture to be recorded and stored, which objectified knowledge and freed up the mind for higher thinking and analysis; and the alphabet was simple enough to make literacy potentially available on a large scale for the first time. Though literacy spread gradually in Greece, by the fourth century it amounted to what Havelock termed a "literate revolution," which was responsible for the development of abstract and analytical thinking in

---

[26] In the wake of Havelock (notes 29 and 30), the simplicity of the phonetic, vowelized Greek alphabet, as opposed to other writing systems, is often stressed. Jahandrie 1999 documents the constant reference to Greece by theorists of orality and literacy, largely under the influence of Havelock.

[27] See Lloyd 1990 for an account and criticism of the concept of mentalities, which goes back to Lévy-Bruhl 1923, 1926.

[28] Goody and Watt 1963 on logic and democracy; Robb 1994 on law and democracy; D. T. Steiner 1994 on tyranny; Wise 1998 on drama. Harvey 1966 argues that Athenian democracy promoted literacy.

[29] Havelock 1963.

[30] Havelock 1982, 1983, 1986 are the key works. Havelock's view of the unique phonetic capabilities of the Greek alphabet is problematic; see Jahandrie 1999: 22–3.

themselves and in various spheres of human inquiry, including history, science, and philosophy.[31]

The breadth and boldness of Havelock's vision still impress. His comprehensive knowledge of Greek culture and forthright style add greatly to his persuasiveness. He opened intriguing questions by moving the focus from Homeric orality in the archaic period to the transition from orality to literacy in the classical period. But Havelock's ideas outstripped his ability to justify them. His grand scheme to account for Greek culture as a whole took on a logic of its own. Students of ancient Greece quickly noticed large fatal gaps in the evidence and argument.[32] Hence Havelock's influence on Hellenists, apart from his students, has been limited. The situation is otherwise among theorists of orality and literacy. In the need to understand the Greek paradigm and, open to the type of argument so persuasively offered by Havelock, a truly learned Hellenist, few have escaped his influence.[33] In this book, we neither follow in Havelock's footsteps nor repudiate him. We take an altogether different approach, relinquishing the grand scheme in favor of specific questions that arise from particular cultural practices.[34]

From ancient Greece to arguments about human beings and human society generally can be a short step, especially when such arguments are supported by data from other (often remote) societies and from psychologists who contrast the cognitive functions of orality and literacy.[35] The dominant figures have been the renaissance scholar Walter Ong, the anthropologist Jack Goody, and the cognitive psychologist David Olson.[36] All three surpass Havelock in the sophistication of their arguments and the awareness of the limits of the evidence. Despite these virtues, their arguments have been perceived as focusing too narrowly on a single cause; that is, it has been claimed that their arguments may be

[31] Cole (a former student of Havelock) 1991 adds rhetoric to this list. Skoyles 1990 proposes a cognitive basis for the argument that the major Greek cultural innovations were due to the alphabet.

[32] See Ford, this volume: 16 with note 4.   [33] See note 26.

[34] Ford, this volume, considers what Havelock still has to offer for the problem of literary analysis.

[35] Jahandrie 1999: 151–97 on the psychological evidence, which is complex.

[36] See especially Ong 1967, 1971, 1977, 1982; Goody 1977, 1986, 1987, 2000; Olson 1994. Summaries of their arguments, which are strikingly diverse, cannot be attempted here; see Jahandrie 1999: 69–130.

inconclusive (or worse) insofar as complex phenomena (e.g., syllogistic logic) that arise in particular circumstances are explained with reference to just one factor (literacy) in those circumstances. This evident problem in orality–literacy arguments has provoked further attempts, especially on the part of anthropologists and sociologists, to examine orality and literacy within cultural contexts rather than to treat them as essential phenomena that can be isolated by themselves.[37] It has also provoked an extreme reaction, the denial that orality and literacy bring about any important differences in themselves or that the differences matter for human capabilities.[38] Indeed, orality and literacy resist simple definition, and oral and written phenomena are found mixed in complicated, unpredictable ways. Students of the subject are still sorting out the arguments and making adjustments.[39] Nevertheless, "the distinction between spoken and written discourse is very real in linguistic, psychological, cultural, and historical terms."[40] And the progress of literacy across time and regions is, ultimately, a massive unavoidable fact, which should put to rest the notion that orality and literacy in themselves have no important consequences.[41]

WRITTEN TEXTS AND CULTURAL PRACTICES IN ANCIENT GREECE

This book takes the inquiry into writing's effect on cultural change in Greece in a new direction. The book is not concerned with orality and literacy in themselves, as social phenomena, or as modes of communication. It is not concerned with cognitive processes, mentalities or states of mind, institutional or cultural memory, intellectual, social, or political revolutions, or overarching interpretations of ancient Greek culture. It is not concerned with the alphabet, the publication, circulation, and physical properties of ancient books, or the levels and rates of ancient literacy.

[37] Finnegan 1977, 1988; Street 1993.
[38] Scribner and Cole 1981 and Street 1984, 1995 take the extreme view. For criticism, see Jahandrie 1999: 267–74, 287–93.
[39] Olson and Torrance 1991 contrast "continuity" theories, which stress what remains the same when oral cultures become literate, and "great-divide" theories, which assert fundamentally different mental states or social existences for orality and literacy.
[40] Jahandarie 1999: 313.
[41] Goody 2000: 1–25, responding to critics.

Introduction: Why Written Texts?

The book is concerned with understanding how specific cultural practices in Greece were affected when the people engaged in those practices began to use written texts. Indeed, all the usual problems of amassing and understanding the ancient evidence are in play, as they would be in any inquiry into the ancient world. Yet neither the practices nor the texts are concepts that need to be defined or adjusted to fit the facts of the real world. The ancient practices differ to some extent from modern ones, hence they need to be identified, but they do not need to be discovered anew. The texts are precisely the ones that, to one degree or another, we have access to and examine ourselves. The phenomena considered in this book are directly represented by the evidence at hand. Interpretation is conducted not at the level of concepts, but at the level of the evidence. Along the way, a number of the most important developments of Greek culture have new light shed on them.

The first two chapters consider the practices that lay at the core of traditional Greek performance culture: song and religious cult. (Much of Greek song in the archaic and classical periods was performed in religious settings.) Written texts of songs originally existed as aide-mémoire or scripts for performance. Andrew Ford examines the manner in which people began to read and study these texts as an autonomous activity distinct from performance. Reading of this kind, discussed by Aristotle, marks the beginning of literature as a literary activity. Greek religion is primarily a matter of actions and utterances; sacred texts are at best a fringe phenomenon. Albert Henrichs looks at the manner in which written texts were gradually incorporated into traditional religious actions in performance. Eventually, writing came to be used to portray, accompany, and regulate religious actions, to the point where the management of public cults depended on written texts and their interpretation.

Two chapters consider how the law developed as written texts were introduced. Michael Gagarin describes the manner in which the Greeks introduced writing into legislation, and thereby created a category of official authoritative social rules to which they gave the name *thesmoi* and, later, *nomoi* (laws). Administration of the law, on the other hand, was left in the hands of the citizens at large; it remained nontechnical, nonprofessional, and largely a matter of oral procedure. David Cohen examines an apparent paradox in Athenian legal practice and demonstrates how written texts were both resisted and embraced. When citizen status and inheritance were disputed in court, social networks and the oral processes of gossip and reputation took precedence over the written texts (citizen rolls and wills) that were used to record and document such matters. In Athens' civic forums, identity was constituted more through what one's friends and relatives were willing to say about one than by official written means. Yet the reliability of documents was upheld over oral testimony, at least in the specialized sphere of maritime courts, which relied on written contracts to define their jurisdiction.

Three chapters consider aspects of science and philosophy (which in the period under scrutiny constitute a single intellectual enterprise). The earliest Greek medical texts (fifth century B.C.E.) are among the earliest surviving technical treatises from Greece. Lesley Dean-Jones considers the role of these texts in medical practice and training. She argues that the texts were intended not for training doctors, which was still mainly oral, but for recruiting medical students. Yet the appearance of medical charlatans, a new phenomenon around the end of the fifth century, can be traced to their use of these texts to acquire the semblance of formal medical training. Geoffrey Lloyd compares ancient Greece and ancient China in considering the role of written texts in scientific instruction and demonstration. The Greek and Chinese texts share certain textual similarities, but insofar as the texts evince differences in the way that scientific activities were carried out, those differences should be traced to the respective social and political backgrounds. Charles Kahn examines the use of prose and poetry in the development of Greek philosophy. Poetry, the inherited mode of formal discourse, gradually gave way to prose under the influence of technical treatises. Yet as the audience broadened, philosophical prose itself continued to develop until in Plato's hands it became a medium of literary art.

Two chapters consider the way new kinds of written texts evolved against the background of oral performance. Rosalind Thomas examines how various kinds of texts of the late fifth century – those of sophists, philosophers, physicians, and others – came to be written down, published, and preserved, many without authorial attribution. The key element is the display performance (*epideixis*), a flexible mode of presentation that accounts for numerous peculiarities of the texts of this period. Harvey Yunis considers how Thucydides and Plato composed texts not just to be read, but to be interpreted by readers. In conscious contrast to the reception of performed poetry and prose, these authors structured the reader's interpretive options for their own didactic purposes.

The final chapter ventures closure by looking back from the perspective of the new (to us postclassical) textual world of the early third century. Richard Hunter considers Theocritus' *Thalysia* (*Idyll* 7) as a dramatization of cultural history, including the consequences of literacy for poetry. Juxtaposing art and nature, inspiration and training, and the literary styles appropriate to each, the poem recalls the evolution of these ideas in normative classical texts, reflects ironically on the poetic practices of the early third century, and foreshadows later discussions of the move from an oral to a literate poetics.

This range of topics is broad, but it is not comprehensive. Rather, the book represents a beginning and points the way to further inquiries into the interaction of specific cultural practices and written texts in Greece.[42] Moreover, two chapters, in which ancient Greece is compared to Rome and medieval England (Gagarin) and to ancient China (Lloyd), show that comparative study pays. Two other cultures suggest themselves for further comparison to Greece. The ancient Near East and ancient India saw cultural innovation in fundamental areas that rivaled in distinction those of ancient Greece. Both saw growth in the use of written texts. Both were, like ancient China, roughly contemporaneous with ancient Greece. Philologists, historians, and historians of science and philosophy can maintain the procedures of their own disciplines while incorporating the comparative impulse that is well established in anthropology. Problems of evidence and scholarly competence can be solved by collaboration.[43]

As a group, the chapters of this book demonstrate that reactions to writing differed from one context to another, and no single pattern or interpretation accounts for the variety of cultural change in ancient Greece. Consider by way of illustration just a few examples. In song

---

[42] At the original conference that lies behind this book (see Preface), Dirk Obbink contributed the paper "Silent Reading and the Origin of Greek Scholarship," and Hilary Mackie contributed the paper "Praise, Performance, and the Past in Epinician Poetry." It was not possible to include these contributions in the volume.

[43] Johannes Bronkhorst was extremely generous in opening an extensive dialogue on ancient India with the editor. Ultimately, it was not possible to include a contribution from Professor Bronkhorst in this volume.

culture and religion (Chapters 1 and 2), writing was used, not unlike a tool, in order to carry out other, higher order activities, namely, song performance and worship. For instance, scripts were created as an aid for performance and names were inscribed on a dedicated object to identify its donor and intended recipient. But once the written texts existed they found uses of their own: song texts came to be studied as literature, written cultic regulations became a means of controlling civic cults. But in another domain (Chapter 4), when the Athenians used written documents to create lists of official citizens, they nevertheless accorded those documents (relatively) little value when citizenship was officially questioned in a court of law. The comparison of scientific texts in Greece and China (Chapter 6) reflects the differing backgrounds of public debate in Greece and hierarchical imperial bureaucracies in China. Yet the rigorous mode of demonstration that is seen classically in Euclid and that became standard in Greek mathematics is far stronger than anything available in the public, political world of Greece; it also did not evolve in ancient China. It required writing to develop. Yet many of the most intriguing texts of Greek intellectuals and scientists of the late fifth and early fourth centuries are texts, so to speak, by default (Chapter 8). They are remnants, preserved under different conditions and for different purposes, of the display lecture performances that were a primary mode of publication of the period.

Throughout the book, the keynote is variation and unpredictability. Over different contexts, written texts are found to pose a number of the same problems. But it is the specific contexts that determine the course of cultural change. Contrary to the expectations prevailing in the learned literature, namely that writing has a uniform effect right across a culture or even across cultures, writing was not taken up by the Greeks as a whole. Within Greece, different groups used writing for different purposes and with different consequences. In this respect, it might be said, writing's introduction into ancient Greek culture is typically Greek.

1

From Letters to Literature

Reading the "Song Culture" of Classical Greece

Andrew Ford

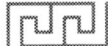

One area of Greek cultural activity that was certainly affected by the introduction of writing was traditional song. It is only thanks to writing that we can study what we call, in a significant divergence from the Greeks, their early "literature." The translation of Greek song into texts is easily taken for granted, but I will try to show how the very creation of "classical" literature and its perennial reuse as a special source of knowledge and pleasure depended upon the ways that song texts were put to use in the latter part of the classical period. My focus will be on how the Greeks *read* what we might call, reverting to a Greek term, their poetry, except that my argument will imply that the very notion of poetry as the production (*poiēsis*) of self-standing works of verbal design, of *poiēmata* rather than of songs, was a new conception of the ancient singer's art and one that was fostered by an increasing tendency through the fifth century to consult and study songs in the form of written texts.

The "song culture" of my title is taken from John Herington's *Poetry into Drama*, which documented the ways in which Greek poetry was regularly presented and often preserved through oral performances rather than through writing and reading. Herington was able to see that, though written texts of poems were far from unknown in early Greece, "texts were no part of the performed poem as such" until well into the fifth century.[1] Modern awareness of the oral dimensions of Greek poetry may be traced ultimately to the work of Parry and Lord on Homer,[2] but recognition of the fact that oral modes of expression and communication permeated Greek culture down through the classical age is due above all to Eric Havelock, who argued in a series of works that literacy was quite restricted in Athens until the second half of the fifth century, when a "literate revolution" transformed its traditional ways of thought.[3] Havelock is not mentioned by Herington, and this is perhaps because classicists have rejected his more far-reaching claims that alphabetic writing sparked the classical enlightenment by setting a paradigm for atomistic, abstract analysis and sequential reasoning.[4] This part of Havelock's theory has drawn legitimate and fruitful criticism: his oppositions between oral and literate mentalities appear overdrawn at times, as if literacy were a single phenomenon easily separable from orality, and as if oral and literate modes of communication had not interacted from our earliest alphabetic writing in the eighth century.[5] In addition, the technological determinism underlying Havelock's account treats the alphabet as an autonomous force in intellectual history, whereas recent studies have shown that the significance of any writing system will depend on the uses to which it is put in particular social contexts.[6]

Having conceded this much, I ask if the reaction to Havelock has not gone far enough.[7] Havelock has strongly influenced important work on archaic lyric by Bruno Gentili and Wolfgang Rösler, both of whom stress the cultural and social functions of early Greek songs that may not survive transcription onto the page.[8] Scholars not affiliated with Havelock have also illuminated cultural changes in the late archaic and classical

[1] Herington 1985: 45.   [2] Parry 1971; Lord 1960, 2000.
[3] Havelock 1982. See also Goody and Watt 1963; Ong 1982.
[4] A recent and sustained critique of Havelock is Nails 1995: 139–54, 179–91, with a survey of earlier critiques at 154 n. 17. Cf. also Burns 1981: 373 n. 18.
[5] See especially Finnegan 1977; R. Thomas 1989.
[6] Bowman and Woolf 1994; R. Thomas 1992.
[7] So also Bowman and Wolf 1994: 1–16, especially 4 with note 6. Cf. Finley 1975: 112: it is "beyond dispute that there is not a single aspect of human behaviour that has not been given new possibilities for development, change, progress, with the introduction of literacy . . . especially literacy that diffuses beyond a small, closed priestly or ruling class."
[8] Gentili 1988; Rösler 1980a. Cf. also Cole 1991, a revisionist account of rhetoric and orality that Yunis 1998 has come to grips with; Svenbro 1993; Robb 1994.

periods by giving attention to the media in which knowledge was stored and communicated.[9] It may be time to speak of a neo-Havelockian approach, one which, without falling into the untenable position of making writing the sole cause of all intellectual transformation, connects specific properties and uses of written texts with significant developments in intellectual activity.

In the study of Greek literature, however, it is more common to find scholars who acknowledge the importance of context and occasion for Greek song only to retreat to texts at the first opportunity. So in the end, Herington looks past the oral performances he so vividly evokes to plant himself on the bedrock of carefully written texts. He ventures that what made Greek song so varied and artful is the fact that "although its *performances* were universally oral, it rested on a firm sub-structure of carefully meditated written texts."[10] In this case, however, it is not clear why we should take early Greek poetry as a "performing act," as Herington urges, before it became a literary text. It is, in fact, irrelevant whether a text was presented orally or not if one assumes that composers were designing works that could be adequately captured on paper.

Progress on this point has been obstructed by focusing on the question of whether poets used writing to *compose* their works. It is usually assumed that writing allows for the kind of careful planning and revision required to produce the complex patterns in word choice and arrangement that we expect of great literature. Homeric studies are an obvious case in which it is frequently argued that the epics are too artfully composed not to be the result of painstaking construction. Pursuing the question from this angle results in predictably neoclassical alternatives. To those who, like myself, find that Homer "reads" differently from Apollonius of Rhodes or Virgil, and that their relation to letters has something to do with this, the answer usually amounts to "Those oft are stratagems which error seem, / Nor is it Homer nods but we that dream."[11] But the question is not whether singers preplan and structure their works; of course they do.[12] What may be questioned is what their planning was aiming at. To the extent that our texts of early

[9] E.g., Lloyd 1979: 239–40, 1987: 70–8; Detienne 1988; Sickinger 1999.
[10] Herington 1985: 41.
[11] Pope (*Essay on Criticism* 1.177–78) glances at Horace, *Ars Poetica* 359, where Homer is contrasted with the writerly poet Choerilus.
[12] Finnegan 1977: 73–6, 183–8.

song represent "scripts" to be embodied in performance,[13] preplanning and artistry would have been more profitably directed at creating a collective experience in which words were but one element in a fabric of music, motion, and spectacle enfolding the audience. A composer of tragedies, for example, owed his success to how his scripts fared when they were performed at the Dionysiac festivals, not to how they read in the hands of actors or in the city's archives. Modern classicists, late plunderers of those archives, may well wonder whether early Greek singers designed their songs to be completely satisfactory, or even fully intelligible, to readers, and indeed to readers like us.

A different path of attack is to ask where song texts were kept and how they were put to use in the archaic and classical periods. My interest, then, is not primarily in the use of writing in the composition of song, nor in its preservation. What needs more discussion is the possibility that the availability of written texts of songs may have influenced their reception and even suggested new ideas of their nature and function.[14] Before this suggestion is dismissed as a vagary, let me offer a small but indisputable example. Acrostics are a verbal effect most readily available to readers. The earliest known acrostic in Greek literature comes from the fourth century B.C.E., when Chaeremon spelled out his name at the beginning of a suite of trimeters (*TrGF* 71 F 14b). This is the Chaeremon whom Aristotle described as a composer in the "readerly" as opposed to "performative" style (*Rhetoric* 1413b13).[15] The trick was taken up by bookish Hellenistic writers such as Nicander, who signed a work in this way (*Theriaca* 345–53). But the habit of poring so closely over texts also allowed readers to "discover" acrostics in Homer, notably the word *leukē* ("white") in the opening of *Iliad* 24 as reprised by Aratus' *leptē* ("subtle," *Phaenomena* 783–87), like the phenomenon itself.

To focus this question, I will ask when did the Greeks begin to read their own "literature," and when do we find them taking up song texts and going through them (silently or aloud) as a way of fully experiencing and enjoying the benefits song was thought to offer? The passage of song from performance event to the object of such reading I call

[13] To borrow a concept from Nagy 1996.

[14] The history of Greek reading has chiefly occupied Italian and French classicists; see the contributors to and bibliography in Cambiano, Canfora, and Lanza 1992 and the bibliography in Detienne 1988: 530–8.

[15] See Hunter, this volume: 218–20, on these stylistic concepts of Aristotle.

"textualization" to distinguish it from transcription, or the simple writing down of the words of a song. The mere existence of song texts does not tell us much about the uses to which they were put. The evidence will suggest that songs were increasingly textualized in the period from Simonides to Plato; this is not to say that songs were being written down with greater frequency in this period, but that their transcriptions were being put to new uses – as works of art to be enjoyed in private reading and not as scripts or promptbooks to be memorized for performance and reused in social contexts. Allowing that our evidence is slim, I shall argue that it is significant that only very late in the fifth century do we find songs being approached, studied, and enjoyed in the form of texts – fixed and isolated verbal constructs demanding a special form of appreciation and analysis.

If Havelock's insistence that written texts were slow to make their way to the center of Greek cultural life remains a significant contribution, the oral–textual transition may be thought a trivial part of larger cultural developments that made classical Greek culture and literature different from archaic – unless some consequence attaches to the specific technology of writing. In my account, writing played a key role in this development in two ways. The most obvious property of written texts is their reductiveness. A written version of a Greek song would have almost certainly omitted its music, and it certainly lacked dance or gesture, to say nothing of costume, and such potent intangibles as the tenor of a maiden's or a boy's voice. Thus, when songs were reduced to words on a page (albeit to rhythmical words that may reflect and refer to their original circumstances and modes of performance), they sacrificed a wealth of appeal and significance. But as these texts, originally contrived as mnemonic aids for prospective performers, came to be used by skilled readers in their private leisure, the formal symmetries that repeated study of a text could disclose came to substitute for the lost meanings of performative context. Put generally, I suggest that texts helped Greeks shift their criticism from evaluating songs in moral and social terms to focusing on their intrinsic formal properties.[16] The second feature of texts that came into play was, equally obviously, that they could preserve old songs. When combined with the formalist

---

[16] Gentili 1988; already *in nuce* in Davison 1968: 113, Havelock 1978: 18–20. Ford 2002 is a fuller account of this transformation.

satisfactions that texts could supply, this gave a new lease on life to songs that were not often re-performed or whose performance modes were dying out. Writing, then, was crucial for the Greeks to construct their classical literature.

The process I am describing is abstract, but can be illustrated by an example from the end stage of the process. Aristotle famously says in the *Poetics* (1453b3–7) that a well-made tragedy should have the same effect when one "hears," or perhaps "reads" (*akouōn*), it as it does when one sees it performed; for "the reader" (*ton akouonta*), as he was called, hearing a well-constructed version of the Oedipus story should be as emotionally engaging as seeing it performed.[17] Here is a Greek who can find full satisfaction in reading a play, and a play that premiered almost half a century before he was born. The survey that follows asks, in effect, how old the attitude of Aristotle is and how much writing came into it. I will review the main evidence that has been adduced in reconstructing Greek literacy, with a special focus on what kinds of song texts were in existence at a given time, where they were kept, and how (little) they were used. It will be seen that different genres underwent textualization to different degrees and at different times, and I can only sketch a large and complex development. But I hope this account, incomplete as it is, may provoke further reflection along these lines.

COUNTING LITERACY

We must assume that some Greek songs were written down as early as the earliest singers of whom we have any substantial knowledge. Putting aside the vexed question of Homer, this means that choral lyric, for example, was already being transcribed in the seventh century B.C.E., from which survive more than 140 verses of a densely symbolic and obscure ritual song known as Alcman's Louvre *Partheneion* ("maiden song," *PMG* 1). It is hard to imagine how Hellenistic scholars came to possess such an abundance of archaic lyric if there were not some copies from a very early time that were preserved by their composers or by those who commissioned the songs, whether individual patrons or cities with temples for storage.[18]

---

[17] On ἀκούειν here, cf. Schenkeveld 1992: 132, 141.

[18] See Pöhlmann 1990 for this argument, though he depicts the archaic age as rather like the Hellenistic *Mouseion*, except with fewer missing volumes.

At the same time, it is hard to see that the manuscript of such a song would have found many readers. The probability is that early song texts lacked colometry (except in the case of stichic verse), music, and other conveniences for reading, including a standard orthography. Altogether, a lyric song text of the archaic period was fairly useless to anyone who had not already heard the song.[19] These considerations are supported by the likely low numbers of people who were skilled enough to tackle such texts in archaic Greece.[20] Some of Havelock's critics have assumed that classical and even archaic Greece was full of readers, but only on the basis of hasty generalizations from the evidence. Just as Havelock may be faulted for lumping all uses of letters under the single category of literacy, those who would infer "widespread literacy" from one or another archaic use of writing neglect the fact that literacy admits of many levels and forms. For example, the use of public inscriptions from the middle of the seventh century has often been cited as evidence of a wide reading public, but Rosalind Thomas has pointed out that inscriptions can serve an array of social and symbolic functions, and we are rash to assume that such monuments stood there to be read by all.[21]

Again, because the unlettered in a society may be surrounded by a wider literacy network, we cannot infer from the use of ostracism in fifth-century Athens that "the ordinary Athenian was a literate person" and that "a widespread ability to read and write is a basic assumption of the Athenian democracy."[22] The design of the institution of ostracism may be owed less to exploiting a generalized literacy among the citizens than to the imitation of the heroic custom of choosing champions by lot. I think particularly of the scene in the *Iliad* (7.175–90) where the Greeks choose who will fight Hector by scratching identifying marks

---

[19] Wilamowitz-Moellendorff 1900: 41 was sensitive enough to such issues to assume that early song texts must have had musical notation in order to function as commercial books; he theorized that such indications were lost when schoolteachers dispensed with them. But school books appear earlier in the record than trade books, and there is no evidence for musical notation before the middle of the fifth century. The grammatists' indifference to such notation as might have existed could signal the fact that the only real way to get a song was by hearing it.

[20] W. V. Harris 1989: Chapter 3, 114–15 finds a relatively rapid expansion in reading and writing between 520–480, with rates remaining relatively low thereafter (5% to 10%) into the fourth century.

[21] R. Thomas 1996; Anderson 1987; *pace* Harvey 1966; Knox 1985: 5.

[22] Turner 1952: 8.

on pebbles and then drawing lots. It remains significant that ostracism required thousands of citizens to cast ballots inscribed with the victim's name, but caches of pre-inscribed ostraca indicate that it worked, at least in part, through the sharing of ballots among the lettered and the unlettered. In addition, we should note, as Havelock does, that ostracism only required an ability to write and recognize names, not the skills to tackle philosophic or poetic texts.[23] Havelock points to Strepsiades reading his accounts in Aristophanes' *Clouds* (18–22), which only requires recognizing names (all in the dative, unfortunately for him) and numbers. To this should be added a passage from Aristophanes' *Wasps* (958–61), where an elementary education in reading and writing is all an unscrupulous politician needs to embezzle public funds. A number of democratic institutions required no more than this level of reading, such as the deme lists of enrolled citizens or the identification tags (*pinakia*) required to get into the courts. In other realms of culture as well, name literacy would have been enough to appreciate the countless *kalos* inscriptions (so-and-so is "beautiful") on vases or to applaud the epigram for Thrasymachus that metrically spelled out his name (DK 85 A8). A wide dissemination of this kind of literacy is all Euripides would have needed to depend on when contriving the famous scene in the *Theseus* (frag. 382 Nauck) in which an illiterate herdsman can only spell out for the audience – by describing the shapes of the letters – the name of Theseus that he discerns on a sail coming into port. If this was the right level at which to pitch a conceit intended to involve the whole theater, we can see why similar scenes were composed by Agathon and Theodectas.[24]

Havelock's picture of restricted early literacy is thus not easily refuted, but its significance for literature may be questioned. After all, a good story needs a good plot, no matter whether it is told or written, and a live performer can bring down the house with *le mot juste* at the right moment as forcefully as a careful writer can by putting it in the right place. Structure, surprise, irony, and even verbal echoes and most figures of speech (e.g., anaphora) are not the monopoly of either written or oral expression. Moreover, a good deal of Greek song is easily memorizable and therefore can be textualized by memory. According to Aelian, Solon once heard his nephew sing a song of Sappho

---

[23] Havelock 1982: 102 n. 32, 191, 199.   [24] *TrGF* 39 F 4, 72 F 6.

over wine and liked it so much he asked the boy to teach it to him.[25] Sapphic stanzas are short enough and metrically constraining enough for us to suppose that the words were transmitted verbatim. Do we have, then, in oral transmission, virtual texts right from the start? If so, what difference could writing down these virtual texts make to verbal art? For Solon also seems to show that it was possible in the archaic age to conceive of a song as a text in the sense of a fixed structure of words. According to Diogenes Laertius (1.60), Solon practiced textual revision on a song of Mimnermus when he bade him to "take out" (*exele touto*) an ethically offensive verse (praying for a quiet death at sixty), "remake" it (*metapoiēson*), and "sing it thus" (*hōde d' aeide*).[26] Oral performers are not thereby indifferent to getting the words "right."

I submit, however, that to focus on the stable text behind such contexts is to impose our textualist values on more complex social practices. When an Athenian aristocrat took on the themes and dialect of a lady from Lesbos, the words were a small part of the show. So, too, Solon's debate with Mimnermus is not so much quotation or citation as conversation in song. The debate is a moral, not a literary one, and Mimnermus' words are less a text than a pretext for Solon's own performance. The game of repeating and varying models will go on.[27] I have no doubt that symposiasts like Solon could run off an impressive stretch of popular songs; indeed, collections of songs suitable for symposia such as the *Theognidea* are likely to be among our earliest collections of nonepic poetry.[28] But the "text" that is "quoted" or reactivated must find its meaning in its relevance to its new situation. If the words of a song may remain the same, their original verbal contexts have virtually no force in determining their meaning in comparison to the contexts in which they are re-performed. It is not only children of rock 'n' roll who will know this, but any who are willing to think of Greek song as analogous

---

[25] Sappho, *Testimonia* 10 Voigt = Stobaeus, *Anthology* 3.29.58.

[26] Solon frag. 20, Mimnermus frag. 6 West. The merit of Calame 1995 is to show the complexities involved in "reading off" references to the "original" circumstances of performance from archaic and early classical Greek texts. Contrast the anecdote about Solon with the facile assumption of Burns 1981: 374 that Sappho is too "intimate" to have been preserved through repeated oral performance. In a similar way, Knox 1985: 3–4 takes a "personal tone" in archaic poetry as evidence that the author used writing.

[27] On early "quotations" of Homeric and other poetry, see Ford 1997.

[28] Ford 1993.

to popular music that is encountered primarily by the ear and not by the eye. We cannot know Greek song except through philology, but we need not therefore make singers philologists, in effect transferring to the text our own relation to the text.[29]

WHERE LITERACY COUNTS: SCHOOLING

An institution that, by contrast, does bear directly on the question of writing and literary culture is education, for it seems that from the first Greek teachers of reading and writing used poetic, especially epic, texts as school books. Schooling in letters is first attested for Ionia in the later sixth century,[30] but there has been a good deal of debate about how rapidly it spread and when *paideia* came to involve not only the traditional lyre teacher (*kitharistēs*) but the letter teacher (*grammatistēs*) as well. Havelock's intellectual history led him to posit that elementary education in reading and writing became normalized in Athens somewhere between the childhood of Socrates and that of Plato (i.e., the 460s and 420s, respectively).[31] But many point to the 480s, when Athenian vases begin to represent school scenes complete with tablets, styluses, and book rolls. It is hard not to connect this with what Rudolph Pfeiffer described as the "sudden appearance" of references to writing and reading in poetry from the seventies of the fifth century.[32]

The vases, however, leave the extent of such education unclear.[33] The fact that they sometimes show book rolls inscribed with poetic phrases does not imply that all their viewers read widely in poetry, for in such representations the writing is often nonsensical, a decorative part of the scene; and when poetic tags can be read they are usually key words for

---

[29] See Bourdieu 1990, a stimulating essay on this theme.

[30] The earliest testimony, Herodotus' account (6.27) of 120 children in Chios learning letters (*grammata*) in 496, is somewhat isolated but is supported by later anecdotes. See Pöhlmann 1989; W. V. Harris 1989: 57–8.

[31] Havelock 1982: 27, 187; cf. Havelock 1963: 40. See Woodbury 1976, 1983 for detailed critique and discussion.

[32] Pfeiffer 1968: 26, citing Aeschylus, *Suppliants* 179 (cf. *Prometheus Bound* 460–61, 788–89); Pindar, *Olympian* 10.1–2; Sophocles, *Triptolemus* (*TrGF* F 597).

[33] Webster 1973: 61 counts 100 school scenes on Attic red-figure vases and judges the sum substantial, but the low ratio (as against, for example, 1,400 athletic scenes) may indicate that formal schooling was a comparatively rare and elite pursuit.

the quick orientation of the viewer.[34] Hence, though the school scroll on the Douris cup (of about 490–80) is inscribed with words that may be construed as an awkward hexameter, they may simply be a melange of two incompatible epic incipits.[35] In addition, there is reason to think that schooling in poetic texts (always privately paid) was a preserve of the elite. François Lissarague points to the surprising presence of drinking vessels in the school scene of the Douris cup; he persuasively explains these as referring to future symposia where this tuition in song will be put to use.[36] More recent studies have in fact pushed the full alliance of education and literacy into the early fourth century.[37]

In the absence of hard figures on the spread of reading in the fifth century, we may ask what students were reading and how. Our earliest discursive account of what the *grammatistēs* ("teacher of letters") taught comes as late as Plato's *Protagoras* (325e–6b), ostensibly describing conditions at around 430 but written almost half a century later. This is late, as are the texts that confirm it, but education is a traditional institution and I will give reasons below for thinking that in its essentials it describes early teaching too.

Protagoras, appealing to commonplace ideas about school, describes how *grammatistai* "set their students on benches and compel them to read and to learn by heart poems by good poets, in which are to be found much valuable advice and many narratives that praise and celebrate worthy men of the past, so that the child may imitate them with enthusiasm and conceive the desire to be like them" (*Protagoras* 325e–6a). Any kind of text can afford practice in decipherment and

---

[34] Immerwahr 1964.

[35] ΜΟΙΣΑΜΟΙ / ΑΜΦΙΣΚΑΜΑΝΔΡΟΝ / ΕΥΡΩΝΑΡΧΟΜΑΙ / ΑΕΙΔΕΙΝ (= Μοῖσα μοι—ἀμφὶ Σκάμανδρον ἐύρροον ἄρχομ' ἀείδειν). "Muse, to me – I begin to sing about wide flowing Scamander." The cup, reproduced on the cover, is Berlin, Staatliche Museen 2285. On the inscribed scroll, see Beazley 1948: 337–8; Immerwahr 1964: 18–19. The best image is that in Kirchner 1948: 11, plate 22.

[36] Lissarague 1987: 130, 132. Such details are not uncommon; a splendid example, an Attic volute crater published by B. Girou in J.-B. Caron et al., eds. *Mélanges d'études anciennes offerts à Maurice Lebel* (Quebec, 1980), shows boys reciting before teachers amidst all the appurtenances of a young man's leisure: walls decked with javelins for sport, a strigil for the gymnasium, and an oil flask for dinners and symposia, all activities in which the boys will join with other youths of similar tastes and education.

[37] Robb 1994, especially 185–97; T. J. Morgan 1999.

penmanship,[38] but the use of poetry was justified ideologically as a form of disciplining students in traditional ethical and political virtue; such a high-minded rationale would also have distinguished the education provided by *grammatistai* from the inculcation of craft literacy. It is also notable that the teacher of letters makes his students memorize the works; this suggests that letter teachers advertised (and perhaps initially chose) song texts less in order to equip students with the ability to read literature than to prepare them to act and perform in the right ways. In this, they would have followed the example of the music teachers, who had always used song to make their charges harmonious and orderly citizens.[39] As Protagoras is marshaling common assumptions to make his case, we can accept his description of parents enjoining teachers to "pay more attention to their children's good behavior (*eukosmia*) than to their learning letters and lyre-playing" (*Protagoras* 325e).

The passage from *Protagoras* goes on, significantly, to contrast the curriculum of the *kitharistai* ("lyre teachers"). They teach "other things" of the same improving character, and here, too, action and performance are the focus. First the student learns to play the lyre in tune and then learns "good poems of other poets, lyric composers, performing them to the lyre" (*Protagoras* 326a–b).[40] It is rarely noted that texts are only mentioned in reading classes, and that these texts are, for understandable reasons, limited to the stichic, recitable verses of didactic hexameter or gnomic elegy and epic, forms that require no music to be adequately performed (e.g., Hesiod, Solon, and Homer). Another Platonic passage on grammatical education, from the *Laws*, confirms this restricted curriculum (810e–11a): "We have numerous poets in hexameters, trimeters, and all the spoken meters, some serious and some humorous, that thousands upon thousands maintain should be crammed into those among the young who are to be properly educated,

---

[38] Turner 1965.

[39] Cf. the emphasis on virtue (σωφροσύνη) and deportment (εὐτάκτως) in the praise of "old" musical education at Aristophanes, *Clouds* 961–4; cf. also Isocrates, *Panegyricus* 159. A practical aspect is not to be overlooked, since epics were likely the most attractive reading matter available at the time, Ionian philosophy being too recherché.

[40] οἵ τ' αὖ κιθαρισταί, ἕτερα τοιαῦτα, σωφροσύνης τε ἐπιμελοῦνται καὶ ὅπως ἂν οἱ νέοι μηδὲν κακουργῶσιν· πρὸς δὲ τούτοις, ἐπειδὰν κιθαρίζειν μάθωσιν, ἄλλων αὖ ποιητῶν ἀγαθῶν ποιήματα διδάσκουσι μελοποιῶν, εἰς τὰ κιθαρίσματα ἐντείνοντες.

making them good listeners through repeated readings and widely learned through getting entire poets by heart."[41] Recitability is obviously the determining consideration, for Plato goes on to add that some teachers compiled key texts (*kephalaia*) from the poets and combined these with entire (dramatic) speeches (*rhēseis*) that had to be memorized to make a student "good and wise" (*Laws* 811a).[42]

The bifurcated curriculum outlined here suggests that lyric texts did not, by and large, become school texts. Thus the textualization of sung lyric took a different course from that of recited verse, and some of its fifth-century turning points are reflected in comedy.[43]

A famous scene in Aristophanes' *Clouds* (1353–90) dramatizes a felt decline in musical culture among the younger generation of the 420s. At a dinner party, old Strepsiades tries in vain to have his son take up a lyre and perform a song (*melos*) of Simonides. A *nouveau riche*, Strepsiades evidently wants his son to take part in the high Athenian culture as described, for instance, by Dicaearchus (frag. 88 Wehrli): at fifth-century Athenian symposia the "most discerning" (*synetōtatoi*) and "wisest" among the company performed not only the customary short drinking songs (*skolia*) as the myrtle branch was passed, but also more difficult songs by the likes of Stesichorus, Simonides, or Alcaeus and Anacreon. When Strepsiades' request is rebuffed, he lowers his standards and asks for a recitation to the myrtle branch of one of the speeches of Aeschylus (*Clouds* 1365). Finally, he is left with asking for a recitation from the younger poets who are so clever (1370). He is at last gratified with a speech (*rhēsis*, 1371) from a discourse of Euripides on incest.

Strepsiades' recalcitrant son finds older lyric "archaic" and suitable for a "dinner for cicadas" (*Clouds* 1360). The "cicada" Athenians, a

---

[41] λέγω μὴν ὅτι ποιηταί τε ἡμῖν εἰσίν τινες ἐπῶν ἐξαμέτρων πάμπολλοι καὶ τριμέτρων καὶ πάντων δὴ τῶν λεγομένων μέτρων, οἱ μὲν ἐπὶ σπουδήν, οἱ δ' ἐπὶ γέλωτα ὡρμηκότες, ἐν οἷς φασι δεῖν οἱ πολλάκις μύριοι τοὺς ὀρθῶς παιδευομένους τῶν νέων τρέφειν καὶ διακορεῖς ποιεῖν, πολυηκόους τ' ἐν ταῖς ἀναγνώσεσιν ποιοῦντας καὶ πολυμαθεῖς, ὅλους ποιητὰς ἐκμανθάνοντας· οἱ δὲ ἐκ πάντων κεφάλαια ἐκλέξαντες καί τινας ὅλας ῥήσεις εἰς ταὐτὸν συναγαγόντες, ἐκμανθάνειν φασὶ δεῖν εἰς μνήμην τιθεμένους, εἰ μέλλει τις ἀγαθὸς ἡμῖν καὶ σοφὸς ἐκ πολυπειρίας καὶ πολυμαθίας γενέσθαι.

[42] On the social practice of reciting *rhēseis*, cf. Theophrastus, *Characters* 15.10, 27.2, and other passages discussed by Pickard-Cambridge 1988: 276.

[43] Cf. the implicit distinction between "learning" a lyric song by ear and having a tragic speech (*rhēsis*) copied out for memorization (Aristophanes, *Frogs* 151–3).

cultural elite in the generation after Marathon, are referred to by Thucydides (1.6.3) and described by Heraclides Ponticus (frag. 55 Wehrli): they pursued a life of elegant leisure (*habrosynē*) and represented themselves as intellectuals (*phronimoi*). The gold "cicada" pins they wore in their hair were one of the ways, along with their ways of singing, their Ionic dress, and their luxurious style of life, that showed them to be distinguished. Aristophanes portrays this high culture on its way out, and Eupolis attests that older lyric performance traditions were in decline during the Peloponnesian Wars: "it's out of date to sing (*archaion aeidein*) the songs of Stesichorus and Alcman and Simonides." Tunes from the tragic poet Gnesippus are more in favor, which the young can sing in their revels "to woo women from their homes." Eupolis also informs us that the same fate befell Pindar, whose works were "already consigned to silence because of most men's failure to appreciate beauty."[44] The fact that Eupolis used Pindar's own trope of "silence" for obscurity indicates he exaggerated, but the last epinician known to have been written in lyric meter was by Euripides. The form was revived in stichic meters in the Hellenistic age.[45]

The diagnostic scene of *Clouds* may be connected with the bifurcated curriculum of the schools if we assume, as Protagoras says, that the wealthy sent their children to school earliest and kept them longest (Plato, *Protagoras* 326c). As grammatical education expanded, the result would be that advanced skills on the lyre were rarer than the ability to recite (as Aristophanes, *Wasps* 959–60); recitations could be got without an instrument, even at a pinch, from a book. Thus, Strepsiades' son is incapable of performing a Simonidean song (*melos*) but can recite trimeters, at least those of the popular Euripides. As their performative modes became less familiar and as the institutions that supported them were fading, texts of lyric songs could become valuable cultural commodities. Some sought to acquire texts of songs that they were no longer likely to meet frequently in social life. These are the kind of people Euripides refers to in *Hippolytus* (451–2), who "possess writings from the ancients and are always among the Muses," and know all the

[44] Eupolis, *PCG* 148, 398.

[45] Fifth-century quotations of Pindar are short, memorable phrases of the sort "water is best," "law is the king of all," or "Athens the violet crowned." Only in Plato does one find Pindaric citations that suggest he used a written text; see Irigoin 1952: 11–26.

stories.[46] Alongside them were collectors of clever and novel lyrics, described by Aristophanes (*Wasps* 1056–9) as collecting the poems of certain poets and putting them in armoires among their sachets, so that they might "smell of cleverness."

Texts of recitable songs, by contrast, were well established in schools and were obtainable in other ways. By the end of the fifth century, educational texts combined nonlyric verse selections and prose writings of an impressive and informative character. In his *Laws*, Plato gives a slightly expanded description of the letter teacher's workbooks. The Athenian describes available school books as the "non-lyric teachings of poets that repose in texts, some metrical, others without meter's articulations, but prose compositions deprived of rhythm and harmony, all slippery texts that have been left to us by such [wise] men" (810b–c).[47] As in *Protagoras*, reading instruction includes only nonlyric songs, but to these have been added extracts of prose wisdom. Xenophon confirms both sorts of education: Nicias' son Niceratus was proud of having learned the entire *Iliad* and *Odyssey* by heart (*Symposium* 3.5), but Euthydemus, who had had the "best" paideia, collected (*syllegō*) "numerous writings of poets and sophists" (*Memorabilia* 4.2.1). A school library described by the comic poet Alexis (*PCG* 140) contained recitable verse – Orpheus, Hesiod, Epicharmus, tragedy, Choerilus – and "all kinds of texts," perhaps a reference to prose. If we construe "tragedy" as referring to tragic *rhēseis* (as in *Laws* 811a), we have the same range of material, both ethically and metrically.

The anthologizing of verse and prose wisdom is attested for the late fifth century in the opening of a work by Hippias the sophist; he advertised that it contained "some things said by Orpheus, Musaeus, Hesiod, Homer, and by many other poets, and by prose writers, some Greek and some foreign" (DK 86 B6). This is important because it supports Havelock's interpretation of an important passage from Aristophanes' *Frogs* (1109–14): just before Aeschylus and Euripides begin attacking each other's verse, the chorus assures them that they need not fear

---

[46] ὅσοι μὲν οὖν γραφάς τε τῶν παλαιτέρων ἔχουσιν αὐτοί τ᾽ εἰσὶν ἐν μούσαις ἀεί, ἴσασι . . .

[47] πρὸς δὲ δὴ μαθήματα ἄλυρα ποιητῶν κείμενα ἐν γράμμασι, τοῖς μὲν μετὰ μέτρων, τοῖς δ᾽ ἄνευ ῥυθμῶν τμημάτων, ἃ δὴ συγγράμματα κατὰ λόγον εἰρημένα μόνον, τητώμενα ῥυθμοῦ τε καὶ ἁρμονίας, σφαλερὰ γράμμαθ᾽ ἡμῖν ἐστι παρά τινων τῶν πολλῶν τοιούτων ἀνθρώπων καταλελειμμένα.

being oversubtle because the audience has shed its former simplicity
and "we're all veterans now, and everyone has a book from which to
learn clever bits" (*ta dexia*).[48] The implications of this line for Athenian
literacy and literate culture depend on identifying the kind of books
referred to. After discarding implausible suggestions that these were
books of poetics or texts of plays, or even a first edition of the *Frogs*,
Leonard Woodbury concluded that the line is a backhanded compli-
ment that the Athenians are "bookish to the extent that they have been
to school and have acquired the skill of reading."[49] Havelock suggested
a "pamphlet of quotations" from tragedy to guide the audience through
the contest:[50] I think it likely that Aristophanes refers specifically to
the popularity of school anthologies, with what Plato (*Laws* 811a) calls
their "key sayings (*kephalaia*) and entire speeches (*rhēseis*)" that one
learned to become "good and wise." Aristophanes' characterization of
these books as containing "clever bits" (*ta dexia*) suggests the quality
one displayed at symposia by "dexterously" handling the exchange of
song.[51] Many in fifth-century Athens were hungry for a snatch of verse
wherever it could be got. In Aristophanes' *Wasps* (580), jurors relish
the prospect of forcing a famous tragic actor "to pick out (*apolexas*) the
finest speech (*rhēsis*) from *Niobe* and recite it."

READING LITERATURE

Whether memorized in school or conned privately as a preparation for
the evening, all these texts remain scripts for oral presentation. As long
as the song text is a device facilitating eventual performance, we do
not yet have "books" for reading alone. This is what makes another
passage in Aristophanes' *Frogs* significant: Dionysus explains why he
has come to seek Euripides in the underworld (52–4): "Indeed when I

---

[48] εἰ δὲ τοῦτο καταφοβεῖσθον, μή τις ἀμαθία προσῇ / τοῖς θεωμένοισιν, ὡς τὰ /
λεπτὰ μὴ γνῶναι λεγόντοιν, / μηδὲν ὀρρωδεῖτε τοῦθ᾽ · ὡς οὐκέθ᾽ οὕτω ταῦτ᾽
ἔχει. / Ἐστρατευμένοι γάρ εἰσι, / βιβλίον τ᾽ ἔχων ἕκαστος μανθάνει τὰ δεξιά.

[49] Woodbury 1976: 353. Wilamowitz-Moellendorff 1907: 120–7 argued for a trade in
tragic texts, but see Sedgwick 1948; on tragedy and writing, see Segal 1982.

[50] Havelock 1963: 55–6, cf. Davison 1968: 107–8.

[51] E.g., at *Wasps* 1222: τούτοις ξυνὼν τὰ σκόλι᾽ ὅπως δέξει καλῶς. Cf. also *Clouds* 548,
Knights 233, Dionysius Chalcus 4.4 West (δεξιότης τε λόγου).

was reading to myself the *Andromeda* aboard ship, a vehement, heart-rattling longing (*pothos*) suddenly overcame me."[52] Here is the first clear example Greek literature affords of a person reading poetry to himself for the satisfaction of reading it, and not for study or rehearsal.[53] Now Dionysus is clearly a ridiculous figure in the scene, and his reading may be of a piece with his effete and unmanly saffron robe.[54] Woodbury, who holds that "literacy had become general by the date of the *Frogs*," yet appreciates that even in 405 "books did not yet fit easily into the general view of life. They were the latest thing, but somehow odd and out of place, and the object of some suspicion and derision."[55]

Some scholars identify as our earliest evidence for silent reading a passage from Euripides' *Erechtheus* (frag. 369 Nauck), usually dated to 422.[56] In view of our sparse documentation, not much hangs on a difference of seventeen years, but this text is worth comparing. The passage from the *Erechtheus* is sung, probably by the play's chorus, old men in a besieged Athens. They use the first-person singular, assuming the voice of a single old man; he longs for peace in which his weapons might gather cobwebs while he binds garlands on his gray head and "unfolds the tablets' voice, which wise men make resound."[57] The word used for peace (*hēsychia*) can also mean leisure, and the garlands (*stephanoi*) suggest that this desired state is being exemplified in that great institution of civilized leisure, the symposium.[58] The metaphor of "unfolding the tablets' voice" means, I suggest, that the old man would like to brush off his old sympotic song book and, as was customary at symposia, lend his voice to songs that in war must lie silent on the

---

[52] Καὶ δῆτ' ἐπὶ τῆς νεὼς ἀναγιγνώσκοντί μοι / τὴν Ἀνδρομέδαν πρὸς ἐμαυτὸν ἐξαίφνης πόθος / τὴν καρδίαν ἐπάταξε πῶς οἴει σφόδρα.

[53] A funeral relief from the same period provides our sole sculptural example of a person reading alone. Immerwahr 1964: 36 suggests the deceased was a poet, but the book, like the hunting dog beside the reader, may be a mark of status rather than occupation.

[54] Dionysus' use of the word *pothos* ("longing") may reflect contemporary literary talk: Gorgias lists "pain-loving longing" (πόθος φιλοπενθής) among the effects of listening to poetry (τοὺς ἀκούοντας εἰσῆλθε, *Helen* 9).

[55] Woodbury 1986: 242.

[56] Knox 1985: 9; cf. Turner 1952: 14 n. 4; Davison 1968: 107.

[57] δέλτων τ' ἀναπτύσσοιμι γῆρυν / ἂν σοφοὶ κλέονται.

[58] Also the model for peaceful retirement at Euripides, *Heracles* 673–7.

page.[59] This old soldier is a traditionalist, not a Euripidean Dionysiac: his book is not a trade paperback but a venerable object (cf. the "folded tablet," *pinax ptyktos*, at *Iliad* 6.169), and it is certified to contain the sort of thing that cultivated men were accustomed to perform or "make resound."[60]

In *Erechtheus*, as in other early references to song texts, a charged metaphorical intensity, when unpacked, has to do with the paradox of translating song to text and text to voice, with the tensions between the world of oral performance and that of reading.[61] In *Frogs*, by contrast, Dionysus reads to himself, and he seems to read an entire play, not just ethically admirable speeches. Yet he also reads as a shipboard marine (*epibatēs*), and while this detail sets up a joke, it suggests the breadth of those who were collecting song texts. Officers in the army had much leisure that had to be filled in a dignified way, and song books would furnish them with materials for their messes. I am partly thinking of the third-century Elephantine papyrus, a collection of drinking songs, some elegiac and some dactylo-epitritic, that was found among the possessions of a soldier stationed there.[62] It is not unlike the text that Euripides' old soldier in *Erechtheus* looks forward to performing.[63] This is also a background against which we may consider Plutarch's story

---

[59] "Unfolding the voice" (ἀναπτύσσοιμι γῆρυν) applies to performing a metaphor appropriate to handling tablets; a complementary metaphor is Euripides, *Alcestis* 967–70, where books of Orphic songs are called "Thracian tablets which the Orphic voice wrote down" (Θρήσσαις ἐν σανίσιν, τὰς / Ὀρφεία κατέγραψεν / γῆρυς). Other references to Orphic books (quoted and discussed in the chapter by Henrichs, 52–4) suggest a tension between performed song and text: their books are insubstantial smoke in Euripides, *Hippolytus* 953–4 and an oppressive "din" (*thorybos*) in Plato, *Republic* 346e.

[60] "Audible" is at the root of *kleomai* here, as of *kleos*, the word for "fame" or "oral tradition."

[61] The first reference to writing connected with poetry is in the mid-century *Prometheus Bound* 461, where Prometheus' gift to humanity of "putting letters together" is called "memory of all things, the handmaiden who gives birth to the Muse" (μνήμην ἁπάντων, μουσομήτορ' ἐργάνην). The kenning (appropriate in a catalogue of inventions, for one must struggle to name what has just come into being) expresses both the low, technical utility of writing as servant and its higher use (via Athena *Erganē*; cf. Chapter 2, 39) as a tool in the production of art.

[62] Ferrari 1989.

[63] One might perhaps take in this sense the peculiar metaphor in *Frogs* 1113 of book owners as clever "veterans" (ἐστρατευμένοι).

of the Athenian captives in Sicily after 413 (*Life of Nicias* 29). Plutarch says that those who managed to escape working in the mines profited from their "mannerly deportment" (29.2).[64] This may mean that they were formally educated. He adds that "some" (others?) were "saved by Euripides" because of the Sicilians' passionate "longing" (*epothēsan*) for the poet. Plutarch's account is not altogether clear in its organization (29.2 and 29.3 seem to tell the Euripides anecdote from two different perspectives) but may be clarified if we apply distinctions with which we are now familiar. He goes on to tell (29.4) how many eventually came back and thanked Euripides for saving them; some of these became teachers (*ekdidaxantes*) on the strength of whatever poems (*poiēmatōn*) of his they remembered (*ememnēnto*), while others remained in the wilds but could sing Euripidean songs (*melōn*) in exchange for supper. I infer that the former got their poems (i.e., *rhēseis*) at school and so were able to function as teachers of letters (i.e., *grammatistai*). Where the others got their Euripidean songs we can only guess; some may have been in choruses, but it was easy for them to pick them up, as many did, by seeking out his songs from those that knew them (29.5). So great was the Sicilians' "longing" (*epothēsan*) for the poet that they would implore passersby for remembered bits and pieces of them, a "sample or a taste" that they would memorize and pass among each other (29.3).

The schooled seem to have fared better in Sicily of 413 than did the listeners, and books were clearly on the way in. A booksellers' quarter in Athens is first attested in 414 in Aristophanes' *Birds* (1288), and Xenophon mentions a wrecked ship full of "written *biblia*" (*Anabasis* 7.5.12–14).[65] Here, too, we should place Plato's reference (*Apology* 26d–e) to the books of Anaxagoras on sale for a drachma (hardly inexpensive) in the "orchestra."

It is also toward the end of the fifth century that we first find a Greek writer producing a discourse designed only to be read: this is Thucydides' famous claim to have written (*egrapse*) an account of the Peloponnesian War that was meant to have permanent interest insofar as human nature does not change (1.1, 22).[66] Hecataeus of Miletus had spoken of "writing" (and of "speaking," *mytheitai*) his work (*FGrH* 1 F 1),

---

[64] ἥ τ' αἰδὼς καὶ τὸ κόσμιον.
[65] Further references in Davison 1968: 108.
[66] See Edmunds 1993 and Yunis, this volume: 198–204.

but Thucydides' text is designed not to please contemporary audiences but to be a "possession for all time" (1.22.4). In implicitly setting his own work off against Herodotus' history lectures (*apodexis*, proem) and in the contempt he shows for the "competition piece" (*agōnisma*) that may win the temporary approbation of a volatile audience (1.22; cf. 3.38), Thucydides adumbrates a contrast that Aristotle drew in his *Rhetoric* (3.12) between the "writerly" style (*graphikē*) and one meant for (competitive) performance (*agōnistikē*).[67]

In the fourth century as well, writing is explicitly associated with carefully working over a composition. Pfeiffer remarked that early fifth-century references to writing most often stress its benefits as a preserver of information, and this idea persists in the rhetorician Alcidamas, who recognizes that written discourses can be left behind as "memorials" of those ambitious for honor. But Alcidamas adds that writing down one's speeches also makes it possible to study progress in eloquence, since written drafts permit comparison more easily than do two orations held in the memory (*Sophists* 31–2). Plato, too, in his discourse against writing in *Phaedrus*, allows that texts may be useful not only as aide-mémoire but for achieving a highly finished style. He dismisses such "poets or speechwriters or law writers" when they lack true philosophical knowledge: they have nothing more worthwhile to show than what they have written, "turning it back and forth, gluing it and taking things away" (*Phaedrus* 278d–e). With this, the first instance of our "cut and paste" terminology, the technology of writerly composition has arrived. The *Phaedrus* is also the first Greek work to mention the idea of organic composition (264c), a notion that governs a whole, stable, and fixed text. The fact that Plato's strictures against poetry in the *Republic* make no allowance for such an approach but focus only on how song seeps into the minds of audiences and corrupts them shows that Havelock's *Preface to Plato* was right to identify Plato's agenda as a cultural critique of Greek song performance traditions.

It was left to Aristotle's *Poetics* to provide a method for coping with tragedies and epics as texts. The reductions in his treatment of tragedy exactly correspond to the qualities a text can and cannot preserve. For example, Aristotle recognizes that music makes tragic pleasures extremely intense (1462a19) and is the most powerful (*megiston*) of its

---

[67] On writing and writerly style, see O'Sullivan 1992: 42–63 and Hunter, this volume.

"seasonings" (1450b18). However, the *Poetics* notoriously neglects both the business of rhythm and harmony and the choral odes that are a defining feature of the genre, and song (*melos*) figures mainly as a formal marker of genre (Chapters 1–3). So, too, Aristotle acknowledges that spectacle can have astounding effects (1453b9) and can provoke the tragic emotions of pity and fear, but he assigns this art to scene painters (1450b15–20) and prefers that poets evoke emotions from the structure of the action (1453b1–3).

Thus does Aristotle bypass the stirring ("psychagogic") effects of performance to find the "soul" of tragedy in its plot, a well-composed "structure of actions" (1450a35–9).[68] Structure is timeless, and so the context of performance is neglected in the *Poetics*, which does not even mention the theater of Dionysus.[69] The variables of performance, of course, may have to be omitted by a systematic theorist, but Aristotle also shows a marked irritability toward performers. The "power" of tragedy remains even without actors and performance (1450b18–19); it can perform its job "even without movement," that is, without acting, simply by being read (1462a11–18). In fact, it is one of epic's few advantages that it has no need of "gestures" (*schēmata*, 1462a3) to be performed; tragic performers can behave like apes and "stir up a great deal of motion," as if without it the audience would not perceive what is happening (1461b29–31). Aristotle's desire to get past performance was not an idiosyncrasy of his age. Sometime around his death, the Athenian politician Lycurgus ordered that official copies be made of the plays of the three great fifth-century tragedians. These texts (according to legend, the ultimate ancestors of our own tragic texts) were deposited in a public archive with the express purpose of preventing actors – that is, performers – from departing from the script as it was determined by a city clerk.[70]

---

[68] Cf. Yunis, this volume: 190–2, on the effect of performance in contrast to reading.

[69] Cf. Hall 1996. Aristotle recognizes the audience in making a purification (*katharsis*) of their emotions the goal (*telos*) of tragedy, but by and large what audiences mainly do in the *Poetics* is interfere with the proper functioning of the art (e.g. 1453a30–9).

[70] [Plutarch] *Lives of the Ten Orators* 841f, on which see Pfeiffer 1968: 82, R. Thomas 1989: 48–9. Pfeiffer 1968: 204 notes that the old inclination to pick out the best writers in a given form, as in *Frogs*, "must have been settled by the second half of the fourth century when Heraclides Ponticus wrote *On the Three Tragic Poets*" (frag. 179 Wehrli).

I thus conclude that it is significant that solitary reading is first attested in the late fifth century. Texts of songs are doubtless very old in Greece, but they do not appear to have circulated widely outside of the archives of professional singers and other specially interested parties before the end of the fifth century. If schooling in letters became a notable pursuit of some Athenians around the time of the Persian wars, at the century's end Aristophanes could still poke fun at mass audiences' pretensions to literary sophistication. A significant body of serious readers of song texts is only clearly visible in the fourth century. What I call textualization was the appropriation of such objects by highly literate minorities who made the primary criterion of their value the play of language, the one aspect of song a text can best capture. Then, as now, fixed written texts allowed interpretation to exploit the precise observation of word usage and formal patterning.

Of course, nothing in principle prevented people from quoting and reflecting on songs without a text at hand. Plato's *Protagoras* dramatizes close readings of a long, complex Simonidean ode that is quoted at length from memory by the participants and then broken down to its minutest elements for analysis (339a–47a).[71] But the intellectuals who gather for conversation in *Protagoras* are hardly typical. Note that it is Simonides they choose to discuss, a favorite of the "cicada" crowd but beyond the reach of Strepsiades' son in Aristophanes' *Clouds*. Their taste in song is as recherché as their methods for making it relevant are novel. The high-flown, technical literary discussion in the *Protagoras* reflects the writerly assumptions of its author and his educated readers. It is noteworthy as well that the conversation switches in the dialogue from discussing virtue by expounding estimable old songs to a dialectical exchange; performing song was no longer the prime way to exhibit quality.[72] In this regard, it is significant that it is from Plato's prose text, and from no other independent source, that we can read as much of this Simonidean song as we can. Given the rage for reading philosophic texts and for dialectic in preference to singing old lyric, Simonides' song had to find a home in the great writing of Plato.

---

[71] On the discussion of Simonides' ode in the *Protagoras*, see Yunis, this volume: 195, 207–8.

[72] Cf. Aristophanes, *Frogs* 1491–5: "There's no charm in talking idly by Socrates' side, throwing poetry away and neglecting the most important things in the art of tragedy."

"In archaic Greece literature preceded literacy," begins a classic account of ancient textual transmission.[73] While it is obvious what the authors mean, it is not quibbling to say that, on any of the usual meanings given to "literature," they put the cart before the horse.[74] I have argued that literacy preceded and fostered the idea of literature, a new way of putting the Greek heritage of song to use as isolated, fixed, and tangible works of verbal design. One implication of this is familiar: the meaning that can be extracted from a song text through the interplay of its lexical items must be subordinated to the entire effects of its situated performance. More generally, I urge that readers of early Greek poetry realize they are dealing with something more than verbal patterning. Like all song, this song had a social life, and that life was its most meaningful presence, however ephemeral, variable, and hard to retrieve it may be.

It would be romantic to evoke all the extratextual aspects of song that gave it its full significance in context – and problematic too, since context is mostly recoverable only from other (contextualized) texts. Circularity threatens any attempt at contextualization, but retreating into a hermetic formalism offers no way out of the difficulty. It is possible to be more realistic about how texts worked in a society. To do so, we take up the tools Aristotle forged, but we need not remain confined to them. For those who wish to consider Greek song in its historical dimensions (and some may not), its meaning is to be derived not simply from textual and intertextual plays of words but also from a contextual and intercontextual meaning-making process. The literally unforgettable songs that we read were surrounded by a untranscribable world that we can only read, but we must find ways to do so if we wish to unfold once again the tablets of song.

---

[73] Reynolds and Wilson 1991: 1.
[74] For a capsule history of the evolution of the concept of "literature," see R. Williams 1976: 183–8.

2

Writing Religion

Inscribed Texts, Ritual Authority, and the Religious Discourse of the Polis

Albert Henrichs

In both literature and art, Greek gods are engaged in a wide range of activities that run the gamut from the domestic and all-too-human to the sublime and often reflect dominant aspects of their character or realm. They eat and drink, have sex and give birth, walk or fly, take a ride or sail aboard a ship, sing and dance, attend weddings and symposia, bear arms or play musical instruments, wage war or hunt animals, perform sacrifice and pour libations, kill or heal, and curse or bless. The one thing they do not do is read and write. To be sure, we know of some exceptions, but they are so few that they prove the general rule: Olympian gods do not appear to be literate, or if they are, they do not flaunt their literacy. In fact, they hide it.[1]

The principal exceptions are the Muses and Athena. On a number of fifth-century vases, one or two Muses are shown holding the ancient equivalent of a book, either a papyrus roll or a writing tablet.[2] Apollo is present in many of these scenes, but he is represented with a lyre, not a stylus. The lyre signals that he is musical rather than literate. In the

[1] Detienne 1989: 104 on the "illiteracy" of the Greek gods: "les dieux grecs sont de parfaits analphabètes: ils vont rester illettrés jusqu'à l'âge hellénistique."

[2] *LIMC* Mousa(i) nos. 13, 19–20, 47d, 95, 103, 106–7; Immerwahr 1990: 99 n. 6. As Michael Gagarin points out, "having the Muses hold a written text may just be a way of illustrating their well-known association with literature and not an indication that they are actually reading or that they can read."

prologue of Callimachus' *Aitia*, Apollo gives advice to the young poet who composes with his writing tablet (*deltos*) on his knees.[3] The patron god of poetry inspires the poet to write, but he does not write himself. Like the Muses, the Moirai and Parcae are groups of divinities whose special tasks require a long collective memory. In Ovid, exceptionally, the Parcae record the human destinies on bronze tablets (*Metamorphoses* 15.807–14). In art, both the Moirai and the Parcae are occasionally shown with scrolls or diptychs, but not before the imperial period.[4] In Attic tragedy, the transgressions of mortals are recorded on the "tablet of Zeus," but the actual bookkeeping is done by subordinate figures like Dike.[5] Of the Olympian gods, only Athena is engaged in writing. On a red-figure Panathenaic amphora from about 480 B.C.E. the goddess stands erect, wears the helmet and the Gorgo, and balances an open writing tablet with her left hand.[6] Her right hand is slightly raised and holds the stylus, as if she were about to write. Her huge shield is temporarily out of service and propped against her body. It looks as if Athena has taken time off from her warlike activities to remember her role as *Erganē*, the divine mistress of domestic skills. But only once, on this vase by the Triptolemos-Painter, is Athena associated with the art of writing.

No other Olympian god is similarly engaged in the act of writing. Nor did the Greeks ascribe the invention of writing to their gods, but rather to mortal heroes like Cadmus, Palamedes, and Orpheus.[7] In view of the overwhelming Greek tendency to separate the gods from the alphabet and from its written application, one wonders why a recent book on the impact of literacy on the Athenian theater was given the provocative but misleading title *Dionysus Writes*.[8] Yet the representations of divinities in art and literature suggest strongly

---

3 Callimachus frag. 1.21–2 Pfeiffer: "For when I put my writing tablet on my knees for the first time, Lykian Apollo said to me."

4 *LIMC* Moira, Parcae. The rare and late representations of the Moirai holding written records are due to Roman influence (S. de Angeli, *LIMC* 6.1.638).

5 Aeschylus *TrGF* 281a.21, Euripides frag. 506 Nauck. At Aeschylus, *Eumenides* 275, Hades records the deeds of men with his "tablet-writing mind" (δελτογράφωι . . . φρενί), a metaphor for memorization that need not be taken literally. See Solmsen 1968.

6 *LIMC* Athena 616. Gloria Pinney brought this vase to my attention.

7 R. B. Edwards 1979; Detienne 1989: 101–15; Gantz 1993: 604; Baumgarten 1998: 73–80.

8 Wise 1998.

that Greek gods did not write and were not expected to write. Their apparent indifference to the art of writing sets them apart from the highly literate gods of the Hittite pantheon, and from Thot, the divine scribe of Egyptian religion.[9] By the same token, since the Greek gods do not rely upon reading or writing to assert their identity or promote their divinity, they can be seen as reflections of the tenuous connection between ritual and writing in Greek religion.

It is well-known that far from being "a religion of the book," the Greek polis religion[10] had no universally recognized sacred texts, lacked a professional clergy, relied heavily on oral tradition, and valued ritual, the "things done" (drōmena), much more highly than the occasional ritual utterances (legomena) that accompanied the rites.[11] In the words of Walter Burkert

> The most important evidence for Greek religion remains the literary evidence, especially as the Greeks founded such an eminently literary culture. Nevertheless, religious texts in the narrow sense of sacred texts are scarcely to be found: there is no holy scripture and barely even fixed prayer formulae and liturgies; individual sects later possess their special books such as those of Orpheus, but even these are in no way comparable with the Veda or Avesta, let alone the Torah.[12]

Under these circumstances, we cannot expect writing to occupy a prominent place in the local systems of divinities, rituals, and beliefs that make up Greek polytheism. Not only were the gods largely indifferent to writing, their human worshipers did not have to be very literate either in order to participate fully in the religious life of their communities. Rituals were performed "in accordance with ancestral custom" (kata ta patria), and ritual knowledge was passed on orally and by example from one generation to the next. As far as we know, during the archaic period no attempts were made to collect and codify the rituals of the polis.[13]

---

[9] Detienne 1988: 13–14 refers to the scribal gods of Hittite culture as "dieux-scripteurs." On the divine scribe Thot, Plato's Theuth (Phaedrus 274c–5b), see Boylan 1922.

[10] On the term and concept, see Sourvinou-Inwood 2000.

[11] Parker 1996: 54–5; Henrichs 1998.

[12] Burkert 1985: 4. On the category of "sacred texts," see Baumgarten 1998, Henrichs 2002. The evidence for "fixed prayer formulae and liturgies" can be found in Porta 1999. On books attributed to Orpheus see 52–4, this volume.

[13] On the codification of sacrificial rites ascribed to Solon, see 54–5, this volume.

Ritual experts such as seers, sacrificers, sorcerers, and itinerant priests specializing in purification rituals must have been familiar figures since the eighth century.[14] But the codification of ritual and the concept of a ritual expertise based on the consultation of written texts rather than on one's own experience are phenomena that emerge for the first time in the fifth century, and even then the best efforts in this regard were mostly confined to local cults and never attained Panhellenic prominence.

At this point, we are faced with somewhat of a paradox. If it is true that Greek religion was predominantly action oriented, nonliterate, self-centered, and reliant on oral tradition, why did it not vanish without a trace? Indeed, if we had no written information about the rituals of Greek religion, the nature of its gods, and the reciprocal relationship between mortals and immortals, it would be hard to imagine that books on Greek religion could be written at all. Let us suppose for a moment that all the relevant texts had perished and that the depictions of gods and rituals in Greek art and the excavated archaeological sites turned out to be our only sources of information. We would still be able to recognize the individual gods, to understand the function of a Greek temple, and to reconstruct major rituals such as animal sacrifice and the pouring of libations. Inevitably, the picture of Greek religion that would result from an examination solely of the visual evidence would remain very incomplete, and any book based on it would be substantially different from anything that has been written on the subject during the past two hundred years.[15]

Fortunately, we have not only the images but also plenty of texts to go with them. Indeed, the true paradox that requires an explanation is the astonishing fact that a religion that relied so heavily on nonliterate forms of communication for the performance of its rituals and for its other activities managed to produce such a large and varied body of texts. Before an explanation can be attempted, we must pause for a moment to take stock of the diversity of the written record of Greek religion and to remind ourselves of the various categories into which these texts fall and of their *Sitz im Leben*, namely, the social conventions and human needs that generated them. The vast majority of these texts are not sacred by any means; in fact, many of them are decidedly mundane.

---

[14] Burkert 1992: 41–87, 1999: 104–11.   [15] Simon 1983.

With the exception of divine oracles issued by a particular shrine in the name and by the authority of oracular gods such as Zeus or Apollo, none of these texts claim to be divinely inspired, to emanate from a supernatural source, or to be anything but products of purely human aspirations.

THE VARIETY OF RELIGIOUS TEXTS

The most straightforward documents for the actual practice of Greek religion do not come from the literature of the archaic or classical period, but from the epigraphical record. The number of texts inscribed on imperishable materials such as stone, metal, or pottery is staggering. For the period from 500 B.C.E. to 400 C.E., a span of almost a thousand years, some 30,000 inscriptions survive from Athens and Attica alone. For the entire Greek world, the number of extant inscriptions is much larger. Although only a small percentage of these shed light on gods and rituals, the total number of inscriptions with a religious relevance runs into the high hundreds or beyond. Texts on stone have produced the richest harvest for the study of Greek religion. They include dedications to divinities,[16] tomb inscriptions,[17] sacrificial calendars,[18] oracles,[19] hymns and other cult songs,[20] cult regulations,[21] temple inventories,[22] contracts for the sale of priesthoods,[23] statutes of religious clubs and associations,[24] records of divine epiphanies,[25] and collections of healing miracles.[26] Certain texts were routinely inscribed on sheets of various metals. This category comprises the questions addressed to the oracle of Zeus Naïos at Dodona, as well as a small number of magical amulets inscribed with spells and prayers.[27] More important, it also includes the leaden curse tablets found in large numbers all over the Mediterranean world and the so-called Orphic gold plates with descriptions of the underworld and instructions for the dead.[28]

---

[16] *CEG*; van Straten 2000.   [17] Peek 1955; *CEG*; Day 1989.

[18] Dow 1968; Parker 1987, 1996: 43–55; Sourvinou-Inwood 2000: 30–2. See also 54–8, this volume.

[19] Parke 1967a, 1967b, 1985; Fontenrose 1978.

[20] Furley and Bremer 2001.   [21] Sokolowski 1955, 1962, 1969.

[22] D. Harris 1995; Hamilton 2000.   [23] Graf 1985: 149–53.

[24] Poland 1909; Sokolowski 1955, 1962, 1969.

[25] Henrichs 1996b.   [26] Dillon 1994.

[27] Parke 1967b: 259–73; Kotansky 1991.

[28] Faraone and Obbink 1991; Gager 1992; Jordan 2000; Riedweg 1998.

Magical papyri form their own category, which ranges from individual texts and collections of spells to entire papyrus books composed of magical incantations and instructions.[29]

Most of these texts talk about, pertain to, or are constitutive elements of various aspects of Greek religion as actually practiced. Some of these aspects were central, such as animal sacrifice and the consultation of oracles; others were more marginal or downright secretive and esoteric, including initiations rites and afterlife beliefs. The majority of these texts refer to ritual practices without being themselves ritual texts or blueprints for rituals. With the exception of some of the magical papyri, most of the hymns, and possibly all of the gold tablets, several of which seem to be initiatory in nature, none of these texts was actually recited in the course of a ritual performance or religious ceremony. In fact, many of them are concerned with practical matters such as the administrative, financial, or economic realities of particular rituals or shrines. Texts that owe their existence to such practical concerns include inventories, calendars, cult laws, contracts, and statutes.[30] The tomb inscriptions and gold tablets deal with death and the afterlife, and appeal more directly to modern religious sentiments. Epitaphs are biographical as well as religious documents. Like dedications, they function as public extensions of the self. Dedications, unlike epitaphs, honor a particular divinity and establish an immediate rapport between the human worshiper and the god, with emphasis on the votive offering as a gift and on the return gift expected from the divinity.[31] Reciprocity requires divine intervention, which often takes the form of epiphanies or healing miracles. Conspicuous instances of such divine epiphanies and healings were recorded on stone, especially in the Hellenistic period.[32]

Now we understand why a religion that was essentially nonliterate in its ritual practices could produce such a plethora of self-referential texts that illuminate so many of its aspects. A small number of these inscriptions preserve hymns and invocations,[33] but these regional documents provide small compensation for the complete absence of Panhellenic

[29] Faraone and Obbink 1991; Graf 1997; Faraone 2000.

[30] Notes 18, 21–4.

[31] Note 44, van Straten 1981. In other cases, the votive offering is itself a return gift for a prior favor received from the gods, for example, a successful childbirth or a miraculous healing.

[32] Notes 25–6. [33] Note 20.

sacred scriptures. From a strictly ritualistic point of view, these are the centripetal texts, so to speak, that reach inward toward the ritual and performative core of Greek cult. Some of the so-called *leges sacrae* – a modern term[34] – contain detailed instructions for the performance of complex animal sacrifices and may be added to the small number of core texts.[35] By contrast, the bulk of the religious inscriptions is centrifugal, I would argue, in that they reach beyond the ritual realm into adjacent areas of polis life, or because they deal with aspects of Greek religion that are peripheral, marginal, or highly personal. That does not diminish their authenticity, source value, or importance for students of Greek religion, but it does put them in their place.

The title of this essay, writing religion, refers to this gradual process by which the Greeks generated written records and testimonials of their cults, temples, gods, and rituals in both their Panhellenic and regional manifestations. It is the interplay of these overlapping constituents that we call Greek religion. The Greeks wrote their religion for themselves, not for us, and their writing of and about their religion is fundamentally different from modern writings on Greek religion. Yet the modern study of Greek religion would not have been able to achieve the results that it did during the past one hundred years if the Greeks had not left us an epigraphic record of their cults and rituals that produces new and important texts year after year and that never ceases to amaze.

The remainder of this essay will discuss the three things that are adumbrated in the title. First, I will retrace the extent of religious literacy in the preclassical period by going over some inscribed texts from the archaic age, specifically from the eighth, seventh, and sixth centuries. This rapid and extremely selective retrospect will prepare us for the explosion of religious writing and the proliferation of religious texts in the fifth century, especially among marginal religious groups. In the next section, I will concentrate on an aspect of Athenian religion that comes into sharp focus at the end of the fifth century, namely, the close connection between written texts and ritual authority as well as the emergence of a select cadre of ritual experts invested with special authority to create and maintain written records of state sacrifices. Finally, I will offer some tentative thoughts on the religious discourse in the polis culture of classical Athens, on the principal

[34] Parker 1996: 54.   [35] Note 18.

initiators of that discourse, and on the role that literature played in this process.

Some of the earliest nonliterary references to Greek religion can be found in the verse inscriptions of the late eighth and seventh centuries. Two of the longest and most informative of these inscriptions are graffiti incised on a Dipylon vase from Athens and on the so-called cup of Nestor from Pithecusae.[36] I have chosen these two inscriptions because they are both performative, and performance as a sequence of actions is a fundamental aspect of ritual.[37] Yet is far from obvious whether or not these two graffiti can qualify as religious texts, or failing that, as texts having to do with religion. Although I defined Greek religion a moment ago as the interplay of cults, temples, gods, and rituals, it is doubtful that any such formula will suffice to capture the totality of the Greek religious experience and of the social and material background against which it unfolded.

The text on the Dipylon vase consists of one complete hexameter and the beginning of another, followed by an unintelligible sequence of letters that some scholars have read and interpreted as an abecedarium. Greek writing was still in an experimental stage and had few practitioners in Athens when the graffito was inscribed on the vase, whose shape and decoration suggest a date from about 750 to 725 for the inscription. This dating makes the graffito on the Dipylon vase the earliest surviving written text from the polis of Athens, and one of the two or three earliest Greek inscriptions anywhere. The vase is a prize for the best dancer, as the inscription makes clear (CEG 432):

> Of all the dancers, he who performs most gracefully here and now,
> this (jug) is his.[38]

---

[36] The two graffiti are often compared because of their early date and verse form, for instance, by R. Thomas 1992: 58.

[37] Emphasized, among others, by Burkert 1979a: 14–18, 36–7.

[38] ὃς νῦν ὀρχηστῶν πάντων ἀταλώτατα παίζηι, | τοῦ τόδε ΚΑΙΜΙΝ. See Powell 1988, 1991: 158–63; Henrichs 1996a: 32–5. The vase is reproduced in Boardman et al. 1984: 80 with plate 56; Powell 1988; Henrichs 1996a.

Each one of the three dance words in this text – *orchēstōn*, *atalōtata*, *paizēi* ("dancers," "most gracefully," "performs") – is also found in Homer, which is not to say that the words are Homeric or that the author of our inscription was familiar with Homeric epic. No deity is mentioned in this inscription, and none of the words contained in it belongs to ritual vocabulary or has a transparently religious meaning.

The text is clearly performative, and if nothing else, it affords us a rare and precious glimpse into one of the earliest and most pristine stages of the archaic song-and-dance culture.[39] In spite of the absence of overtly ritual or religious markers, I am inclined to argue that this important text deserves a place of honor not only in the history of Greek dance and performance culture, but also in Greek religion. In the case of the Dipylon vase, writing about the dance is tantamount to writing religion because dancing was a ritual invariably tied to religious festivals. It would be difficult to imagine a dancing contest in the archaic period unconnected with a divinity, a sacred location, or a festival. This is especially true for choral performance, but it applies to solo dancers as well. Unfortunately, the epigram does not explain the type of dancing it refers to, nor does it explain the relationship among the dancers. The "dancers" of the graffito could be competing solo performers or members of a chorus; competition between choruses must have been the norm, but competitive rivalry between the individual dancers of a Greek chorus is not unheard of.[40] And it should be recalled that the Dipylon vase was found in Athens, not far from the Acropolis and the site of the Theater of Dionysus, where two hundred years later competitive dancing still flourished, performed on a large scale at various Dionysiac festivals.

The second graffito has received even more attention since its publication in 1955, thanks to its exquisite epic diction, mixed meter, preoccupation with wine and sex, and the intriguing reference to Nestor – is it the Homeric figure, or a real-life namesake? The graffito promises good sex to anyone who drinks from the cup on which it is inscribed

---

[39] Henrichs 1996a.

[40] Henrichs 1995: 83–4. The initial *hos* ("he") of the Greek text points to a single winner, which suggests a competition between solo performers, but it does not conclusively rule out competition between individual dancers in an ensemble performance.

(*CEG* 454, ca. 725 B.C.E.):

> I am the cup of Nestor that is good for drinking.
> Whoever drinks from this drinking cup, straightaway
> shall desire for/of fair-crowned Aphrodite seize him.[41]

Like the Dipylon graffito, this is a performative text, but the intended performance is not choral but sexual. As has long been recognized, the text is in fact a magical text, a love charm that promises immediate gratification.[42] The desire is caused by wine and aimed at Aphrodite. It is a desire for intercourse, because Aphrodite stands metonymically for the works of Aphrodite, that is, for sex. The idea seems to be that Dionysus and Aphrodite join forces and that one compels the other. From a Greek point of view, magic and religion are not at odds but perfectly compatible, although the magical charms are powerful enough to force even the hands of the gods. Aphrodite herself has magical powers, but in our text she seems to be prompted into action by the power of the spell, which functions as a performative utterance that activates the potency of the wine. Such a scenario is surely not a major manifestation of mainstream religion, but it is religious to the extent that it is predicated upon divine forces and supernatural agency.

SOME ARCHAIC DEDICATIONS

So far we have explored the inscribed fringes of archaic religious culture. We now turn to a series of inscriptions from the archaic period that are also in verse and represent one of the most common types of inscribed religious texts, namely, dedications on objects offered to the gods. More than half of the 465 verse inscriptions collected in the first volume of *Carmina Epigraphica Graeca* are dedicatory epigrams. The three that I have selected range in date from 700 to 500 B.C.E., and comparing them illustrates both the consistency of, and the deviations in, their generic features.

---

[41] Νέστορός ε[ἰμ]ι εὔποτ[ον] ποτήριον. | ὃς δ' ἂν τοῦδε πίησι ποτηρί[ου] αὐτίκα κεῖνον | ἵμερος αἱρήσει καλλιστε[φά]νου Ἀφροδίτης. See Watkins 1994; Carratelli 1996: 192, 665 with photograph.

[42] Faraone 1996.

The standard dedicatory inscription contains at least two names, that of the human dedicant and that of the divine recipient. The highly archaic Mantiklos inscription, probably found in Thebes, is written on the thigh of a bronze *Kouros* (*CEG* 326, ca. 700–675 B.C.E.):

> Mantiklos dedicated me out of a tithe to the Far-Shooter with the silver bow.
> May you, Phoibos, give (him) a pleasing return gift.[43]

The epigram delivers both names in the first line, and it does so by elegant circumlocution without ever mentioning the actual name of Apollo. Instead of using the theonym, the author of the text employs two standard epithets of the god, "Far-Shooter" (*hekabolos*) and "with the silver bow" (*argyrotoxos*), followed in the next line by Phoibos. More remarkable than the well-balanced tripartite use of divine epithets is the explicitness with which Mantiklos goes to the heart of the matter and asks Apollo for an unspecified return of the favor. *Do ut des*, "I give to you so that you may give to me" – the reciprocal principle of mutual gift giving as an exchange of favors between god and mortal is here formulated for the first time outside epic literature with an aplomb and immediacy that illustrate the ease with which Greeks could talk to, and interact with, their gods, at least within the relative safety of cult.[44]

More than 150 years later, Peisistratus the Younger, the grandson of the tyrant whose name he bore, dedicated an altar in the sanctuary of Apollo Pythios in the southeast area of Athens, between the Olympieion and the Ilissos.[45] The dedication is preserved on a piece of marble that once belonged to the monumental altar that Peisistratus describes as a "memorial (*mnēma*) of his rule/archonship." By a rare coincidence, the same stone epigram is also quoted by Thucydides (6.54.7). The two principal parties in this transaction, the god and the mortal, are fully

---

43 Μάντικλός μ' ἀνέθηκε Ϝεκαβόλωι ἀργυροτόξωι | τᾶς δεκάτας· τὺ δέ, Φοῖβε, δίδοι χαρίϝετταν ἀμοιβ[άν]. See Day 2000: 42–54. Photograph in Stewart 1990: vol. 2, plate 11; drawing in R. Thomas 1992: 79.

44 On reciprocity, see Burkert 1987; Parker 1998.

45 On the sanctuary of Apollo Pythios and its altar, see H. A. Shapiro 1989: 50, 59–60. The date of the archonship of Peisistratus the Younger appears to have been 522/1 B.C.E.

and elegantly named (*CEG* 305):

> Peisistratus, the son of Hippias, dedicated this memorial of his
> rule in the sacred precinct of Pythian Apollo.[46]

The tyrant's name and patronymic fill the better part of the hexameter following the masculine caesura, whereas the god's name and epithet frame the diaeresis in the middle of the pentameter. (These and the other aspects of the verses' artistry are partly obscured in translation.) God and mortal are assigned separate but interdependent realms in a playful separation of religion and state: Peisistratus and his political ambition occupy the hexameter; Apollo and his temple inhabit the pentameter, while the *mot propre* for dedications, *thēken* ("dedicated," literally "set up"), is strategically positioned at the boundary between the two realms. After all, it is the act of dedicating the altar that brings god and mortal together in mutually beneficial self-interest. The author of this poem knew the religious conventions as well as he knew his craft.

The third dedication, which is also from Athens, dates from the beginning of the fifth century B.C.E. and introduces a new feature, a first-person declaration of ownership (*CEG* 251):

> I belong to the goddess Pallas. Dexitheos, son of Eudikos,
> dedicated me as a first offering, a share of his possessions.[47]

Monuments and other physical objects often speak in the first person in Greek epigrams.[48] It is much rarer for them to declare so emphatically − "I belong to the goddess Pallas" − that they are the property of a particular divinity.

The three dedicatory epigrams were all composed with considerable literary skill, inscribed on works of art, and put on conspicuous display. Taken together, they bear witness to a central category of worship, namely, gifts to the gods. When read separately, they are eloquent examples of the close collaboration of dedicant, divine recipient, and poet

---

[46] μνῆμα τόδ᾽ἧς ἀρχῆς Πεισίστρατος Ἱππίου υἱὸς | θῆκεν Ἀπόλλωνος Πυθίου ἐν τεμένει.

[47] [Π]αλλάδος εἰμὶ θεᾶς· ἀνέθηκε δέ μ᾽ Εὐδίκου υἱὸς | Δεξίθεος κτεάνων μοῖραν ἀπαρξάμενος.

[48] Svenbro 1993: Chapter 2; R. Thomas 1992: 63–4.

in the perpetual chain of exchange that connects gods and mortals. All three epigrams are highly literary creations and models of their kind. Although they exhibit the art of composing and writing on the highest level, they do not refer to themselves as written compositions. But other inscriptions do, and it is to these that I will now turn.

CULT AND LITERACY

Important evidence for a dynamic relationship between writing and religion in the early archaic period comes from a rather unexpected source, a treasure-trove of vase inscriptions discovered since the 1920s in a sanctuary of Zeus near the summit of Mt. Hymettos in Attica and securely dated between 700 and 575 B.C.E.[49] Incised on the outer and in some cases the inner surface of Phaleron cups and subgeometric *skyphoi*, these graffiti constitute our earliest specimens of Attic writing after the Dipylon vase (if, indeed, the lettering on that vase is Attic and not the work of a non-Athenian scribe, as some specialists believe). Those graffiti that could be read and identified fall roughly into two groups. The first group consists of dedications of the type "To Zeus Semios," "So-and-so dedicated me to Zeus," and "I belong to Zeus [Semios]."[50] Dedications of this type are fairly standard, but the name Zeus Semios, that is, Zeus of weather signs (*sēmata*), is special and distinguishes the Zeus of Hymettos who presides over the local weather from similar manifestations of Zeus' power elsewhere. As far as I know, the Zeus Semios of the Hymettos graffiti is the earliest nonliterary instance of the interplay of divine names and cult epithets that ranks as one of the defining features of Greek polytheism. The epithet Semios is not attested elsewhere. Its nearest namesake is Zeus Semaleos, whose altar is located by Pausanias (1.32.2) on Mt. Parnes, another Attic mountain that produced inscriptions and graffiti. Cult names like Zeus Semaleos and Zeus Semios derive their message from their complete transparency – the name of the sky god, his meteorological epithet, and the mountaintop location of the cult place reinforce one another and articulate a fundamental function of Zeus that was of great concern to the farmers and herdsmen who frequented his mountain shrine and to those

---

[49] Langdon 1976: 10, 41.

[50] Σημίωι Δί, Δὶ Ση[μίωι], ἀνέθηκε Δί preceded or followed by the name of the dedicant, [‐ ‐εἰ]μὶ τοῦ Διὸς τοῦ [Σημίου] (Langdon 1976: inscriptions 2–8, 11–18).

Athenians who interpreted the cloud formations over the surrounding mountaintops as signs of divine favor or disfavor.[51]

The second group of Hymettos graffiti affords a rare insight into the early days of Greek writing and into the mentality of some of the first practitioners of the new art. The potsherds from this group contain fragments of eight different abecedaria.[52] These alphabet lists suggest that some of the earliest visitors to that shrine knew how to write but lacked experience, an impression that is confirmed by the crudeness of some of the hands. As if to compensate for such inexperience, the inscribers of several other graffiti express pride and joy in their skills by insisting that the writing is their own handiwork. "So-and-so wrote this himself" proudly proclaims one of the texts.[53] Another sherd contains the isolated phrase "as he wrote."[54] Since the pots found in the shrine of Zeus are glazed but not painted, we can be absolutely sure that in all these instances the verb *graphein* means "write" and not "paint."[55] Uniquely, then, we are dealing not with painters' signatures but with the names and signatures of the inscribers. Such self-conscious preoccupation with the act of writing is so unparalleled that Merle Langdon, the editor of the graffiti, concluded twenty-five years ago: "Writing must have been still so new that its accomplishment was being stressed."[56] In fact, according to Langdon, the worshipers dedicated to Zeus not the plain pottery that served as their writing material, but the very specimens of their newly acquired skill: "It was writing itself which was the gift."[57]

Langdon's suggestion is attractive, but remains speculative. Still, there can be no doubt that in the shrine of Zeus on Mt. Hymettos the idiosyncratic emphasis on autography as a performance and the worship of the gods through gift giving were closely connected. This connection is confirmed by another graffito, which has been restored, with near certainty, from three separate fragments: "I belong to Zeus. So-and-so inscribed me."[58] The vase *qua* votive offering speaks in the first person, which is standard convention and also describes itself as the property of Zeus, thus providing a crucial link between the gift and the

---

[51] Parker 1996: 29–33.   [52] Langdon 1976: inscriptions 20–6.

[53] τάδ' αὐτὸς ἐγ⟨ρ⟩αφ[σε] (Langdon 1976: inscription 30).

[54] ὥσπερ ἔγραψεν (Langdon 1976: inscription 27).

[55] Langdon 1976: 46.   [56] Langdon 1976: 46.

[57] Langdon 1976: 46, followed by R. Thomas 1992: 60, Parker 1996: 33.

[58] [τοῦ Διός] εἰμι. [– – –]ας δέ μ' ἐγραφ[σε]ν (Langdon 1976: inscription 29).

inscriber. The latter, identifying himself as the writer, thereby identifies himself also as the dedicant of the vase. As we have seen, writing and religious gift giving often go hand in hand, and votive offerings were often inscribed to identify the divine recipient as well as the human donor. But nowhere else do we find anything like the autographic self-reference that characterizes these graffiti from Mt. Hymettos and makes them such unique records of one of the earliest Greek alliances between religion and writing.

WRITING AND RITUAL AUTHORITY

As we move into the classical period, connections between religion and writing become more frequent as well as more nuanced. They can be found in tragedy, comedy, and a variety of prose writers from Heraclitus to Herodotus, Lysias, and Plato. The earliest datable reference to religious writings in tragedy is a notoriously mysterious and controversial passage in Euripides' *Hippolytus* (428 B.C.E.), in which Theseus vilifies Hippolytus as a religious outsider (952–5):

> Go on, posture, advertise your meatless diet,
> play the possessed devotee with Orpheus as your master,
> honoring your many vaporous screeds (*pollōn grammatōn* . . .
>   *kapnous*):
> you are found out! (trans. West, adapted)

Vegetarianism, Bacchic rites, Orpheus as a spiritual master, and a pile of books whose contents dissipate into thin air – this is a powerful mix of ritual ingredients that has exercised the imagination of many a modern scholar.[59] It is anybody's guess whether Euripides intended to describe the Orphic way of life as he knew it or borrowed tantalizing bits and pieces of initiation rituals from various esoteric groups that may have included Pythagoreans, Orphics, and the Dionysiac margin. Given Euripides' syncretistic tendencies elsewhere (e.g., the chorus of initiates in the *Cretans*), I would be reluctant to look for a uniform pattern of authentic ritual in this passage. One element that *is* authentic, however, is the association of written texts or books – papyrus

---

[59] Barrett 1964: 342–5; West 1983: 16; Graf 1986; Bremmer 1991: 23–7 (Orpheus as "guru").

rolls – with the obscure and sectarian margin of Greek religion.[60] Another aspect that finds confirmation elsewhere is the link between texts of a religious nature and ritual authority invested in initiatory figures such as Orpheus or in ritual experts such as the legendary Boeotian seer named Bakis, whose name was attached to collections of oracles.[61]

In the *Birds* of Aristophanes (414 B.C.E.), Peisetairos is in the process of performing the foundation sacrifice for his new city when he is interrupted by a succession of intruders, one of whom is a "collector/ reciter of oracles" (*chrēsmologos*). Experts on the use of oracles, the *chrēsmologoi* played an important role in Greek religion and Athenian society.[62] In modern scholarship, they are often referred to pejoratively as "oracle mongers," a term likely inspired by this scene in Aristophanes. This *chrēsmologos* indeed peddles the oracles that he quotes from a papyrus (*biblion*)[63] and attributes to Bakis. The *chrēsmologos* has just recited several hexameters from a purported oracle of Bakis that fits the occasion when the following exchange takes place between him and Peisetairos (980–9):

> PEISETAIROS: That's in there as well?
> CHRĒSMOLOGOS: Take the book (*biblion*).
> PEISETAIROS: The oracle, I see, doesn't at all resemble this one,
> which I wrote down from the words of Apollo:
>
>> "But when a quack of a fellow shall come uninvited,
>> annoy the sacrificers, and desire to share the inwards,
>> even then must thou strike him between the ribs –"
>
> CHRĒSMOLOGOS: I think you're making it up.
> PEISETAIROS: Take the book (*biblion*).
>
>> "– and show no mercy even to an eagle 'midst the clouds,
>> not if he be Lampon nor if he be the great Diopeithes."
>
> CHRĒSMOLOGOS: That's in there as well?
> PEISETAIROS: Take the book (*biblion*).
>
> (trans. Sommerstein, adapted)

---

[60] "The association between bookishness and irregularity is at its clearest in Orphism" (Parker 1996: 55).

[61] On Bakis, see Trencsényi-Waldapfel 1966: 232–50; Fontenrose 1978: 145–58; Baumgarten 1998: 50–2.

[62] Fontenrose 1978: 152–8; A. Shapiro 1990; Dunbar 1995: 542; Baumgarten 1998: 38–48.

[63] The *biblion* is either a sheet of papyrus or a papyrus roll.

In their hilarious display of oracular one-upmanship, the *chrēsmologos* and Peisetairos exchange fake oracles that they read out from a written text and that were allegedly composed by no less an authority than Bakis and Apollo. As in the *Hippolytus*, ritual marginality is associated with written texts ascribed to false prophets. Further confirmation for this nexus can be found in Plato's *Republic*. According to Plato, "itinerant priests and prophets" went from door to door "offering a hubbub of books (*biblōn homadon*) by Musaeus and Orpheus" that contained sacrificial instructions (*Republic* 364e). At the same time, the emphasis on written copies of religious texts indicates that writing was being recognized as a status symbol that facilitated the consultation of these texts and enhanced their authority.

I do not mean to suggest that the use of writing and written texts for religious purposes was entirely confined to marginal groups; they can also be found in the center of the polis. In the troubled years towards the end of the fifth century, the polis of Athens on two separate occasions appointed a commission of legal experts called "inscribers" (*anagrapheis*), whose task it was to produce a new copy of the "Solonian" law code, "to inscribe the laws of Solon" (Lysias 30.4).[64] One of these "inscribers" was Nicomachus, who labored long and hard – from 410 to 404 and again under the restored democracy from 403 to 399 – in two successive attempts to revise and reinscribe the ancestral laws of Athens, including the sacred laws that regulated the Athenian state sacrifices. It took Nicomachus and his colleagues several years to execute the two revisions of the sacrificial calendar and to inscribe them on walls erected inside the Stoa Basileios in downtown Athens, a task that was completed "in or near the year 401."[65] Substantial portions of the calendar survive on a series of marble slabs and provide unique information on the cost and nature of the sacrifices performed by the polis.[66]

---

[64] See Parker 1996: 43–55 on "Solon's Calendar"; Sickinger 1999: 94–105 on the revision conducted by Nicomachus and his colleagues; Dow 1963: 38–9; Todd 1996: 108–15 on the *anagrapheis*, Athenian officers appointed to "write up," "record," or "publish" (*anagraphein*) laws and decrees by having them permanently inscribed on stone. The codifiers of the late fifth century must be differentiated from the secretaries or city clerks of the same title who are first attested in 321/20 B.C.E.

[65] Parker 1996: 43.

[66] Dow 1953–7, 1960, 1961; Healey 1984; Parker 1996: 43–4 n. 3.

Nicomachus was ill rewarded for his efforts. He was indicted on technicalities and dragged into court (it was Athens, after all). Lysias, writing for the prosecution, accuses Nicomachus of tampering with Solon's laws by "inserting some laws and erasing others" (30.2, cf. 30.5). Lysias is more explicit as he reaches the climax of his accusation (30.18):

> But of course, gentlemen of the jury, we are not to be instructed in piety by Nicomachus, but are rather to be guided by the ways of the past. Now our ancestors, by sacrificing in accordance with the tablets (*kyrbeis*),[67] have handed down to us a city superior in greatness and prosperity to any other in Greece; so that it behooves us to perform the same sacrifices as they did, if for no other reason than that of the success which has resulted from those rites. And how could a man show greater piety than mine, when I demand, first, that our sacrifices be performed according to our ancestral rules, and second, that they be those which tend to promote the interests of the city and also those which the people have decreed and which we shall be able to afford out of the public revenue? But you, Nicomachus, have done the opposite of this: by inscribing (*anagrapsas*) a greater number than had been ordained you have caused the public revenue to be expended on these, and hence to be deficient for our ancestral offerings.   (trans. Lamb, adapted)

In the persona of the speaker, Lysias in fact argues that Nicomachus turned his assignment on its head and put his ritual expertise and writing skills to a perverted use. Instead of transferring the ancient laws of sacrifice faithfully and scrupulously from one writing surface to another, he erased some of the old sacrifices and substituted new ones of his own making that were more costly than the state coffers could afford. Although Lysias' argument is more concerned "with the relation between writing and law" than with that "between writing and religion,"[68] two conclusions can be drawn from it: first, that the perpetration of an alleged forgery abetted by writing is here perceived as a serious threat to the ancestral religion; and second, that written codification does not in and of itself bestow a seal of authenticity on ritual practice.

[67] We are ill-informed about the physical appearance of the *kyrbeis* and the material from which they were made. See Stroud 1979.

[68] Parker 1996: 50.

We have reason to believe that Nicomachus had a political agenda and designed sacrifices that benefited some of his own associates. His opponents, including Lysias' client, clearly had legitimate financial concerns.[69] Sacrificial animals were expensive, and Nicomachus' generosity cost the city dearly.[70] Similar considerations must have been voiced in the demes. The demes had their own sacrificial calendars, several of which survive.[71] These calendars are ritual as well as financial records, and Lysias expresses concern over their economic aspect.

However, religion is not completely absent from Lysias' argument. He poses as a ritual conservative who defines piety (*eusebeia*) as strict compliance with ancestral custom (*kata ta patria*) and with the sacrificial schedule allegedly codified for the first time under Solon some two hundred years earlier.[72] Nicomachus' distinction between appropriate and inappropriate forms of piety is a nice example of what I mean by the religious discourse of the polis. Legal experts like Nicomachus and his colleagues may have had the authority to set ritual parameters for the entire polis, but that does not mean that their opinions and rulings went unchallenged. The rituals and the religious beliefs of the polis were subject to continuous debate in democratic Athens. This debate took place in the law courts (the impiety trials are a case in point),[73] on the tragic and comic stage, in political speeches, and in other settings of civic discourse. The debate was largely performed *viva voce* on public occasions before an audience of fellow citizens. Nevertheless, pen and papyrus played an important role in this process. Playwrights, "orators" (that is, politicians), and forensic speechwriters depended on the written medium for the composition and transmission of their work. First composed, then committed to writing, and finally delivered from memory (i.e., performed orally), their plays and speeches confirm

---

[69] Parker 1996: 52–3; on the legal case, see Todd 1996.

[70] van Straten 1987, 1995: 170–86; Rosivach 1994.

[71] Parker 1987; Henrichs 1990: 260–4.

[72] Todd 1996 is concerned with the legal and constitutional issues raised by Lysias' speech; he barely touches on the "rhetoric of religious traditionalism" (112). The Solonian connection remains obscure. Michael Gagarin comments: "There must have been some *kyrbeis* with some written laws on them, even if the writing could no longer be understood and even if the *kyrbeis* were not Solonian" (oral communication). On the *kyrbeis*, see note 67.

[73] Yunis 1988: 59–72; Winiarczyk 1990.

that orality and literacy existed side by side in classical Athens; they also show that the discourse among citizens remained predominantly oral.[74]

In practicing their religion, the Greeks followed ancestral custom, which for the most part was handed down orally: "Writing was not . . . used to build up a complicated specialized corpus of ritual knowledge."[75] Yet numerous cult regulations were recorded on stone or metal between 600 and 300 B.C.E. throughout the Greek world. Dozens of examples are extant.[76] Like the sacrificial code associated with Nicomachus previously described, the majority of the cult regulations from the classical period are sacrificial calendars that specify the ritual requirements for various animal sacrifices in meticulous detail, including the date of the sacrifice, the name of the divine recipient, the species and price of the animal, and the ritual privileges of the officiants.[77] Texts of this nature reveal next to nothing about the actual performance of sacrificial rites. As Parker observes, "much traditional usage remains unexpressed in the early calendars, and must have been left to collective memory or the memory of priests."[78]

Not every surviving cult regulation follows this pattern. A lead tablet from Selinous (ca. 450 B.C.E.) reveals a remarkably different *lex sacra*. Not a cult calendar, it contains precise, step-by-step instructions for the performance of sacrifices and libations to Zeus Eumenes, the Eumenides, Zeus Meilichios, and various ancestral spirits such as the Tritopatores and the Elasteros.[79] Exclusively concerned with the ritual process, the Selinous inscription preserves a rare written record of those practical aspects of ritual lore that were normally transmitted orally. When the anonymous author of the Derveni papyrus, who wrote around 425 to 400 B.C.E., refers to the type of person "who makes a craft out of rites"

---

[74] Cf. R. Thomas 1992: 3–5, 88–93, 117–27, and this volume.

[75] Parker 1996: 54. With a different emphasis, W. V. Harris 1989: 83: "It is likely, however, that the religious practices of most ordinary Greeks were touched by the written word lightly or not at all."

[76] Notes 18, 21.   [77] Notes 18, 71.

[78] Parker 1996: 52.

[79] Jameson, Jordan, and Kotansky 1993. Parker 1996: 51, 53 describes the lost *Exegetika*, manuals compiled by the Athenian "expounders" (*exēgētai*) of sacred lore, as "do-it-yourself guides to various forms of ritual." The text from Selinous falls into a comparable category.

(20.3–4),[80] he must have been thinking of ritual experts who recorded their rites and circulated them as normative texts similar to the tablet from Selinous.

With few exceptions, however, the entire oral dimension of Greek religion – cult songs, public prayers, ritual utterances and exclamations, the so-called sacred tales (*hieroi logoi*), and other elements – has vanished without a trace.[81] Only the texts that made it into writing survive. These survivals include not only documents as functional as cult regulations or curse tablets, but also the more imaginative and fictional accounts of burial rites, choral dancing, and other ritual activities in literature. The literary representations complement and enrich the cultic record. How much poorer would our perception of Greek religion be if we did not have the Homeric scenes of sacrifice, the rich ritual repertoires of the tragedians, the prayers and hymns of Aristophanes, or the comparisons of Greek and non-Greek religions that we find in Herodotus?[82] Greek poets and prose authors wrote religion with their own agendas in mind, but exploring all those would require another essay.[83]

---

[80] ὁ τέχνην ποιούμενος τὰ ἱερά. See Burkert 1992: 41–6 on ritual "craftsmen." On the Derveni papyrus, see Yunis, this volume: 195–6 with note 21.

[81] What remains is collected in Porta 1999; on the elusive *hieroi logoi*, see Henrichs 2002.

[82] Homer: Seaford 1989. Tragedy: Easterling 1988; Sourvinou-Inwood 1997; Krummen 1998; Lloyd-Jones 1998; Henrichs 2000. Aristophanes: Bierl 2001. Herodotus: Burkert 1990; Harrison 2000.

[83] For advice and suggestions, I am indebted to Maura Giles and Gloria Pinney.

3

Letters of the Law

Written Texts in Archaic Greek Law

Michael Gagarin

he use of writing in connection with Greek law has attracted a
good deal of interest in recent years. Several papers in Marcel
Detienne's collection on writing bear on law,[1] and law has had
a significant place in Rosalind Thomas' work on orality and writing.[2]
Others have considered writing and early legislation primarily from
the political perspective of the role of written legislation in the development of the polis.[3] My own interest centers on the legal effects of
writing, and in particular its role in shaping the legal systems of ancient
Greece and its effect on the Greeks' thinking about law. I will begin by
sketching the picture we have of Greek law from our earliest evidence,
the poems of Homer and Hesiod, and will then consider the ways in
which written texts were introduced into this system. Comparison with
other premodern legal systems will help us appreciate the unusual way
in which writing interacted with law in Greece.

[1] Note especially Ruzé 1988 on writing by officials, Camassa 1988 on early codification,
Maffi 1988 on writing in classical Athens, and Canfora 1988 on Demosthenes' written
assembly speeches.
[2] R. Thomas 1989, 1994, and especially 1996. Like me, Thomas is particularly interested in the interplay of oral and written aspects, though from a rather different
perspective. Although in this chapter I note primarily issues on which we disagree,
there is much in her work with which I agree and which has helped shape my own
views.
[3] Stratton 1980; Eder 1986; Hölkeskamp 1992, 1995, 1999; Whitley 1997.

Michael Gagarin

EARLY GREEK ADJUDICATION

The poems of Homer and Hesiod, which probably reached their more-
or-less final shape around 700 B.C.E., show that by this time a standard
procedure for settling disputes between members of the community was
well established in Greece. This suggests that the procedure probably
had reached this form before the introduction of alphabetic writing,
around 750. The procedure is most fully illustrated by the famous trial
scene on the shield of Achilles.[4] The people are gathered in the agora to
hear a dispute between two men. Heralds keep order, as the people shout
their support for each side. Each litigant presents his case to a group
of elders sitting in a circle. Each elder then rises and in turn proposes
a solution (the verb is *dikazō*) to the dispute. The elder who proposes
the best solution (*ithyntata dikē*, literally, the "straightest settlement")
is awarded a prize of two talents.

I will not here enter into the fierce debate over many details of this
scene, but will stick to what is clear. The procedure involves two litigants, a group of respected elder members of the community, and
a crowd of ordinary folks, together with heralds to keep order. All
these people participate in the process orally: the litigants "affirm" or
"deny" something (*eucheto, anaineto*), the people "shout out their support" (*epēpyon*), the elders "give judgment" (*dikazon*), and at the end the
prize will go to the elder who "speaks" the best solution (*dikēn ithyntata
eipoi*). Even the heralds are said to be "loud voiced" (*ēerophōnōn*).

The placing of this scene on the shield indicates that the process
for settling disputes was important for the community, and that by
being good at judging, a person earned honor and respect. This same
message is conveyed by many other references to, and scenes of, dispute
settlement,[5] but nowhere is it more evident than in a passage from the

---

[4] *Iliad* 18.497–508: "Meanwhile a crowd gathered in the agora, where a dispute had
arisen: two men contended over the blood price for a man who had died. One swore
he'd pay everything, and made a public declaration. The other refused to accept
anything. Both referred the matter to a referee for a decision. People were speaking
on both sides, and both had supporters; but the heralds restrained them. The old
men took seats on hewn stones in a sacred circle; they held in their hands the scepters
of heralds who raise their voices. Then the two men rushed before them, and the
elders in turn gave their judgments. In the middle there lay two talents of gold as a
gift for the one among them who would give the straightest judgment."

[5] Collected in Gagarin 1986: 19–50.

proem to Hesiod's *Theogony* describing how kings benefit from the gift of the Muses (80–92):

> And whichever of the divinely nourished kings (*basileis*) are honored by the daughters of great Zeus [i.e., the Muses], who look upon him at birth, on his tongue they pour sweet honey and soothing words flow from his mouth. And all the people behold him, deciding the issues with straight settlements (*itheiai dikai*). And he, speaking surely, quickly and skillfully puts an end to even a great dispute. Therefore there are intelligent kings, in order that in the agora they may easily restore matters for people who have suffered harm, persuading them with gentle words. And as he comes to the hearing, the people honor him as a god with gentle reverence, and he is conspicuous among those assembled.

The association of Muses with kings has puzzled many.[6] It has been argued that the Muses help a king memorize and recite laws that have been transmitted to him orally by his predecessors in much the same way that epic poets recited verses learned from their predecessors;[7] but Hesiod does not say this. Rather, the Muses cause "soothing words" (*epea meilicha*) to flow from the king's mouth – a description that does not suggest the text of a law. Similarly, kings "persuade them with gentle words" (*malakoisi paraiphamenoi epeessin*). Again, this is not a description of someone reciting the text of a law. In fact, Hesiod is showing that a king's success depends on his ability not just to find a settlement that will be fair, but also to persuade the litigants themselves, and the rest of the community who are present, that it is fair and that they should accept it. The process must be voluntary at some level, and unless the king's decisions over time are perceived as fair and acceptable to all sides, people will lose confidence in his judgment and will no longer come to him to have their disputes settled. This is why the Muses' gift – the ability to speak persuasively – is so valuable.

Other examples of legal procedure found in early poetry differ in some of the details, such as whether the dispute is heard by a single person or by a group. But there is enough uniformity to recognize an established procedure. The procedure is not autonomous – those who hear cases are the same as those who sit in council – and there is no

---

[6]   The following remarks are more fully elaborated in Gagarin 1992.

[7]   See Roth 1976.

separate profession of judge.[8] The vocabulary for judging is still quite fluid, and several verbs are used: *krinein, diakrinein, diagignoskein,* and the most general term, *dikazein,* which has the sense of "settle" or "decide" and then takes on a more precise meaning depending on the specific juridical context.[9] But in all contexts, *dikazein* designates an speech act[10] and essentially means "speak so as to resolve a dispute."[11]

Early Greek legal procedure, then, consists of litigants who deliver their pleas orally before judges who give their judgments orally, often in the presence of a crowd of onlookers who also comment orally on the proceedings. None of the speech acts that constitute this procedure is constrained to take a specific form. A litigant can plead however he wants: there are formularies found in Roman law and elsewhere, and even when someone proposes an automatic procedure such as an oath, the precise wording of his proposal does not appear to be specified. After the chariot race in Book 23 of the *Iliad,* for example, Menelaus, a litigant, assumes the role of judge (23.579: "I myself will decide") and proposes that Antilochus swear an oath in order to win second prize: "lay your hand on the horses and swear by him who encircles the earth and shakes it that you used no guile to baffle my chariot" (23.584–5). The oath Menelaus proposes may use the formulaic language of epic, but it is not a formulaic oath; it is tailored to this specific dispute and would be different in another situation.

Another feature of early Greek legal procedure is that it is normally public. Zeus may be said to decide in secret, but the Greeks decided disputes in a public place, usually in the agora in the presence of a large crowd. In the scene on Achilles' shield, the elders sit on polished stones

---

[8]   The word *dikaspolos,* sometimes translated "judge," is only used as an adjective applied to a person "when he gives judgments" (*Iliad* 1.238, *Odyssey* 11.186). Another word – *istōr* – is found in the shield scene (*Iliad* 18.501: the litigants are seeking an *istōr*), but in the one other occurrence of the term (*Iliad* 23.486) it is not a professional but Agamemnon, who just happens to be present, who is asked to be the *istōr*.

[9]   Talamanca 1979.

[10] Benveniste 1969: 2.107–10 (s.v. *dikē*) connects *dikazein* with the Latin *dico* ("speak") and understands the judge's speech to be a recital of the texts of laws. As argued above, this is wrong, but *dikazein* may nonetheless have a connection with speaking. Etymologically, *dikazein* is probably connected with Greek *deiknumi* ("show") and means something like "mark" a settlement (see Palmer 1950), but *dico* may also be part of this complex.

[11] Allen 2000: 317.

in a circle in the agora; this may be a special part of the agora set aside for hearing disputes, but other kinds of meetings or assemblies may have been held here too. "Kings" (*basileis*) participated in this process on a regular basis, and certain days or times may have been set aside for hearing disputes. Even in Hades, Minos, king of the dead, is pictured hearing disputes brought by a crowd of dead spirits (*Odyssey* 11.569–72).

As legal matters grew more complex over the course of the archaic age, this oral procedure also became more complex, though it retained its fundamentally oral nature. One feature of this complexity was the addition of an official called a *mnamōn* (or *mnēmōn*) – "rememberer" – whom we know from inscriptions from all over the Greek world. This official assisted judges in remembering proceedings in court[12] and had other duties, such as remembering ownership of property.[13] At Gortyn, the *mnamōn* continues to remember oral judicial proceedings even after writing has been established in the community for a century and a half.[14] The *mnamōn* may later have acquired other duties that involved writing (as we shall see in the case of Spensithios), but *qua mnamōn*, his task was to remember, not to record. Thus, when the *mnamōn* participated in the judicial settlement of disputes, his participation, like that of others, took the form of speech acts.

Finally, the importance of settling disputes well and the oral nature of the Greek process are illustrated by a story from Herodotus (1.96–100), which will also introduce the subject of writing. The story concerns

---

[12] See the Great Code at Gortyn (*ICret* 4.72) col. 9.24–37: "If one dies who has gone surety or has lost a suit or owes money given as security or has been involved in fraud or has made a promise or another (be in like relationship) to him, one must bring suit against that person before the end of the year; and let the judge give his decision according to the testimony. If the suit be with reference to a judgment won, the judge and the *mnamōn*, if alive and a citizen, and the heirs as witnesses (shall testify), but in the case of surety and money given as securities and fraud and promise, the heirs as witnesses shall testify" (trans. Willetts, adapted). Here the *mnamōn* is expected to remember the earlier trial, and the text implies that if he is dead, his recollection dies with him; he puts nothing in writing. The *mnamōn* is also mentioned in the code in connection with paying a deposit to an adopted son who is being renounced (11.16) and hearing a declaration (11.53).

[13] A fifth-century inscription from Halicarnassus (ML 32) provides that a plaintiff has eighteen months in which to challenge a previous court decision, and "what the *mnēmones* know shall be binding."

[14] The earliest inscriptions from Gortyn are generally dated to the early sixth century (Jeffery 1990: 311–13). The code is generally dated to the middle of the fifth century.

Deioces, the first king of the Medes, who of course are not Greek but whose early history is recreated here according to a Greek model. In early days, the Medes lived scattered in small villages, in one of which Deioces judged disputes brought to him by the villagers. He was so good at this that soon everyone from the whole region would only bring their disputes to him, and he thus gained a monopoly over dispute settlement. One day, however, he stopped hearing disputes. As a result, violence and lawlessness (*anomia*) broke out everywhere. Finally, the Medes decided they needed a king. Naturally, they chose Deioces, who promptly restored law and order – but of a very different kind. Like an oriental despot, he removed himself from public view and all access to him was controlled by his advisers: "People had to put their cases in writing and have them sent in to him; then he made his decisions and sent them back" (presumably in writing).[15]

Clearly, the Medes' premonarchic procedure is Greek: people bring disputes to a respected judge for settlement. The entire process is oral and public. The monarchic system is very different: people still bring disputes to Deioces for settlement, but they now put their pleas in writing and a decision is made in private (indeed, in isolation) and then conveyed to the disputants in writing. Whether this latter system is seen as characteristic of oriental monarchy or of Greek tyranny (extreme forms of which in Herodotus' portrayal closely resemble oriental monarchy), it emphasizes by contrast the oral and public nature of the traditional Greek judicial process and shows that by the middle of the fifth century, the Greeks were aware that writing could play a different, more central, role in judicial proceedings than its traditional use in Greece, which was largely confined to writing down laws.

WRITTEN LAW

After writing was introduced in Greece, around 750 B.C.E.,[16] it was first used for private purposes – dedications, declarations of ownership,

---

[15] Herodotus 1.100.1: τάς τε δίκας γράφοντες ἔσω παρ᾽ ἐκεῖνον ἐσπέμπεσκον, καὶ ἐκεῖνος διακρίνων τὰς ἐσφερομένας ἐκπέμπεσκε.

[16] The dispute about just when alphabetic writing was introduced to Greece (contrast Isserlin 1982: 816–18 and Jeffery 1982: 823) is of little relevance for this chapter (see Introduction, 3–4). Legal inscriptions do not begin until about a century after our earliest inscriptions, and it is highly unlikely that if earlier inscriptions are found, they will contain legal material.

and other sorts of graffiti.[17] The earliest public inscriptions, which are mostly laws, begin in the second half of the seventh century.[18] Of course, the surviving evidence may not fairly represent the actual use of writing, but for law, at least, the inscriptions are consistent with evidence from the literary tradition, which dates the earliest lawgivers, Zaleucas, Charondas, Lycurgus, and Draco, to the seventh century. Although most of the early legal inscriptions that survive are from Crete, especially Gortyn, they are also found all over the Greek world;[19] and Greek traditions about early lawgivers, even if distorted and exaggerated,[20] indicate that the practice of writing laws was becoming established throughout Greece during the late seventh and sixth centuries. Moreover, despite Hölkeskamp's repeated claim that archaic legislation consisted of isolated responses to specific crises or problems,[21] there is evidence even in the earliest inscriptions from Gortyn and in Draco's seventh-century homicide law, that legislators organized and grouped provisions on the same subject, inscribed them on the same stone, and made them as accessible as possible to members of the community. What survives of Draco's law indicates that a considerable amount of thought went into organizing the provisions and anticipating possible problems.[22] The first four lines of a fragmentary early inscription from Gortyn, though sometimes thought to be inscribed by different hands, seem to consist of an organized series of provisions for public sacrifices.[23]

Now, if we consider that the surviving archaic inscriptions probably represent fewer (perhaps far fewer) than 1 percent of the texts originally inscribed, it becomes clear that the archaic Greeks devoted considerable resources to the writing down and public display of laws. And this

---

[17] Powell 1989.   [18] Jeffery 1990.

[19] See the collections of van Effenterre and Ruzé 1995 and Koerner 1993. Fell 1997 provides a useful concordance to these two works.

[20] Szegedy-Maszak 1978.

[21] Hölkeskamp 1992, 1995, 1999; cf. R. Osborne 1997.

[22] Gagarin 1981. Whether the reinscribed text of IG I³ 104 represents the original beginning of Draco's law (as I think) or not, the language is archaic and the surviving provisions were almost certainly part of the original law of 620.

[23] ICret 4.3: "... sacred rites [to be] performed ... on the fifth day of the month Welkanios ... / ... a full-grown [bull?] and a goat on [the sixth day?] a female sheep to Apollo ... a bull ... / ... to Hera a female sheep, to Demeter a pregnant sheep ... / ... two females and two males and a goat ..." Perlman 2001 questions the common assumption that the lines were written by different hands.

abundance of written laws was matched by an almost complete lack of any other written legal material. Besides legal statutes, archaic inscriptions include quasi-legal material such as decrees, treaties, religious rules, and curse tablets, perhaps written in the hope that they would influence a legal case, but no other legal matter. It also appears that writing was sometimes used in the administration of law, though no actual texts survive. For instance, Solon apparently created a new judicial procedure, called a *graphē*, which evidently involved writing, to supplement the traditional procedure called a *dikē*. In a *graphē*, the initial complaint or "indictment" was written down by the magistrate.[24] There is also a puzzling report that many years after the establishment of the first three archons "the Thesmothetae were instituted in order to write down *thesmia* and keep them for deciding disputes."[25] If there is any historical basis to this report (which is doubtful), my guess is that these *thesmia* were notes recording information about earlier cases, which the Thesmothetae then used as a guide for later cases.[26] But there is no sign that this practice, if it ever existed, lasted into the classical period.

We may conclude that for more than two centuries after the discovery of writing, the Greeks used writing to record a great deal of legislation, but writing played only a peripheral role in the judicial process during this period.[27] This somewhat paradoxical situation – an abundance of written laws matched by an almost total absence of writing in the judicial process – is illustrated, in my view, by a recently discovered inscription from Arcades in Crete honoring a certain Spensithios, who is called a *poinikastās* – generally translated as "scribe" (though this meaning is not certain). Spensithios holds a position of honor and power: he and his descendants pay no taxes and are given a monopoly on writing. His specific duties, however, are not just scribal, for his charge is "both to write and to remember (*poinikazein te kai mnameuwein*) for the polis all

---

[24] In the fourth century, the plaintiff himself wrote down the complaint (Calhoun 1919).

[25] Aristotle, *Constitution of the Athenians* 3.4: ἀναγράψαντες τὰ θέσμια φυλάττωσι πρὸς τὴν τῶν ἀμφισβητούντων κρίσιν.

[26] See Sickinger 1999: 10–14, who argues that the report deserves more credence.

[27] In the fifth and fourth centuries, writing for administrative purposes undoubtedly increased (though we know little of the details), and the texts of laws, contracts, and other evidence could be brought into court, but these texts were all read aloud by the clerk, so the trial itself remained a set of oral performances.

public matters, human and divine."[28] Thomas observes that the pairing of these verbs does not indicate a change from remembering to writing but rather two simultaneous activities. If so, since writing is largely used to record laws, it is likely that Spensithios wrote (*poinikazein*) the rules or decisions the city wished to have publicly displayed as laws. At the same time, like the Gortynian *mnamōn*, he remembered (*mnameuwein*) the proceedings in court.[29] Spensithios thus exemplifies the duality of writing and orality in archaic Greek law.

THE EFFECTS OF WRITING

The introduction of writing in general has various effects, but primarily it sets standards: standards for language, education, commercial practices, and even morality.[30] Thus, in Greece, writing helped standardize legal rules so that the penalties for offenses or the distribution of an estate became more consistent in each community. More important, writing down rules conveyed the idea that there *are* fixed standards, and this helped create the idea that some rules existed as standards or laws. Thus, writing made it possible to separate a group of rules – laws – and to distinguish them clearly from all other rules. The step from a collection of rules, like Hesiod's *Works and Days*, to a collection of (written) laws, such as Solon's, is conceptually very large. The former includes rules that resemble laws (such as advising against aggression towards one's neighbors), and they may have the authority of tradition and community support. But Solon's laws, although treating many different subjects, included only those rules that applied to matters regulated by the community. By writing down these and only these rules, and by displaying them in public apart from the other sorts of rules we find in Hesiod (traditional moral rules, advice on farming, etc.), Solon identified these rules as a separate category, thereby giving them a special status and authority as laws. He and Draco also gave these rules a new name, *thesmoi*, to confirm their separate status.

---

[28] *SEG* 27.631.A.3–5: ὡς κα πόλι τὰ δαμόσια τά τε θιήια καὶ τἀνθρώπινα ποινικάζεν τε καὶ μναμονεῦϝεν. See van Effenterre and Ruzé 1995: 1.102–7; R. Thomas 1996: 21–5.

[29] As we saw in note 12, in the Gortyn Code, the *mnamōn* remembers the outcome of a previous trial as it affects further litigation on the matter. He is not asked to cite laws, which others (including the litigants) could do simply by reading them.

[30] Clanchy 1985.

A number of years ago I argued that, for the most part, without writing there is no law. Collections of oral laws may have been recognized in some societies, such as early Iceland, but there is no evidence for similar collections in Greece. If *oral law* designates simply the traditional customs and rules of conduct that are preserved and transmitted orally, then these might exist in, for example, *Works and Days*, but they are not laws. The idea of oral law in Greece, however, has attracted many scholars, among them Thomas, who cites evidence for sung laws, and also for *mnamones*, who (she claims) remembered laws. But as we have seen, there is no evidence that the *mnamones* remembered oral laws. They remembered the proceedings and outcomes of trials and certain other matters, but they did not remember rules, which were now preserved in writing. Nor is there any evidence that they remembered the outcomes of earlier cases as precedents or rules for new cases.

As for sung laws, the main evidence is Athenaeus' report (619b) that "at Athens even the laws (*nomoi*) of Charondas were sung at symposia." But this and other such reports[31] raise more questions than they answer. Why, for instance, are the Athenians singing the laws of Charondas, lawgiver for the city of Catana (in Sicily), rather than their own laws of Draco and Solon? Charondas' laws were certainly not valid in Athens. Why, moreover, did they sing these while drinking? We know a fair amount about behavior at a Greek symposium, but the recitation of laws is unattested and seems improbable. Even the idea of setting an archaic Greek law to music is problematic, for the legal texts we know from inscriptions or literary preservation are prosaic in the extreme. Can we really imagine anyone putting the Gortyn laws or Draco's homicide law to music? And even if the Greeks did put the laws of Charondas to music for the purpose of entertainment or education, this would not make them "oral laws" any more than the Constitution of the United States would become an oral law if someone were to write music for it.

Part of the confusion may lie in the vocabulary. Many scholars understand the word *nomos* in this and other reports as designating written laws, but *nomos* is not used for the written text of a law until the fifth century.[32] Before that, it broadly means "rule" or "custom," the sort of rules that would be found in Hesiod. It is thus more likely that reports

---

[31] Strabo 12.2.9; Aelian, *Varia Historia* 2.39.
[32] Ostwald 1969.

of sung *nomoi* refer to general rules and customs, such as are found in *Works and Days*.[33] Thomas has it the wrong way around when she writes:

> In the archaic period what *we* call law and custom were barely distinguished from each other as concepts. What is distinguished . . . is "what is laid down," *ho thesmos* (as Solon refers to his laws), or "what is announced," the *rhetra* and very often simply "the writing" (*ta grammata*), to distinguish what is written down from other norms and rules. The idea of law as a body of written rules seems to have developed in close conjunction with the political and legal experiences of fifth-century Athens.[34]

It is precisely in the archaic period that the Greeks distinguished laws as written text from "other norms and rules" (*nomoi*) by giving them a new name (*thesmos, rhētra, grammata*). The writing down and the naming of this special category of rules was the crucial act in distinguishing laws from a wide array of other unwritten rules, customs, norms, and traditions. In this way, in the archaic period the Greeks used writing to create the idea of laws as a special category of rules. In the fifth century, the use of *nomos* to designate these written laws was probably intended to make it appear that they arose out of the customary rules of the community and were not imposed by a legislator.[35] This development had important consequences for the rhetoric of litigation in the classical period, but the basic concept of law is a creation of the archaic period. Thus, "the idea of law as a body of written rules" did not develop in the fifth century (as Thomas would have it) but in the seventh century, when someone first used the new technology of writing to record certain rules and thus to mark those rules as having a special status (laws) and a special name (*thesmos*, etc.) distinct from the rest of the community's *nomoi*.

The broad range of meanings of the English word *law* may tempt us to think of a broad spectrum encompassing oral and written rules, but the archaic Greeks themselves recognized a difference in kind, not

---

[33] Ruzé 2001 reaches a similar conclusion, citing Solon's elegies as a possible example of sung *nomoi*.

[34] R. Thomas 1996: 19.

[35] Ostwald 1969 argues that this extension of the use of *nomos* was motivated by the growth of democratic government in Athens. This is a plausible thesis, but unprovable.

just degree, when they gave new names, and thus a new status and authority, to these written rules. Orally transmitted rules and customs are not part of this "law." Some archaic poetry may have achieved quasi-official status as a guide to conduct and may have been cited in judicial proceedings (as we know it sometimes was in later trials), but this did not make poems into laws. The expression "oral law" may be a convenient metaphor for referring to certain kinds of rules, but we must draw a clear distinction between these and the written laws of archaic Greece.[36]

As Thomas has shown, writing also conferred authority on these statutes, not just by the fact of their being written but also because they were then publicly inscribed and displayed, often monumentally and in places of special significance.[37] Moreover, writing and public inscription together strengthened the sense that a more permanent, impersonal institution – the polis – existed as the authority for what was written and displayed. But beyond the sense that this larger entity was the authority behind the laws, it appears that the act of writing down laws did not have one single kind of political effect. Athenian ideology generally saw written law as democratic. As Euripides' Theseus puts it, "when the laws are written down, then he who is weak and he who is rich have equal justice" (*Suppliants* 430–4).[38] Herodotus, on the other hand, associates writing with tyranny in the story of Deioces and elsewhere.[39] And since archaic written laws are best attested for two cities, Athens and Gortyn, which developed democratic and oligarchic forms of government, respectively, it appears difficult to associate writing with just one of these forms of government. Written law, it seems, could have different political effects in different circumstances. We might tentatively conclude only that it strengthened the authority of whoever held power in the community.[40]

---

[36] I pass over here the interesting and difficult issue of "unwritten law." The concept seems to be a fifth-century creation, later than, and dependent on, the use of *nomos* for written law; see Ostwald 1973.

[37] R. Thomas 1996. We should resist the tendency to assume a polarity between writing meant to be read and writing meant to make a visual impression. The two functions are not exclusive.

[38] γεγραμμένων δὲ τῶν νόμων ὅ τ' ἀσθενὴς / ὁ πλούσιός τε τὴν δίκην ἴσην ἔχει.

[39] D. T. Steiner 1994.

[40] Derderian 2001: 110–13 reaches a similar conclusion about the effects of inscribed funeral monuments: "The political role of writing on the funerary monument

As for the specifically legal aspects of the effect of writing, the evidence from Gortyn has some interesting implications. First, the laws inscribed at Gortyn are true legislation. This may seem unsurprising, but it needs to be said because scholars are beginning to see that superficially similar collections of laws outside Greece, including Hammurabi's laws and the laws of the Anglo-Saxon kings, were not true legislation but a king's ideal formulation of the justice of his reign.[41] By contrast, the Gortyn laws were evidently intended to regulate actual legal disputes in the city. This is most clearly shown by provisions that state explicitly that a law is or is not retroactive. Retroactivity is of concern to those who use the law, but is of no concern if the laws are intended only to illustrate a king's views of justice, and such provisions are not found in these non-Greek laws.[42]

The provisions on retroactivity also suggest that all legal inscriptions at Gortyn were seen as part of a single legal system: legislators understood the need to integrate new legislation with earlier laws and to address potential conflicts between new and earlier legislation. A sense of unity was also conveyed by the fact that the Gortynians referred to their laws by forms of the expression "what is written" (*ta grammata*).[43] Since virtually all their publicly inscribed texts at this time were laws, the Gortynians had no need to specify what type of document was in question; everyone understood that "what is written" was equivalent to "the law." "What is written" implies, moreover, that a specific set of texts exist − those that are written down − and that all written laws at Gortyn thus belong to a single, self-contained set of legal rules. As an early fifth-century treaty between

---

thus evades any exclusive association with democratic or elite advances. Rather, it shows itself as an adaptive medium with potential for use in both democratic and aristocratic spheres" (112).

[41] For Hammurabi, see Bottéro 1992: 156–84; for early England, see Wormald 1999.

[42] See Westbrook 1989, who notes that Draco's homicide law also includes a provision for retroactivity.

[43] E.g., *ICret* 4.72.12.1–4: "If a son gave property to his mother or a husband to his wife as was written before these writings, there shall be no legal action" (ματρὶ υἰὺς ἒ ἀνὲρ γυναικὶ κρέματα αἰ ἔδοκε, ἆι ἔγρατto πρὸ τōνδε τōν γραμμάτον, μὲ ἔνδικον ἔμεν). Similar expressions for written laws were widely used in archaic Greece.

Gortyn and Rhittena put it, "Let what is written be valid, but nothing else."[44]

Writing thus created the sense of a self-contained set of legal regulations that fixed substantive standards of conduct in many areas as well as standards and rules for judicial procedure. As a single cohesive set, existing at a specific time and place, written law also conveyed the sense of a fixed, stable institution – the Law. New legislation could change the law, but at any given time it was fixed by the words on the stone. No matter how few people could or did read these texts,[45] the potential existed for knowing with certainty what the law was. And the sight of a law physically inscribed on a stone monument would add to the sense of its solidity and permanence. We might contrast the praetor's edict in Rome, which was reissued every year. Even if most of a new edict's regulations were unchanged from the previous edict, the knowledge that this edict was not permanent but valid for only one year would not have produced the same sense of stability.[46]

Outside Crete, the inscriptional evidence for legislation is widely scattered, but it is supplemented by various traditions of early lawgivers that are consistent with the appearance of inscribed laws all over the Greek world at this time. And the evidence for Solon's wide-ranging legislation in Athens is quite secure.[47] We may thus conclude that in the archaic period Greeks everywhere wrote down and publicly displayed a great deal of legislation, that this was true legislation meant to be read and used by members of the community, and that besides legislation, writing was little used in connection with law, and judicial procedure remained very largely oral. Even as greater use was made of writing in all aspects of life during the fifth and fourth centuries, written laws and other documents were never presented to the jurors in writing but were always read aloud to the court. The central judicial process thus remained essentially oral.[48]

---

[44] *ICret* 4.80.12: τὰ ἐγραμμέν', ἄλλα δὲ μέ.

[45] The degree of literacy in Greece is hotly debated; see in general W. V. Harris 1989, and specifically for Crete, Perlman 2001, who challenges the conclusions of Whitley 1997. The percentage of the total population who could read was undoubtedly small (in modern terms), but may have included a large percentage of those who were active politically. The situation may have been further complicated by various degrees of partial literacy.

[46] Ruschenbusch 1966.   [47] Frier 1985: 57.

[48] Cf. Cohen, this volume.

GREEK LAW COMPARED WITH ROMAN AND
ENGLISH COMMON LAW

This combination of written legislation and oral procedure, it should be stressed, is highly unusual in premodern legal systems,[49] whose use of writing is generally different.[50] Like the Greeks, the Romans used writing to record laws very early, probably about 450 B.C.E., with the publication of the Twelve Tables. But apart from this, written laws were relatively unimportant during the republic.[51] Another important source of law was the praetor's edict, though we do not know how early it was put in writing. A third source of law in Rome was interpretation, which was first practiced by the *pontifices* around the time of the Twelve Tables and was continued later by the jurists,[52] who may have been issuing *responsa* in writing as early as 300 B.C.E.

Judicial procedure at the time of the Twelve Tables appears to have been entirely oral.[53] Unlike the Athenians, however, the Romans from the beginning specified precise forms of procedure (*legis actiones*). At first, they allowed only three or four *actiones*, and litigants had to conform strictly to these. One wrong word could invalidate a person's case. The Twelve Tables do not indicate that these *actiones* already existed in written form, but this step must have been taken at an early date. A collection of *actiones* was said to have been published around 300 B.C.E. by Gnaeus Flavius, and they were apparently available in writing for the magistrates earlier. With the development of the formulary system in the third and second centuries, writing became even more central to the judicial process. Early formularies may have been simple enough to be issued orally and then remembered during the proceedings *apud*

---

49 There are some interesting parallels in the legal system of the United States, which now relies on juries more than most systems. Here, most, but not all, material is presented to jurors orally, who then decide on the facts of the case. But decisions about legal issues, made by a judge at the trial or on appeal, are based largely on written documents.

50 There is evidence in Hammurabi's laws for much legal writing other than legislation (contracts, property transfers, a judge's verdict, etc.), but the degree to which these were used in the judicial process is impossible to determine.

51 See Jolowicz and Nicholas 1972: 87, and in general Schulz 1946: 5–37.

52 Jolowicz and Nicholas 1972: 88–97; see also Frier 1985.

53 The Twelve Tables mention a will (*testamentum*, V.6), but this is not a written document at this time. In certain cases (e.g., VI.1a), it is explicitly said that an oral statement is valid.

iudicem ("before the judge"), but as their number and complexity grew, they must have been written down in addition to being spoken orally.[54] Similarly, verdicts were at first issued orally, but at some point these began to be collected in writing for use by jurists, just as jurists' opinions had long been available in writing. Thus, by Cicero's time, although written laws were not as numerous as in Greece, written *responsa*, *legis actiones*, formularies, and verdicts, many of which were not published but were kept for the use of magistrates and jurists, all played a role in Roman trials. And with the *actiones* and formularies in particular, writing found its place at the heart of the judicial process.

Although precise causes and effects are difficult to determine, it seems very likely that the increasing use of writing in the legal process was connected with the increasingly technical nature of the law and the growing importance of legal professionals in Roman law. Nonprofessionals remained a part of the process, in particular the judge, who was supposed to be a layman, and the advocate, who did not need to have specialized training in law (but often did). However, as the importance of writing increased, Roman law became more and more a scholar's law, knowledge of which was increasingly confined to a relatively small group of specialists. There are early indications, especially in the *legis actiones*, that Roman law from the beginning was inclined to be more technical and formulaic than Greek law ever was, and the mention in the Twelve Tables of a *vindex* (perhaps an early form of the advocate), who could assist a litigant, may indicate that at that time the Romans already saw litigation as beyond the ability of some members of the community. Even so, a Roman trial of 450 B.C.E. must have resembled an Athenian trial of 600 B.C.E. in being primarily oral. After 450, however, the increasing use of writing within the legal process influenced Roman law to develop in a different direction.

The influence of writing on the development of English common law was equally large. Before the Norman conquest in 1066, law in England was almost entirely a matter of local jurisdictions deciding cases according to local customs and traditions. Common law was administered by the king's court, which traveled around the country hearing cases, but it had little importance and most cases continued to be heard in local courts. After the conquest, as feudalism disappeared, the

---

54 Jolowicz and Nicholas 1972: 201 with note 6.

common law tailored itself to fit the needs of landowners, who responded by making more and more use of it. By the end of the thirteenth century, the common law had almost completely replaced the local courts.

Because common law was rooted in the customs and traditions of the people, for a long time legislation played a very small role in its history. Disputes and the rules for adjudicating them were decided by courts, not legislatures. Written decrees and proclamations addressed specific situations, such as the taxes to be paid that year, and only occasionally set out general principles, as in the Magna Carta of 1215. However, during the period of the formation of the common law – roughly from the Conquest to the death of Edward I in 1307 – the quantity of writing and its impact on the law increased dramatically, not in the form of legislation but in the system of writs.[55] As the name indicates, a writ was a written document, originally an order from the king commanding a person to appear in the king's court to answer a complaint, or commanding a royal magistrate, such as a sheriff, to take action on a complaint.[56] In order to initiate litigation in the king's court, an individual had to have the king, or in practice his chancery, issue a writ. Gradually, the issuance of writs was standardized, and the chancery issued them for a fee upon request, provided the request followed the proper form. The writ then constituted an order to the accused to answer the charge in court. The writ thus controlled the course of the trial and, like the Roman *legis actiones*, was central to the judicial process.[57]

Though very small at first, the number of different writs increased rapidly, and the common law became ever more complex and technical. One consequence was the rapid growth of the legal profession, since most Englishmen, even if they were able to read and write, and even if they knew the language of writs (which was generally Latin or an archaic form of French), were not able to determine which of the many specific writs was appropriate for the damage or injury suffered. Thus, the increasing complexity and technicality of the law and the

[55] Clanchy 1993.

[56] See Pollock and Maitland 1898, especially 150–1; Baker 1990, especially 63–83.

[57] "The choice of original writ governed the whole course of litigation from beginning to end and the plaintiff selected the most appropriate writ at his peril" (Baker 1990: 66).

growth of the legal profession went hand in hand with the growth of writing.

In Greece, by contrast, writing was never central to the legal process. In classical Athens, a trial consisted of litigants presenting their own pleas orally, in whatever words they chose, punctuated from time to time by the reading aloud of documents by a clerk. There was no need and no place for legal experts, and so there were none. We know of a body of *exēgētai* ("interpreters"), but they offered information and advice on religious matters and were not legal authorities. The logographers, or "speechwriters," were experts in presenting a case to the jurors, but they too were not legal authorities. Any litigant could give a legal opinion and could even pose as an expert on the meaning of the law or the intentions of the lawgiver, as Demosthenes often does, but his views had no legal validity, except to the extent that they were accepted by a jury. Thus, the Athenian legal process remained essentially oral, nontechnical, and nonprofessional to the end, and the absence of writing in the legal process was, I suggest, an important reason why Athenian law could develop without the concomitant growth of a legal profession.

In sum, writing had a significant impact on archaic Greek law both by its presence and by its absence. Widely used for legislation from early times, it helped bring the concept and the reality of law directly into the lives of many citizens, but writing was almost entirely excluded from the judicial process, which retained its traditional oral form. Unlike other similar legal systems, Greek law did not become technical and did not see the growth of a legal profession. The important factor in this development was not the total amount of legal writing in Greece, which in the form of legislation was large, but the place of writing, which remained external to the legal process. Both written laws and oral procedure helped make Greek law part of the public discourse of the polis; the presence of writing brought the city's legislation directly to the people, and the absence of writing ensured that the judicial process would remain in the hands of the people. Writing thus created a recognized body of written statutes that provided a fixed, stable framework within which the fluid discourse of oral procedure negotiated its way.

We can only study the interplay between written legislation and oral procedure in detail in classical Athens, but one could argue that this same interplay may have characterized the law of all Greek cities, except perhaps Sparta, which was different in its attitude toward writing as in so many other ways. We have abundant evidence that, with this one exception, writing was used for legislation all over Greece. Although we have very little evidence for judicial procedure outside Athens, the Gortyn Code reveals a procedure that appears also to be entirely oral.[58]

Both these features – written legislation and oral procedure – helped to preserve the public and communal nature of law in Greece. Written laws brought more order and predictability to the previously existing legal process, and also brought the people into more direct contact with the rules by which the polis was governed. And the exclusion of writing from the judicial process kept Greek citizens directly involved in the law and prevented the development of legal professionals, who in most other legal systems tend to form a barrier between the law and ordinary people. Thus, the discourse of Greek law – including the written texts of the laws and the oral discourse of the courts – remained open and communal. The discourse of most other legal systems is a specialized, technical language, controlled and authorized by a relatively small number of professionals. The discourse of Greek law, whether written or oral, remained the language of ordinary people.

As we noted, this basic structure seems to be independent of any particular form of government. It is a general feature of Greek society, not limited to law, that even communities with hierarchical social structures, such as Homeric communities, give a significant voice to some who are not members of the ruling class. Even Thersites has a right to speak. Thus, the open and communal nature of legal discourse at Athens and the concomitant nonprofessional nature of the law may not be special consequences of Athenian democracy, as is often thought, but basic features of law in most Greek cities, whatever their form of government. Legal historians have often scorned Greek law, especially by comparison with the great system constructed by the Romans. But Greek law, both oral and written, was perfectly suited to the Greek desire for open, public discourse by the members of the community. Written texts had a limited, and from a Roman perspective inadequate, role in Greek law, but both their presence and their absence helped preserve just the qualities the Greeks found desirable in a legal system.

---

[58] Dareste, Haussoullier, and Reinach, 1891–1904 observed more than a century ago that judicial procedure at Gortyn "est entièrement orale" (1.432). See Gagarin 2001.

4

Writing, Law, and Legal Practice in the Athenian Courts

David Cohen

One way to approach the subject of writing and law in classical Athens would be from the standpoint of legal theory. One might begin, for example, with the famous contrast, invoked by Antigone in Sophocles' play (450–70), between a ruler's pronouncements and the unwritten, unchanging, timeless divine laws. One could then turn to the resolution adopted by the Athenians during the law reform after the end of the Peloponnesian War, which provided that magistrates could only enforce laws that had been inscribed (Andocides 1.85–9). Significantly, Andocides treats this prescription as a legal principle (to use a modern term) to which the Athenians resolved to bind themselves. Other principles entailed that laws should be universal in application and not applied to individuals and that no decree of the Assembly or Council was to override a law. Thus, while acknowledging the central importance of fixed, written laws as an anchor of democratic government, the Athenians were by no means bewitched by the notion of law as eternal, divinely mandated, or immutable – beliefs that are familiar from a variety of other legal cultures.

In the *Laws*, Plato tries desperately hard to secure for the law code of his hypothetical city an immutability based on divine mandate, but his very effort to construct a tradition of reverence and permanence for the written code reveals his awareness of contrary dispositions in contemporary Athens.[1] The enactments in connection with the law reform at the end of the Peloponnesian War reflect a society with a positivist understanding of law as embodied in the written statutes of the polis.[2] They also suggest a legal culture with an instrumental understanding of law as the creation of human beings, that is, that laws are created by a political community to satisfy its particular understanding of its values and needs.[3] Because, on this view, what human beings can make they can just as easily unmake, law is a creation that needs institutionalized protection from the inclination to change, override, or circumvent it according to the exigencies of the moment.

The most eloquent testimony to this recognition of the mutable, manmade, instrumental quality of law – beyond all the reverence for ancestral lawgivers and time-honored traditions – is found in Demosthenes' oration *Against Meidias*. This remarkable passage pierces the collective fiction found in so many societies, ancient and modern, about the permanence and sovereignty of law and the independence of its origin from the realm of the political. Demosthenes asks the judges as citizens of Athens, as the embodiment of the *dēmos*, to consider this elemental question of the nature and source of written law (21.224–5):

> And what is the strength of the laws? If one of you is wronged and cries aloud will the laws run up and stand at his side to defend him? No. They are written texts (*grammata gegrammena*) and incapable of such action. In what, then, resides their power? In you, if you support them and make them effective whenever anyone asks. So the laws are strong through you and you through the laws.

---

[1] See especially *Laws* 772cd, and, for discussion, D. Cohen 1995: 49–51.

[2] Among other things, the Athenians decided that legal actions could only be based upon the written statutes and not upon "the unwritten law." This seems to reflect a conviction, similar to that of contemporary legal positivism, that the *only* source of law is the written statutes enacted by whoever is legally empowered to do so. The enactments mentioned by Andocides coincided with the effort to transcribe anew the Solonian law code; see Henrichs, this volume: 55–6.

[3] Aristotle and Plato both make the point, for example, that laws will differ according to the kind of constitution present in a particular society. Oligarchies will enact laws that suit them, and democracies will do likewise. In this way, laws are shaped to suit the interests of the dominant group. See, for example, Aristotle, *Politics* 1279ab, 1282b5–10, 1289a13–25, 1291b7–13, 1296a22–b3.

A full commentary on this passage would involve nothing less than a complete exploration of Athenian political and legal theory.[4] My subject, however, is not the realm of theory, but that of legal practice. This brief excursus was simply intended to suggest that in some Athenian conceptualizations of law and of the rule of law, the idea of law as written, as statute, had a central place.[5] Let us now turn to the far less lofty realm of the Athenian courts and to the role of writing in Athenian litigation. I will take up the role of writing in three areas of legal practice: lawsuits involving claims about citizenship and civic identity, inheritance litigation, and commercial loans, all of which, in modern practice, may depend crucially upon written documents. Examining these cases will, I believe, reveal a good deal about Athenian cultural ambivalence about writing in legal contexts.

WRITTEN DOCUMENTS, CITIZENSHIP, AND CIVIC IDENTITY

In the democracy of classical Athens in which a privileged minority of adult male citizens governed a city where the vast majority of the inhabitants were strictly excluded from political participation, perhaps no issue was more fundamental than that of establishing claims to citizen status.[6] The basic mechanism for doing so was the enrollment of new members in the written register of their deme when they attained the age of eighteen. At that time, they could be presented by their fathers to the demesmen, who had to certify their claims to citizenship. As Aristotle recounted the procedure (*Constitution of the Athenians* 42.1–2), the name of a new citizen would be added to the deme register when the deme members had voted on oath in favor of the young man both having attained the age of eighteen and having met the requirement of birth from citizen parents as specified by the statute. In the event that the vote went against the recognition of his claim to citizenship, he could appeal to the court. In the case of such an appeal, the deme sent five men to make the case against him. At the trial, both sides address the judges. If the deme's representatives succeed, the young man is sold into slavery. If he prevails, he is inscribed in the deme register as a citizen.

---

4 Ober 1989: 300–3.
5 On the rule of law in Athens, see Ostwald 1986; D. Cohen 1995: Chapter 3.
6 On the law of Athenian citizenship, see Patterson 1980; Davies 1977–8.

This legislative scheme appears to have located the fundamental responsibility for enrolling and vetting citizens in the demes. The huge risk that one runs in appealing the decision of the deme – being sold into slavery – underscores this responsibility and serves as a serious disincentive to litigate against the deme's decision. The vote of the deme members is the statutory mechanism that enables a young man to attain the legal status of a full Athenian citizen. That vote is memorialized not merely in the collective memory of the deme members but also in writing. In a context in which many foreigners and Athenians of illegitimate birth were clearly seeking the significant advantages of citizenship, the written record of the deme register would have provided, at least formally, a definitive written record of the deme members. On the one hand, since anyone trying to insinuate his way into citizen status would have to conduct his fraud through a deme, the registers presumably provided a check against deme members who might support such an attempt. (However, as we will see, this check might not be so effective in very small demes, where collaboration in fraud might involve many deme members.) On the other hand, since it was a staple of Athenian forensic rhetoric to try to blacken the character and standing of one's opponent by claiming that he was of servile or foreign birth, the deme registers would provide a fixed reference point for testing or rejecting such claims.

The underlying problem is that citizenship was a highly prized commodity, and there were a variety of reasons why some deme members would be prepared to help those illegitimately seeking to obtain it. First, there is simple venality. As will be seen below, accusations of selling citizenship appear to have been commonplace, especially in regard to particular demes. Second, Athenian metics (free resident aliens), many of whom were prominent members of commercial circles in Athens, might have lived in Athens for generations. Since they were permanently barred from citizenship no matter how long they lived there (because they could not fulfill the statutory requirement of citizen birth on both sides), they might well seek a way around the legal prohibition, and their friends, neighbors, and business associates might well be sympathetic. Helping a well-to-do friend become a citizen would also enable potentially advantageous marriage alliances that would otherwise be legally prohibited (since under Athenian law both parties had to enjoy citizen status in order to form a valid marriage). Finally, in cases where an Athenian had an illegitimate male child (for example, with a noncitizen woman), he might well seek to persuade (through a variety of means) his fellow demesmen to enroll the boy.

For reasons largely unknown to us, the middle of the fourth century saw an increasing concern with the composition of the citizen body. Although we tend to think of Athenian citizenship as determined by the very exclusive laws familiar to us, citizenship in fact seems to have been more porous and fluid than the formal rules suggest.[7] In any event, a resolution of the Athenian Assembly, probably on the basis of a proposal by Demophilus in 346 or 345, called for a reexamination of the citizen rolls. The demes were required to vote about the citizen status of all their members; that is, they were required to purge their own ranks.[8] The fact that this task was delegated to the demes points up their authority in matters of citizenship as well as the practical fact that only they were realistically in a position to carry out such a task. In the absence of centralized political records, the deme registers were the only authoritative documentation of citizenship. If there had been no doubt as to their veracity and integrity, the problem never would have arisen. The crisis, however, seems to have arisen because of the belief that the deme registers could not be trusted. In this case, when the registers' contents themselves were called into question, there were no other means to verify citizenship except to entrust the demes with examining their own ranks. As one might expect, the aftermath of this enactment and the ensuing purge of the citizen rolls seem to have involved a great deal of legislation, some of which has been preserved for us in the corpus of the Athenian orators. All such orations must be read, of course, with the understanding that they are entirely partisan accounts, the veracity of which we have no way to check. They do reveal, however, the kinds of arguments that were thought to be plausible to judges in the highly charged atmosphere of the scrutiny of the citizen rolls. This, in turn, reveals a good deal about the attitudes and expectations that a randomly selected group of Athenian citizens would bring to bear in judging such cases.

The oration *Against Eubulides* (speech 57 in the Demosthenic corpus) is an appeal to the court. The speaker, Euxitheus, seeks to defend himself

---

[7] On naturalization as a means of obtaining citizenship outside of these strictures, see M. Osborne 1981–2.

[8] On this episode, see Demosthenes 57; Whitehead 1986: 106–9.

against the charges that have resulted in his expulsion from the deme list. The way in which he seeks to do so and the story he recounts reveal the tension in Athens between, on the one hand, an administrative, document-oriented understanding of civic identity, and a much more powerful oral culture of informal knowledge, social networks, and, ultimately, social control on the other.

Before even recounting the tale of his expulsion, Euxitheus must first legitimize the very act of appeal. That is, he anticipates that the judges will be disposed to accept the opinion of the demesmen as sufficient in itself: "I beg you, men of Athens, not yet to take my rejection by the demesmen as proof that I am not entitled to citizenship, for if you thought that the demesmen would be able to decide all cases justly, you would not have allowed the appeal to yourselves" (Demosthenes 57.6). It is, of course, the written record of the deme register to which one might have appealed to settle such disputes, but when the community represented by the demesmen rejects that record, the speaker antici-pates that the natural reaction of the judges will be to accept their word as coming from the parties who know. The logic of this expectation is explained by a passage from Aeschines' speech *Against Timarchus*, where Aeschines talks about the nature of informal communal knowl-edge. Referring to the ongoing litigation over the revisions of the citizen lists, Aeschines comments (1.77–8): "Whenever I am in the courts lis-tening to the pleas I see that the same argument always prevails with you. When the prosecutor says, 'Judges, the men of the deme have ex-cluded this man based on their own collective knowledge, even though no one accused him or testified against him,' you immediately applaud, assuming that the man you are judging has no claim to citizenship. For I suppose you are of the opinion that, when one has clear *personal knowledge*,[9] there is no need of argument or testimony."

It suits Aeschines' rhetorical purpose to characterize informal com-munal knowledge this way, but the underlying assumptions well match those of Euxitheus. It is interesting that nowhere does Euxitheus try to justify the fact that his name is inscribed in the deme register. Of course, if his name did not appear there his position would be far worse. But in this context, where the authenticity of the register has been called into question, the best he can do is to rely on personal knowledge to

9   ὅσα τις σαφῶς οἶδεν αὐτός. Emphasis added.

support his claim that *his* name was not fraudulently inscribed. Thus, his central argument will be to place the personal knowledge of his relatives over against that of the demesmen while calling the motives of the latter into question. Before he can do this, however, he must attempt to counteract the natural tendency of the judges to accept the demesmen's story as conclusive. So, to legitimate his opposition to the deme, the speaker adopts a two-pronged rhetorical strategy in the opening of the speech. First, he affirms the importance of expelling those who are justly accused, those who "by stealth and violence come to participate in your religious and public affairs;" then he asks the judges not to let their understandable anger at such rascals prejudice their judgment of those honest Athenian citizens who, like himself, have been the victims of enmity and rivalry (Demosthenes 57.3). Having thus established his character, he recounts his version of how the deme came to reject him.

Euxitheus explains that Eubulides, a member of the Council and clearly influential in the deme, hates him because of testimony he had given against Eubulides in a previous lawsuit. (In fact, this feud was inherited from the previous generation, and Euxitheus was involved in more conflicts within the deme than he here suggests.) According to Euxitheus, Eubulides called a meeting of the deme to review the register, which was in his custody (57.8). He deliberately prolonged the meeting until, evening coming on, the older men left to return to their farms. Instead of adjourning the meeting, since they could not finish going through the roster that day anyway, Eubulides, without calling any witnesses, accused Euxitheus and called for a vote. Euxitheus asked for the vote to be postponed until the next day so that he could have people present to speak on his behalf (57.12). Eubulides persisted, since the whole affair had been rigged, and handed out ballots. Despite the fact that only thirty demesmen were now present (the other forty-three having left), more than sixty votes were cast against Euxitheus. As he succinctly puts it, "we were all astounded" (57.13).

Now, this is a very strange story. Here is a man whose father had, on his account, held public office, submitted to the attendant examinations of his status and conduct, and had himself passed a previous review of the deme register (about which more follows). Beyond his father's record, Euxitheus himself had been nominated and drawn lots for the priesthood of Heracles, held civic office, dedicated shields to Athena and been honored by his fellow demesmen for doing so, and, finally, served as both phratriarch and demarch in the deme. Though he was duly enrolled on the deme register, he finds himself unanimously rejected by his demesmen and fighting for his freedom and status before a court. He believes that the judges will find it at the very least plausible that the vote in the deme could be rigged in the most transparently fraudulent manner. In his defense, he brings into court a host of citizen witnesses who swear to be his relatives, as well as other witnesses from his *genos*, phratry, and deme who also support his account of his identity. Moreover, Halimus, the deme in question, is very small – only 73 members were present to vote on the scrutiny of the register. How is it possible that in such a face-to-face community, which possessed written records of membership, there could be so much controversy as to the most fundamental social question of who one was? To answer this question, let us look closer at both the arguments against Euxitheus, the speaker, and the strategy he employs in his defense.

The arguments employed by Eubulides against Euxitheus attack his parentage on both sides. Eubulides apparently claims that Euxitheus' father was not Athenian because he spoke with a foreign accent. Of his mother, his opponents claim that she was of servile status because she peddled ribbons in the agora and had also worked as a wet nurse. Euxitheus employs both defensive and offensive strategies to combat these allegations.

In regard to his father, Euxitheus responds that his father had been captured while fighting for Athens abroad, and after long servitude was ransomed and brought back to Athens, hence the slight accent. He supports this allegation with witnesses and then brings forward additional testimony from his father's surviving relatives on both sides, who all swear that he was Athenian on both sides of his family and of citizen status. To reinforce this argument, Euxitheus introduces what he claims is decisive testimony from members of his *genos*, phratry, and deme (Demosthenes 57.24):

> You have heard the testimony given by my relatives and members of my *genos*, phratry, and deme, who are the proper persons to be called to testify. And from this you may learn whether a man who has this support is a citizen or alien. . . . Since my father while he was living and I myself at present were clearly put to the test before all the groups to which each one of you belongs [viz., phratry, family,

deme, *genos*], how can it be, how can it be possible that all these
men have been suborned and are not in truth my relatives?

As to his mother, Euxitheus defends against the insinuations of ser-
vility based on her economic activity by pointing out that poverty has
forced many women to take up menial work in the agora and fields
(57.35). He notes that the law protects them from abuse on this account
by establishing penalties for reproaching any male or female citizen with
working in the agora. He asks the judges not to let their prejudices about
poverty and citizenship cloud their judgment and repeatedly reminds
them that poverty has nothing to do with birth: "For even if a nurse
is a lowly thing, I do not avoid the truth. For it is not our being poor
that would mark us as wrongdoers, but our not being citizens. And
the present trial has to do not with our fortune or money, but with
our descent" (57.45). These passages are extremely interesting from a
variety of social historical perspectives, but of importance for present
purposes is the way in which reputation, gossip, and inferences from
everyday behavior can be used to support judgments about one's civic
identity. If one or one's parents are seen doing such and such, then one
cannot be a citizen. The speaker clearly expects this kind of argument
to have a powerful appeal to the judges, and he devotes a substantial
part of the oration to trying to counter it.

As he did with his father, Euxitheus rehearses his mother's genealogy
on both sides and introduces the testimony of many witnesses to support
his claims. He then goes on the offensive and attacks Eubulides' motives
and character in rather interesting ways. Having already argued that
Eubulides had corrupted the scrutiny of the deme registers, he next
explains how this was part of a larger pattern of questionable activity
that goes back to the previous generation. Having claimed that his father
had held office, Euxitheus asks how the demesmen would have passed
him in his scrutiny if they had known him to be an alien. Further,
he argues, when Antiphilus, Eubulides' father, was demarch, the deme
register disappeared and a scrutiny was held in which no one questioned
his father's citizenship (57.26–7). This disappearance, we are told, was
part of a plot to admit certain aliens to the deme (for money) and to expel
certain others – all of whom the courts supposedly restored, save one
(57.59–61). Euxitheus continues this diatribe with an argument from
probability: even though Eubulides' father was his father's enemy, the

vote for the citizenship of Euxitheus' father was unanimous in favor. Is it likely, he implies, that an enemy would have desisted from voting against someone he knew to be an alien? Then, in the next generation of this inherited feud, when Eubulides saw the *dēmos* in a stir about those who had bought their way onto the citizen roles, he saw his chance to take vengeance on *his* enemy.

This enmity may explain Eubulides' action, but how does it explain the unanimous vote against Euxitheus' citizenship? Euxitheus claims, first of all, that Halimus is the most corrupt of all Athenian demes and that many men have been unjustly expelled. The manifest injustice of these expulsions is revealed, he claims, by the fact that they were expelled even while many of their closest blood relatives remained in the deme untroubled (57.58). Then Euxitheus explains that when he was demarch, he incurred the enmity of many influential demesmen because he forced them to pay rents they owed for using sacred land and because he prosecuted them for embezzlement of deme funds. The way he delays this accusation until quite late in the oration reveals, perhaps, his reluctance to admit that he may have been as active in pursuing vendettas against his enemies as they were against him. He caps his argument in an interesting way when he asserts that in revenge, his enemies chiseled out his name from the honorary decree passed by the deme when he dedicated shields to Athena (57.64).

This, like the whole argument about corruption in the deme, calls into question the value of written records. They can mysteriously disappear, they can be subverted, and, finally, they can be fraudulently altered and effaced.[10] In a way, the cumulative argument of the whole oration is that the only reliable and definitive evidence of identity is what people are willing to say about one under oath. As Euxitheus says to the judges, "Let each one of you consider in what other way he could prove that people are his kinsmen than in the way in which I have proved it: by having them give testimony under oath and showing that they have been my kinsmen from the beginning" (57.56).

The typical reaction to questions of status and identity (marriage, citizenship, public service, etc.) in our society is to refer to documents and official records, fingerprints, DNA, dental records, and to scientific

---

[10] Of course, although written records are, as this oration shows, by no means foolproof, those who wish to falsify the past must nevertheless find a way of dealing with them.

proof of their accuracy. In this case, however, where the documents that are supposed to resolve controversy about identity are suspected of being subject to the very social forces that bring identity into question, the only sure solution is to fall back on the principle that one is who one's associates say one is. Reputation and communal knowledge, the media of an oral culture, are the ultimate arbiters of citizenship even where an administrative process and official records exist to provide a formal, public answer to such questions. In his peroration, Euxitheus imagines for the judges a conversation in which he enacts the interrogation of a public scrutiny: "Sir, who was your father? – My father? Thucritus. – Are there relatives to testify for him? – Certainly: first, four cousins; then, the son of a cousin; then, those who are married to female cousins," and so on, through deme, phratry, *genos*, and then the same on the mother's side. Euxitheus asks the court, "How could I prove my case more justly or convincingly?" (57.67).

How, indeed? In the demes of Athens, at least as portrayed in this oration, one is utterly dependent upon one's standing in one's community to maintain one's claims to membership in the polis. Rivalry, enmity, and conflict could lead to attacks not only upon one's conduct but also upon one's identity and status as a citizen. Despite written records, despite a lifetime of living in and serving the community, one could find oneself fighting to preserve one's name, identity, social existence, and freedom. In that struggle the only hope one has is that one's kin, friends, and associates will speak on one's behalf. These mutual dependencies create a powerful nexus for social control and the repression of deviant behavior. One may not rest secure by the mere fact that one's name appears on the roll of citizens, for ultimately one's identity rests upon one's reputation and relations with one's peers. Euxitheus' entire case rests upon the claim that there is no other valid means of proof.

That the argumentative strategies of *Against Eubulides* are not idiosyncratic appears from the only other surviving oration dealing with the same issue. Oration 12 of Isaeus, *In Defense of Euphiletus*,[11] apparently arises out of the same review of the deme registers. In the small deme of Erchia, the demesmen had excluded a man named Euphiletus.

---

[11] Preserved only by Dionysius of Halicarnassus (*Isaeus* 17), this speech appears to represent just part of the defendant's case.

According to the speaker, the case was twice arbitrated and both times Euphiletus won. The demesmen persisted in their refusal to recognize him as a citizen and Euphiletus appealed, hence this trial. The speaker acknowledges that many citizens adopt aliens as their children, either because they are childless or because of poverty they accept money and anticipate future benefits. Neither of these conditions obtains in the present case, we are told, because Euphiletus' father has two other sons and is well off. Hence, the speaker (Euphiletus' half brother) argues, is it likely that his father would do such a thing or that he, the half brother, would support Euphiletus if he were a stranger, thereby diminishing his own share of the patrimony?

This is also a strange case, in part because of the apparent obstinacy of the demesmen, in part because it seems bizarre that someone in these circumstances could be disenfranchised. Of course, as usual, we only hear one side of the case, but Euphiletus' brother tells us that Euphiletus was inscribed as a citizen, and that his father, mother, brothers, and all his other relatives and fellow phratrymen support his claim. Furthermore, unlike the speech *Against Eubulides*, there appears to be no question as to the citizenship of the parents. The opponents admit that the speaker's stepmother, Euphiletus' mother, is a citizen. Nonetheless, Euphiletus finds himself before the court, having wagered his freedom to try to prove his identity. His brother tells the judges that in such a case there is only one valid method of proof, and that is the testimony of the family: "I should like to hear from the most respectable of our opponents whether he could produce any sources of evidence to prove that *he* is an Athenian other than those which we have introduced in support of Euphiletus. I do not think that he could argue anything other than that his mother was a citizen and married a citizen. And he would produce relatives to testify on his behalf that he was speaking the truth" (Isaeus 12.7). In this case too, the speaker alleges that enmity within the deme is what actually accounts for the conflict. Whether this is true, or whether the opponents' argument, namely, that Euphiletus is illegitimate, is true, we cannot know. What does appear certain, however, is that the written documentation of citizenship was not independent of the social and political force field within which citizenship was contested according to particular patterns of rivalry and conflict. Ultimately, litigation over civic identity could only boil down to – as usual in Athenian litigation – whose story the judges found more persuasive. Citizenship, we might claim with only slight hyperbole, was not legally inscribed, but rather rhetorically constructed.

WRITTEN DOCUMENTS AND INHERITANCE

I want now to survey two inheritance cases where wills play an important role. We will see how these cases also raise issues of status and identity similar to the ones already discussed.

In Isaeus 4, *On the Estate of Nicostratus*, the deceased was a mercenary who had been absent from Athens for many years. A number of claimants apparently rushed forward, but the present suit involves the two finalists in the struggle over the inheritance. One of these, Chariades, alleged that he had served with Nicostratus and produced a will under which he was adopted and made heir. Hagnon and Hagnotheus, on the other hand, claim that the will is a forgery and that they, as first cousins of the deceased, are the next of kin. How is the status of the will resolved? We only have the case made on behalf of Hagnon and Hagnotheus, but this at least indicates what Isaeus considered the best rhetorical strategy that could be adopted in such a situation. Apart from suggesting that it is unlikely that Nicostratus knew Chariades well enough to make him his heir, Isaeus attacks the very possibility of verifying the authenticity of a will; that is, he suggests that documents are by their very nature unreliable, whereas kinship can be independently verified. When it is a matter of wills, how can the court evaluate who is telling the truth, "since the party against whom they bear witness is dead, the relatives know nothing of the facts, and the method of refuting the evidence is by no means exact" (Isaeus 4.12–13)? He then talks about how easy it is to alter a will or substitute another: "For the witnesses will have no more knowledge than anyone else whether the will produced is that which they were summoned to attest. Since it is possible to deceive those who were present when the will was made, how much easier to attempt to deceive you who know nothing of the matter?" (4.14).[12] Isaeus adds other arguments, all of which go to show that writings may be forged or tampered with and that there is no reliable method of authenticating them. Better, then, to give an estate to kin, for their identity can be readily established. Or can it?

[12] On the role of witnesses in such litigation, see Humphreys 1985.

The problem is that identity can be almost as readily contested. In fact, Chariades argues that not only does he have the will, but Hagnon and Hagnotheus are not actually related to the deceased. They are, he claims, in reality the sons not of Thrasymachus, the relative of Nicostratus, but of a man named Smicrus. Both sides will, of course, produce witnesses to confirm under oath their respective proposed genealogies. This is not surprising. Among previous claimants to the estate, a certain Demosthenes had claimed to be a nephew, and another man had produced a three-year-old "son" of Nicostratus, although Nicostratus had not visited Athens for eleven years (4.8). What Isaeus really means, I think, is not that identity can be definitively proved, since identity, too, he tacitly admits, can be established only by witnesses. Rather, the judges are in a far better position to evaluate the veracity of testimony offered about identity, whereas the authenticity of a will is necessarily much more indeterminate.

In speech 9, *On the Estate of Astyphilus*, Isaeus again attacks the authenticity of a will. The speaker, half brother of the deceased, claims to inherit the estate as next of kin, but he is opposed by Cleon, a cousin of the deceased, who claims that the deceased made a will adopting his son. The speaker introduces witnesses who claim that Cleon went around looking for collaborators, offering to produce a will naming anyone who would share the estate with him. Apart from this, the case is largely based upon arguments from probability. The central thrust of the case is that Astyphilus could not have made this will because he summoned none of his *philoi* as witnesses to the will. He extends this argument by saying that those who were witnesses were unknown to the family and, moreover, Cleon himself was in a state of enmity with Astyphilus, so his son was a very unlikely object of benefaction. The part of the oration that is of particular interest here is the argument about the witnesses. Isaeus raises the issue of how someone who wanted to make a will might ensure that his testamentary wishes would be upheld by a court. That is, the starting point of any testamentary act should be the recognition that the status of the document will be attacked. How, then, to prepare for this? If Astyphilus had wanted to make a will, "he would be assured that all those intentions would best be effected not if he made his will without the attestation of his relatives, but if he summoned first his kin, then his fellow demesmen and members of his phratry, and, finally, as many as possible of his friends and acquaintances" (Isaeus 9.7–8). This would be quite a crowd, as Isaeus acknowledges later, when he says that "no one ought to be ashamed of summoning the largest possible number of witnesses" when the law allows for testamentary disposition (9.13). Since Astyphilus did none of this, but summoned, allegedly, a few chance persons, "is there any probability that the will is genuine?" (9.12–13).

In these inheritance cases, there is evidently considerable insecurity about how the validity of a document can be established. The only way envisaged of establishing validity is by embedding the document in a web of social relations that can give it social meaning and make it appear real. The document cannot stand alone. To recognize it as valid requires authentication by oral testimony of the deceased's familial and social network. Furthermore, this testimony must concern not just the document but the whole familial context out of which the document arises – these factors appear in all seven speeches of Isaeus where inheritance on the basis of a will is contested.[13] But what this really means is that the will must be supported by the family not as just a legal document but as the right way to dispose of the estate. If the family is unhappy with the provisions made by their deceased relative, their denial of the will's authenticity will act to "correct" his decision simply because *they* are the ones who know. Hence the conflict among kin groups that we find in so many orations. In Isaeus 5, *On the Estate of Dicaeogenes*, where two wills are in play, both are rejected by the courts.

Inheritance cases often extend beyond discussions of the authenticity of documents to the authenticity of claims about social identity. For both documents and social identity, as in the controversies over citizenship, the ultimate recourse is to the persuasiveness of what one's friends, relatives, and associates will say about the web of relations and transactions in which the particular legal matter at issue is embedded. The spoken word as the medium of informal knowledge, reputation, social control, and legal argument overshadows the official or private legal document.

WRITTEN DOCUMENTS AND COMMERCIAL TRANSACTIONS

A brief examination of another, very specialized, legal context may help to complicate usefully the analysis of attitudes towards legal documents advanced thus far. By the fourth century, Athenian commercial law,

---

[13] Isaeus 1, 3, 4, 5, 6, 9, 11.

particularly in the area of maritime loans, had developed a considerable degree of sophistication.[14] This is not surprising given Athens' role as a major commercial center and its dependence upon imported foodstuffs to feed its large population. Maritime loans were the principle legal and financial mechanism by which the trading ventures upon which such commerce depended were facilitated. Because of the increasing complexity of such maritime loan contracts, it is natural that those involved in such endeavors appreciated the advantages that writing offered to help mitigate the risks and uncertainty that inevitably attached to maritime trade. It is fairly clear that by the end of the fifth century or the beginning of the fourth, written contracts had become the foundation for these transactions.[15]

In light of the analysis offered above of the reception of written documents in Athenian courts, one might well ask how such written contracts could have significantly increased the security of lenders. The fact is that in order to do so the juridical evaluation of such contracts had to be removed from the normal context of litigation and anchored in a more receptive and secure setting. Although it is not possible to determine precisely when they were established, special maritime courts (*dikai emporikai*) were functioning in Athens by the beginning of the fourth century.[16] These courts, employing judges who specialized only in these maritime transactions, provided a venue where, with the necessary speed and rigor, commercial disputes could be adjudicated in a manner that would facilitate rather than obstruct this lifeline of Athenian commerce. It is a striking characteristic of the Athenian legal system that, seemingly recognizing its own shortcomings, it was able to construct specialized legal institutions, like the maritime courts or the homicide court of the Areopagus, where different rules and procedures applied commensurate with the perceived importance of the subjects of litigation. The maritime courts were also unique in that foreigners could litigate there as well, provided that their cases met normal jurisdictional requirements.

---

[14] On Athenian commercial practices generally, see E. E. Cohen 1992. On the system of maritime transactions and the courts which adjudicated disputes about them, see E. E. Cohen 1973.

[15] E. E. Cohen 1973: 129–36.

[16] On the development of these courts, with full references to the sources and secondary literature, see E. E. Cohen 1973: 158–98.

The way in which the maritime courts used writing to enhance the security and sophistication of financial transactions is evident from one of their defining characteristics: the jurisdiction of these courts was limited to cases in which a written maritime contract had been employed by the parties.[17] Not only was this requirement reflected in legal practice, but it tended to ensure that written instruments were used in all such transactions. To see how such contracts fared in the crucible of litigation we may turn to one of the handful of maritime cases that have been preserved.

Against Lacritus (Demosthenes 35) involves, like most of the surviving maritime loan cases, a challenge to the jurisdiction of the court. In this case, it is based upon the fact that the contract had been made by the deceased brother of the defendant, Lacritus, who is being sued as his brother's heir, having taken over his brother's estate and, hence, his obligations. In other words, it appears that where a party is being sued for nonperformance (i.e., failure to repay) the best defense strategy is to try to get the case out of the maritime courts in the first place. The reason is clear. In a court whose jurisdiction is based generally upon the universal commercial practice of employing written loan contracts, and in particular upon the existence of a written contract in the case at hand, arguments casting doubt upon the reliability of written documents, as opposed to the oral testimony of friends and colleagues, are not likely to be terribly persuasive. Accordingly, Androcles, the prosecutor and speaker in *Against Lacritus*, bases his whole case upon the authority of the written document and displays none of the insecurity about the status of writing that we saw in the citizenship and inheritance contexts. Unlike the orations discussed above, where written records or documents were treated as inferior to the testimony of friends and relatives about the parties and their transactions, in *Against Lacritus* the written contract is practically the sole focus of the argument from the beginning to the end of the oration.

Early on in the oration, Androcles has the whole document read to the judges (Demosthenes 35.10–14). This is followed immediately by the reading of two brief depositions that affirm that the contract had been duly deposited for safekeeping. The ensuing argument again and again insists upon the written document as the sole criterion by which the

---

[17] E. E. Cohen 1973: 129–36.

behavior of the defendant must be evaluated. Reviewing the provisions
of the contract in detail, Androcles affirms that "they stand written in
the agreement" (35.19).[18] Having completed his review of the contract,
he claims that in the case of maritime contracts, the provisions "are
considered by all men to be final" (35.27). Having the agreement read
in its entirety again (35.37), he argues that the only recourse available
to the defendant is to claim that he did not borrow the money at all
or that he paid it back, or to assert that "maritime contracts are not
binding" (35.43). In other words, he expects the judges to agree that
the written terms completely define the relations of the parties. What
his opponent in fact argues is that the case does not belong before the
maritime court at all because he was not a party to the contract. What
Androcles does not anticipate is that his opponent will challenge the
status of the document.

In the inheritance and citizenship cases discussed above, written
documents were subsidiary to the oral testimony that the parties used
as the principal foundation for their claims. It was asserted that the most
reliable way of arriving at a just verdict was to judge the testimony of
friends, neighbors, relatives, and so on. In *Against Lacritus*, on the other
hand, there is no felt need to introduce testimony that claims personal
knowledge of the details of the transaction and its obligations as a way
of showing that those obligations in fact had been incurred. It is the
document itself, read out twice to the judges and discussed provision by
provision, that "speaks" authoritatively. That the document "speaks"
is not just my account of the matter; in his conclusion, Androcles claims
that "the written contract ... testified" that he lent the money for the
venture in question (35.50).[19] In a sense, we have come full circle: a
written document "speaks as a witness" because the spoken claims of
human witnesses are unnecessary.

In the final section of the oration (35.50–6), Androcles argues that a
man who nullifies written contracts harms the entire polis as well as the
aggrieved individual, for it is the authoritative validity of these agree-
ments that makes maritime commerce possible. In the maritime courts
in particular, whose very existence and jurisdiction depend upon the

---

[18] γέγραπται μὲν ταῦτα ἐν τῆι συγγραφῆι. Cf. 35.18, 21, 24, 52, etc. for similar
statements.

[19] ἡ συγγραφὴ ἐβοήθει ... καὶ ἐμαρτύρει.

institution of writing, such claims were likely to be persuasive. The emergence of these specialized courts at the same time as the development of the legal instruments that were the basis of their exclusive jurisdiction testifies to the way in which the social and legal appreciation of the role that writing might assume was circumscribed and emergent rather than general and complete. These courts could not have functioned if they allowed doubts about the reliability of written documents to undermine the definitive status of contracts. The narrowness and uniqueness of this legal sphere in which writing might prevail underscore both the ambivalence that reigned in other contexts and the advantage that ambivalence gave to litigants whose cases depended upon nullifying the authority of written documents. At the same time, the fact that such divergent practices in regard to the status of writing could coexist in the same society and the same legal system testifies to the complexity of the role of writing in this society, whose culture still revolved so centrally around the force and persuasive potential of the spoken word.

5

Literacy and the Charlatan in Ancient Greek Medicine

Lesley Dean-Jones

O
utside of the medical treatises themselves, the existence of untrained individuals posing as doctors in ancient Greece is not attested before the fourth century B.C.E. I argue that their appearance in the fourth century is due in part to the early and widespread use of writing among the bona fide medical profession and that the success of some of these charlatans, however circumscribed or short-lived, contributed to the suspicion of medicine that arose among some in the ancient world. The ancient Greeks expected their *iatroi* – "physicians" – to have undergone extensive medical training with an experienced physician, and most *iatroi* did so because it was difficult to make a living as an *iatros* without such training. This is true notwithstanding the fact that many educated laymen took an interest in medical matters, that nonphysicians wrote and spoke on physiology and

---

Note on citations and translations of the Hippocratic treatises: Many, but not all, of the treatises of the Hippocratic Corpus are readily available in English in the Loeb Classical Library. My references are to the Loeb editions where they exist; I cite the gynecological treatises by the book and chapter divisions of the complete edition of Littré (Paris, 1839–62; reprinted in Amsterdam, 1962–73). The translations used here come from the Loeb series. They are based on, or have been modified to reflect, the text of the *Corpus Medicorum Graecorum* (Berlin, 1927–), the standard edition where available.

pathology, and that some individuals without medical training could pose as doctors and dupe patients for a greater or lesser period of time, circumstances that exist in our own culture.[1]

In particular, my argument is the following:

1. Natural, empirical medicine was accepted as a *technē*, and *iatroi* were respected from the earliest times and not just in surgery. Natural medicine was mainstream in the fifth century.
2. The status of medicine increases in the fourth century to that of a *technē* par excellence, but at the same time criticism of medicine first appears in nonmedical texts.
3. This is due, in part, not to a greater failure rate among physicians because they were beginning to deal more widely with nonsurgical cases, but to the appearance of individuals who could pose as *iatroi* with some success without undergoing the traditional extensive training.
4. The traditional medical training was intrafamily, oral, and difficult to convey in written form, yet technical medical treatises are amongst the earliest prose works in Greece. Many of these, however, are insufficient for training without oral supplementation, and their appearance is to be explained by the fact that in the fifth century more individuals from nontraditional medical families started to enter the profession and needed aids to mitigate their lack of training from childhood.
5. Making a living as a teacher of medicine was new in the fifth century because previously not enough nonfamily members wanted to be apprenticed to make it feasible. In the hope of attracting pupils, not patients, the new breed of teachers produced treatises that do not need oral supplementation and were intended for a general audience.
6. Most people who wanted to be *iatroi* wanted the best training available because increased efficacy led to a larger clientele, and

---

[1] A fair number of patients in the Western world seek out alternative medicine and deny the efficacy of scientific medicine without seriously jeopardizing its mainstream status. A recent study found that 75 of the 125 medical schools in the United States offer some form of education on alternative medicine (Wetzel, Eisenberg, and Kaptchuk 1998). I do not claim that ancient Greek medicine functioned just as it does in our own society, but the attempt to correct this naive view has led to a depiction of the social status of ancient medicine as differing more from that of our own scientific medicine than is the case.

having teachers of a high status meant a greater chance of winning a position as a public physician.

7. The availability of previously restricted knowledge led some to try to practice medicine simply on the basis of book learning. This kind of charlatan was not possible before literacy. Generally, he would not be as successful as a properly trained *iatros*.

WRITTEN TEXTS AND THE STATUS OF MEDICINE IN GREECE

Earlier work on literacy in ancient Greek medicine has supported the conclusion reached by Cornelius Celsus in the first century C.E., namely, that one of the most far-reaching effects of literacy was the development of internal medicine.[2] Modern scholars trace this development to the capacity of literate doctors to keep lists of symptoms and syndromes that could be ever added to, refined, and subdivided. But Celsus suggests a rather different cause (*De Medicina*, proem 5–7):

> No distinguished men practiced the art of medicine until literary studies (*litterarum disciplina*) began to be pursued with more attention, which more than anything else are a necessity for the spirit, but at the same time are bad for the body. . . . Healing was needed especially by those whose bodily strength had been weakened by restless thinking and night-watching.

From Celsus' point of view, there was no *need* for internal medicine before the advent of literacy.[3]

Of course, as Celsus himself knew, medicine had been acknowledged as a *technē* for several centuries before writing appeared, though he says it was used solely for the treatment of wounds. Most references to medicine in early literature are indeed surgical in nature,[4] but arguments from silence are risky at best, and there are sufficient allusions to internal medicine in early poetry to suggest that the activities of *iatroi* were not entirely surgical in nature. Homer says that everyone in Egypt is a "knowledgeable physician" (*epistamenos iatros*) because the land yields so many drugs (*Odyssey* 4.230–31). The poet Arctinus of the

---

[2] Kudlien 1967; Jouanna 1974; Lonie 1983; Miller 1990.

[3] The idea that sophisticated lifestyles in general led to increased medical intervention is a frequent motif in the medical literature.

[4] See Kudlien 1967 for the argument that internal medicine developed comparatively late in ancient Greece.

middle to late seventh century is said to attribute surgery to Machaon and a "knowledge of hidden diseases" to his brother Podalirius.[5] At the beginning of the sixth century, Solon describes *iatroi* as "those who undertake the task of Paieon with all his drugs" (13.57–62 West), and at the end of that century, Democedes is recorded as treating a spreading tumor (*phyma*) in Atossa's breast (Herodotus 3.133–4). Early in the fifth century, Pindar has Asclepius initiate the art of medicine using drugs to treat internal ailments as well as performing surgery (*Pythian* 3.52–3). It should also be noted that at least some Greeks of the classical period believed that internal medicine had had a long history. From the vantage point of the end of the fifth century, the author of the treatise *On Ancient Medicine* argued that medicine had a continuous history beginning in the distant past, when men lived as beasts. Therefore, although literacy may have promoted the elaboration of internal medicine, treating internal ailments had been part of the job of *iatroi* from a much earlier period.[6]

An *iatros* was distinguished from other sorts of healers in employing only natural therapies.[7] The separation of natural from supernatural healing is represented among the gods themselves in the *Iliad*. Paieon, the divine doctor of the gods and the god of medicine, heals the wounds of Ares and Hades in the manner of a human doctor rather than by the divine touch of his hand, as Dione heals Aphrodite.[8] After describing

---

5 Scholium to *Iliad* 11.515, Eustathius on *Iliad* 11.514.

6 Indications of natural explanations for internal pathology can also be found in early poetry, for example, the symptoms deployed by Sappho to describe the intense emotions of unfulfilled desire (frag. 31 Campbell), and Alcaeus' recommendation to "keep lungs moist at the rising of the Dog Star" because the Dog Star "withers men's brain and knees" (frag. 347 Campbell). Drying diseases are among the seasonal ailments associated with the Dog Star in Chapter 10 of the Hippocratic treatise *Airs, Waters, Places*.

7 This excludes priests, seers, soothsayers, or anyone else who, whatever else he did, healed by supernatural as well as natural means; see Lonie 1983: 147; King 1998: 40. Dodds 1951: 167–8 n. 72 says that already by Homeric times the roles of *iatros* and *mantis* were distinct, and calls the figure of the shaman a "throwback." Aeschylus uses the term *iatromantis* of Apis and Apollo precisely to indicate that they are functioning as something more than *iatroi* (*Suppliant Women* 264, *Eumenides* 62). Herodotus 4.68–9 calls the healers summoned to treat the Scythian king *manteis*, "seers," rather than *iatroi*, because they use divinatory rather than natural means.

8 *Iliad* 5.401–2, 416–17, 899–904. The *pharmakon* that Paieon uses is described as acting as fig juice does on milk, that is, as a clotting agent. This is an accurate

doctors as being of the race of Paieon, Solon says that "the simple touch of a hand" can sometimes succeed where *iatroi* fail. Sophocles has Ajax state, "No wise *iatros* sings incantations over a wound that needs the knife" (*Ajax* 582–3). Empedocles is sometimes cited as an example of a shamanlike figure who would be considered an *iatros* by the ancient Greeks, but it seems unlikely that he ever actually practiced as a doctor.[9] Recounting an example of Empedocles' healing, Heracleides called him "both a doctor and a seer" (*kai iētron kai mantin*), and the fragment in which Empedocles claims to teach "all the drugs which are a defense to ward off evils and old age" is introduced by a reference to his sorcery (*goēteuonti*). Empedocles' supernatural methods are linked to something other than his being an *iatros*.[10]

Scholars agree that in the preliterate period physicians were held in high esteem as craftsmen.[11] In the *Iliad*, Idomeneus gives voice to the respect in which doctors were held (9.514–15): "an *iatros* is a man worth many other men in cutting out shafts, dressing arrow wounds."[12] An inscribed epitaph of about 530 B.C.E. reads "the memorial to the skill of Aineias, best of physicians,"[13] and when the Greek physician Democedes was captured in 522 B.C.E. and held with Darius' other prisoners, he did not want it known that he was a doctor lest he be deemed so valuable that Darius would never let him go (Herodotus 3.130–1). It was his profession, not his name, that he thought would make him attractive.

By the time we get to the classical period, however, we are faced with something of a paradox. In some ways medicine is, if anything, held in even higher regard. In Aeschylus' *Prometheus Bound* (478–83) Prometheus says he has shown men remedies to ward off all illnesses

---

empirical observation that is used by the author of *Diseases* 4.52 as an analogy for the clotting of bodily humors and of which Aristotle makes much use in his embryology. Fig juice is used in the Hippocratic treatise *Regimen in Acute Diseases (Appendix)* 59 to staunch a nosebleed, though in fact the latex in fig juice causes it to act as an anticoagulant (Majno 1975: 152).

[9] Inwood 1992: 7.

[10] DK 31 B111, Diogenes Laertius 8.61, 59.

[11] "The Greek doctor . . . did not *need* to become literate in order to win professional and social status" (Lonie 1983: 148).

[12] The fact that other men can do the same things *after a fashion* does not detract from the status of medicine as a *technē*, pace Nutton 1995: 15.

[13] *Journal of Hellenic Studies* 29 (1909): 154.

and this was the greatest of the *technai* he bestowed. Sophocles has his chorus sing that man "has contrived refuge from illness once beyond all cure" (*Antigone* 361–2). Xenophon says any effective general has to have some knowledge of medicine (*Education of Cyrus* 1.6.14–17), and every cultured layman was supposed to know its basic principles.[14] Many doctors too seem to have a higher status than simple craftsmen. In Plato's *Symposium*, the physician Eryximachus is depicted as being a member of the Athenian elite. Cities are paying for public physicians; doctors are exempted from civic and military service.[15] Yet at the same time, it has been felt that the status of medicine as a craft comes under challenge. The Hippocratic treatise *Law* opens with this claim:

> Medicine is the most distinguished of all the arts, but through the ignorance of those who practice it, and of those who casually judge such practitioners, it is now of all the arts by far the least esteemed.

And *Regimen in Acute Diseases* 8 says:

> Yet the art as a whole has a very bad name among laymen, so that there is thought to be no art of medicine at all.

In the early classical period, evidence for the precarious status of medicine is found almost exclusively in the Hippocratic Corpus itself. *On the Art*, avowedly composed to refute those who denigrated medicine, is perhaps the most oft-cited text to show that medicine's social status was in crisis in the fifth century. However, the treatise begins

> Some there are who have made an art of vilifying the arts, though they consider not that they are accomplishing the object I mention, but that they are making a display of their own knowledge. . . . As for the attacks of this kind that are made on the other arts, let them be repelled by those who care to do so and can, and with regard to those points about which they care; the present discussion will oppose those who thus invade the art of medicine.

The passage shows that the attacks on medicine envisaged by the author are not motivated solely, or even primarily, by a concerted attack on *medicine's* claim to be a *technē*. It is simply one among many *technai* that provide grist to the mill of polemical speakers. The first argument the author deploys against the detractors of medicine is simply that the existence of the art of medicine is sufficient rebuttal in itself, and

---

[14] Jaeger 1944: 3.3–45.   [15] Cohn-Haft 1956; Pleket 1983.

he ends his text by saying that the achievements of doctors are a better defense of medicine than his words.[16] Many scholars believe that the treatise was written by a sophist rather than a practicing physician, and it is known that Protagoras published model speeches demonstrating how to deal with criticisms against wrestling and other fields that the Greeks generally accepted as *technai* (Plato, *Sophist* 232d). That is, Protagoras apparently demonstrated how one could use the *technē* of rhetoric (i.e., the field that was fighting hard to establish itself among the more traditional *technai*) to defend the more traditional *technai* should they be attacked by rhetoric.[17] The adversaries of *On the Art of Medicine* may well have been composed more of straw than of flesh.

Outside of the medical literature itself, negative portrayals of *iatroi* do not appear until the fourth century. When Aristophanes mentions the Athenian physician Pittalus, he does so without any hint of sarcasm. For instance, Philocleon, after citing the proverb "let each man practice the *technē* he knows," tells a man he has assaulted to go to Pittalus with his injuries rather than bring a lawsuit (*Wasps* 1431-2). When Aristophanes does make a joke against doctors, it is to comment on their greed rather than their incompetence, as when the blind god of wealth is only taken to Asclepius' shrine to be cured because there are no *iatroi* left in Athens since the curtailment of their fee.[18]

---

[16] In light of the derogatory comparison of those who write about medicine to those who actually practice it, it is interesting to note the frequency with which writing is used as an analogy for medicine. *Regimen* 1.23 compares medicine to writing, as does *Places in Man* 41. *On Ancient Medicine* 20 says, "All that has been written on nature has less to do with medicine than with writing"; see Craik 1998: 77, 200. Unlike medicine, writing does not require a knowledge of the opportune moment, *kairos*. Isocrates 3.12–13 opposes rhetoric, which must consider *kairos*, to writing; cf. also Empedocles DK 31 B23.

[17] Mann (forthcoming) revives and augments Gomperz's thesis that *On the Art of Medicine* is in fact a work of Protagoras. He demonstrates that the treatise can be seen as a series of rhetorical *topoi* that with a minimum of revision can be pressed into service to defend other *technai*.

[18] *Plutus* 406–8. *Plutus* was performed in 388; the cult of Asclepius had been introduced into Athens in 420. Whatever this passage may or may not imply about public physicians, it implies that at the beginning of the fourth century a patient would normally seek treatment from an *iatros* before going to Asclepius. Cf. Parker 1996: 184: "The truest explanation for the rise of Asclepius may be that he was, as it were, in partnership with Hippocrates." See Wickkiser forthcoming for a detailed examination of these issues.

In contrast, doctors in New Comedy are often depicted as buffoons and charlatans.[19]

Similarly, in forensic oratory, there are no clearly negative allusions to *iatroi* in the early period. At one point, Antiphon considers whether a victim of an assault may have died from the incompetence of the attending physician rather than as a result of the assault itself (4.2.4). But this is not a general distrust of doctors; the speaker adds that other doctors had beforehand warned against treatment at the hands of this particular doctor. Two generations later, however, Aeschines and Demosthenes do make disparaging comments about the profession as a whole.[20]

The distrust of medicine in the fourth century is by no means universal. Plato invokes medicine with increasing frequency as the paradigm *technē* to provide an analogy for true statesmanship and philosophy. Aristotle, arguing that one should not claim to be wiser than the laws even if they occasionally seem to be mistaken, cites a proverb and explains (*Rhetoric* 1375b20–3): "There is no advantage to being smarter than the doctor; for a mistake by a physician does not do so much harm as becoming accustomed to disobey one who is in charge."

The argument that internal medicine was a development of literacy has been used to explain the contrasting views of physicians in the fourth century.[21] As long as it stayed with the tried and true methods of surgery, the argument goes, medicine retained the respect of its public; once it ventured into uncharted territory where opinions on causes, effects, and remedies multiplied exponentially, it ceased to retain the unity of a *technē*. At the same time, it was this very examination of causes that raised medicine's intellectual profile. But while the physician–author of *Regimen in Acute Diseases* ascribes medicine's unpopularity to the fact that doctors disagree (8), he does not imply that this is something that had come about recently, anymore than it had in divination.[22] And the complaints against medicine and doctors

---

[19] See Jacques 1998: xxxix.   [20] Demand 1996.

[21] Kudlien 1967; cf. Lonie 1983: 160.

[22] Divination and medicine are two of the earliest *technai* to be referred to with terms using the -*ikē* suffix (*mantikē*, *iatrikē*), which indicates the noun *technē*, and there are close ties between them. But skepticism of seers appears much earlier and is more widespread than that of doctors. This is due, I think, at least in part to the fact that some *iatroi* could be consistently better than others in a way that no seer could be.

recorded by nonphysicians focus on competency and greed (and, in the *Philogelos*, bad temper), not on the multiplicity of opinions. Nor, with the exception of the author of *On Ancient Medicine*, is there any indication that *iatroi* were perceived as offering a new type of healing or expanding their traditional domain. All indications are that most people accepted the idea of a continuum in medicine from ancient to contemporary times, which does not, of course, preclude the possibility of new developments and improvements. Far from medicine's status being in jeopardy because it was a newcomer in the fifth century, struggling to find acceptance, it would seem that the other traditional forms of healing made opportunistic inroads into caring for the sick by adopting some methods from natural healing. *On the Sacred Disease* 2 comments that, while seizure-type illnesses are the only ones ascribed to divine or supernatural agency, many of the prohibitions advocated by magical healers are those that *iatroi* would prescribe, though the magical healers lack the knowledge and courage to give positive directions. In the fourth century, about two hundred temples of Asclepius were founded,[23] and a large part of his popularity can be traced to his association with natural medicine. Nevertheless, by the end of the fourth century, skepticism of the abilities of ordinary mortals who wielded these methods is expressed more often than it was in the fifth century.

Now, even had physicians in the preliterate period concerned themselves exclusively with surgery, which we have seen was not the case, they could never have expected or achieved a 100 percent success rate. In fact, the scourge of infection, which can kill patients suffering from otherwise nonfatal wounds even today and against which the ancient Greek doctor was powerless, would seem to render survival from a battlefield wound no more likely, in fact less likely, than survival from an internal complaint, many of which are self-correcting. The status of *iatroi* in the preliterate period was not dependent upon complete effectiveness. Solon admitted that their *technē* was not complete and that Aineias could not be called "the best of physicians" if it were not thought possible for some *iatroi* to exceed others in skill. Likewise, the doctors of Aegina whom Democedes was said to have excelled were not always unsuccessful (Herodotus 3.133). The Egyptian doctors who treated Darius unsuccessfully before Democedes intervened were

---

[23] *Princeton Encyclopedia of Classical Sites*, s.v. "Epidauros."

applying what they learned in a bona fide medical training; nobody thought they were *pretending* to be doctors because they were unsuccessful. Similarly, authors in the Hippocratic Corpus refer to doctors who disagree with them or who make mistakes without denying them the status of doctors.[24] In fact, both *On Ancient Medicine* 1 and *On the Art of Medicine* 5 cite the range of ability within the ranks of physicians as evidence that medicine is a *technē*. If all practitioners were similarly effective, these authors say, it would imply that medicine was a matter of chance. And there is room for even a good doctor's success rate to be increased by luck (*Diseases* 1.8).

However, in the Hippocratic Corpus, there are many complaints not only against bad or inexperienced doctors[25] but also against frauds, quacks, and charlatans – called *hoi mē iatroi* or *aniatroi* (literally, "nondoctors") or *alazones* (literally, "boasters").[26] Aristotle defines the *alazōn* as one who pretends "to have distinguished qualities which he possesses either not at all or to a lesser degree than he pretends," and he further subdivides these into those who are *alazones* either because they enjoy boasting for its own sake, desire the glory attached to whatever they boast about, or desire a profit. The latter lay claim to skills "such as both convey some advantage to their neighbors and can escape detection as being nonexistent – e.g., prophetic powers, or philosophical insight, or medical skill."[27] Of course, Aristotle is not saying medicine does not exist any more than he is denying the possibility of philosophic insight. His father was a successful doctor, and he himself wrote a treatise on medicine (unfortunately not extant). He means that people pretend to be doctors if *they* think there is really no skill involved and that they can therefore get away with it.

It has been claimed that in the ancient world it was possible for individuals to assume the status of *iatros* purely on the basis of rhetorical skill because there were no institutionally recognized credentials that

---

[24] E.g., *Regimen in Acute Diseases* 7, *Precepts* 8, *Glands* 14.

[25] E.g., *Epidemics* 2.1.7, 5.95, 7.123, *Joints* 1.

[26] *Regimen in Acute Diseases* 6, *Precepts* 7, *On the Sacred Disease* 2.

[27] *Nicomachean Ethics* 1127a–b. See MacDowell 1990 on the term *alazōn*, confirming that "charlatan" gets closest to the common meaning of the term in the fifth and fourth centuries. It should be noted that Aristophanes never uses this term of doctors, though he does of ambassadors, politicians, sophists, and oracle mongers.

marked off individuals as bona fide doctors.[28] It is the existence of such credentials today that marks off doctors, who may make mistakes and can be sued for malpractice, from charlatans who knowingly pretend to medical knowledge and thereby risk criminal charges, though the actions of both groups could result in the same consequences for the patient. But credentials can be, and with surprising frequency are, forged, and some modern-day charlatans have had successful practices before they were discovered.[29]

The view that there were no charlatans as such in the ancient world rests on the assumption that medical training made little or no difference to an individual's practice and effectiveness as a physician – a view that would be surprising to almost everybody in the culture we are discussing. A physician might not be able to nail a diploma to his wall, but he had to be able to substantiate his training by naming his teachers. Xenophon shows the absurdity of laying claim to a skill without being able to name one's teachers by using the most extreme example he can imagine: applying for the post of public physician while admitting that one had no teachers (*Memorabilia* 4.2.5). It may have been easier for a charlatan in ancient Greece to lie than for a modern charlatan to forge records, but we must assume the ancients recognized the possibility of fraud as well as we do and took steps to corroborate claims when they felt it necessary. The lack of institutionalized credentials meant that it was not illegal for anyone to "hang out a shingle" and make a living as an *iatros*. But it was no more feasible to do that than it was for an untrained individual to make a living (at least for very long) through navigation, though there was no such thing as a pilot's license, or as an architect, though nobody could produce a Bachelor of Architecture degree.

Similarly, although only the best pilots could weather the worst storms (or the best architects build a Parthenon), only the best doctors were successful in the face of the worst illnesses. Lack of such skill

---

[28] Lloyd 1987: 103–4, Nutton 1995: 26.

[29] Of course, patients who feel that they have been cured by these people might object to the label "charlatan" and insist they were true doctors even if they had not received traditional medical training. In this case, the category "charlatan" collapses in our own culture just as it would in ancient Greece, but the general expectation of both cultures is that such success would be atypical.

means one is a poor doctor, not that one is a fraud.[30] Educated people in
the ancient world undoubtedly knew more about ancient medicine than
we do, yet many, if not most (to judge from the existence of public physicians
and the fact that epilepsy is singled out as *the* sacred disease in
comparison to all others), seem to have preferred seeking out the services
of an *iatros* to those of magicians or to treating themselves. The fact that
some people tried and, to a point, succeeded in posing as *iatroi* without
the requisite training does not undermine the utility of such training.[31]

<h3 style="text-align:center">WRITTEN TEXTS AND MEDICAL TRAINING</h3>

Prior to the production of medical texts, other doctors were the only
source of medical training. For the most part, this would be an intrafamily
affair, but nonfamily members could learn the craft either by apprenticing
with a local practitioner, by traveling to a center of medicine
such as Cos, Cnidos, or Croton, or by seeking out a teacher elsewhere.[32]
When Democedes is unable to hide from Darius the fact that he has some
medical knowledge, he pleads that he has a poor knowledge of the art,
having spent some time (*homilēsas*) with a doctor (Herodotus 3.130.2).
By this, he meant not just that he had some acquaintance with a doctor

[30] "I should most commend a physician who in acute diseases which kill the great
majority of patients, shows some superiority" (*Regimen in Acute Diseases* 5). "That
physician who makes only small mistakes would win my hearty praise" (*On Ancient
Medicine* 9). It has been noted to me that medical degrees are not awarded with
varying amounts of honor because patients would not want a physician who did
not graduate first class or summa cum laude.

[31] Or at least no more than it does in our own day. It is indeed difficult to see from our
point of view exactly how ancient medical training made a difference, apart from
making a doctor better able to tell when a case was hopeless and refuse to treat it.
But it seems more likely that there was something in the practice of ancient Greek
medicine that we do not as yet fully understand than to dismiss the view, held
by an intellectually sophisticated culture over many centuries, that training in the
treatment of illness by natural means made some men more successful than others.
The fact that Greek medicine eventually became established in Rome, which had
no tradition of professional medicine and which was originally deeply suspicious
of Greek rational methods (Jackson 1988: 10), suggests it had some efficacy.

[32] When Socrates mentions the possibility of studying medicine with Hippocrates
himself, Hippocrates was probably in Thessaly (Plato, *Protagoras* 311b; Jouanna
1999: 26–30). In the second century C.E., a young man from Cythera traveled to
Sparta and Boiae to learn medicine (Nutton 1995: 21).

but that he had spent time as a doctor's pupil without completing his apprenticeship.

Traditional medical training was expected to be very long, preferably beginning in childhood (*Law* 2). The individualistic nature of ancient medicine would make the necessary accrual of detail best taught in this way. For example, *Prognosis* is a treatise that explains in considerable detail the signs that a doctor can use to forecast the outcome of an illness. It covers the patient's face, position in bed, movements during sleep, sores, hand gestures, breathing, sweating, hypochondrium, bodily swellings, nosebleeds, pus, dropsy, warmth of hands and feet, state of nails and fingers, sleep patterns, stools, flatulence, urination, vomit, sputum, empyemata, abscesses, pain, fever, headaches, earaches, and sore throats. Chapter 14, detailing the different types of sputum, can stand as an example of the variety in just one of these areas that a doctor has to look out for:

> In all diseases which affect the lungs and sides, sputum should be brought up early and, in appearance, the yellow matter should be thoroughly mixed with the sputum. It is not so good if it only comes about some while after the beginning of the pain, that the sputum is brought up and it is yellow, or light brown. It is a sign of danger if the yellow matter is not diluted; and white, sticky, and nummular sputum is not beneficial. It is worse if it should be a marked pale green and frothy. If it should be so undiluted as to appear dark, this is even worse still. It is also bad if the lungs are not clear and nothing is produced, but the throat remains full of bubbling matter.
>
> In all diseases of the lungs, running at the nose and sneezing is bad, whether it existed before the illness or supervened during its course. But in other diseases which are likely to prove fatal, sneezing is beneficial. In cases of pneumonia, the production at the beginning of the illness of yellow sputum mixed with a little blood is a good indication of recovery. But when this occurs on or after the seventh day, it is less certainly good. All sputa are bad which do not relieve the pain; the worst are those which are dark in color as stated above (*diagegraptai*). The production of any sputum which relieves pain is rather better.

Even if a lay reader could assimilate all this detail from the text alone, to be able to apply it he had also to learn how each sign was affected by the patient's age, sex, constitution, and habits and appearance when healthy (*Places in Man* 41). And finally, at the end of *Prognosis*, the author says:

> He who would make accurate forecasts as to those who will recover and those who will die, and whether the disease will last a greater or less number of days, must understand all the symptoms thoroughly and be able to appreciate them, estimating their powers *when they are compared with one another.* (emphasis added)

So even here, where the author is able to write down with impressive clarity a comprehensive list of symptoms that a doctor should look for, it still falls far short of the practical experience of working at the side of a competent doctor.

Transmitting the necessary medical knowledge simply by precept (written or oral) without extensive practical training is even more difficult in the area of surgery, especially without the aid of clear diagrams. *On Joints* 33 says, "It is not easy to give exact and complete details of an operation in writing; but the reader should form an idea of it from the description." To teach surgery, this treatise would have to be used in conjunction with practical demonstration. The same is true for venesection. *Places in Man* 13, for example, explains the incisions to be made around the eye in the case of a phlegmatic flux, but it assumes a certain skill in advising the reader to cut to the bone, and in Chapter 32, the reader is told to trephine, but no instructions at all are given. Craik argues, apropos of the frequent instructions to cauterize in the same treatise, that "explicit directions are rare . . . , doubtless because cautery was generally learned by practical demonstration rather than from a manual." She believes that this treatise was written for a readership with some specialized knowledge, but not yet as much as the teacher who will be overseeing their attempts.[33] Although cautery is considered a more severe remedy than venesection (*Aphorisms* 7.87), it is easier to apply and is therefore learned first. Nevertheless, despite the absolute necessity of studying with a physician to learn surgical technique, competency in this area is still not the surest sign of a well-trained doctor. *Breaths* 1 says of medicine:

> Whenever surgical treatment is called for, training by habituation is necessary, for habit proves the best teacher of the hands;

[33] Craik 1998: 198, 18.

but to judge of the most obscure and difficult diseases is more a matter of opinion than of art (*doxēi mallon ē technēi*), and therein lies the greatest possible difference between experience and inexperience.

Perhaps the area where the Hippocratics seem least forthcoming in their texts is their pharmacology. Sometimes, authors write as if they assume their readers already have the required pharmacological knowledge. For example, *Places in Man* 13 says that a phlegmatic flux (with no indication what distinguishes a phlegmatic flux from any other sort of flux) can be treated by a laxative, without specifying any such drug. It then goes on to say that a slight flow should be treated with a drug that simultaneously dries the eye and induces slight watering, again with no suggestions of what drug to use. Lists of ingredients and compound medications do occur in the Corpus, particularly in the gynecological writings, but "there is hardly a hint of appropriate dosage."[34] Plato comments, "If you were to remove from any of the *technai* calculation, weighing, and measuring, what would be left would be fairly worthless" (*Philebus* 55e). It is not that the dosage was irrelevant, but that it was frequently left to the individual doctor's considered opinion.[35] The decision would proceed from consideration of a plant's age, size, location, soil, how long ago the plant was picked and the time of day and year, climactic conditions, what else grew nearby, and so forth, as well as the nature of the particular patient and disease.[36] Again, a working familiarity with these variables is best inculcated through hands-on experience, but that does not mean there was no standard to be learned. When illustrating that exceptions to generalizations can often themselves be generalized and are therefore not accidental, Aristotle chose a pharmacological example (*Metaphysics* 1027a20–7). Variations in dosage could be generalized, but listing them each time a drug was named would make a medical text unusable. We do not need to assume, therefore, that doctors kept their herbal knowledge deliberately secret, as has been suggested.[37]

---

[34] Craik 1998: 17.
[35] Craik 1998: 149. But Lloyd 1987: 250–2 cites several passages in which dosages are given.
[36] Lloyd 1987: 253 n. 133.   [37] Craik 1998: 180.

THE INTENDED AUDIENCES OF THE EARLY MEDICAL TEXTS

Despite the difficulties inherent in teaching medical knowledge in written form, it is widely believed that parts of the technical medical treatises of the Hippocratic Corpus are among the earliest, if not the earliest, prose works we possess. The author of the pseudo-Galenic *Definitiones* says that there were pre-Hippocratic texts, albeit very few.[38] *Airs, Waters, Places* could well be earlier than Herodotus.[39] Evidence for the reworking of early, pre-Herodotean material has been discerned in *Diseases* II, in *Places in Man*, and in the gynecological texts.[40]

Why would a craft so dependent on practical training produce so many technical texts so early? The *Law*, when listing things that make a man "truly suited to the practice of medicine," makes no mention of literacy, though it does list a natural disposition, necessary instruction, favorable circumstances, education, industry, and time.[41] And given that other technical treatises were being produced at the same time, why is it that medical treatises, of little practical use unless combined with training, circulated and survived? We know that nautical almanacs were produced,[42] and it is perhaps significant that pilots and doctors are used as analogies of one another by Plato, at least two Hippocratic authors (*On Ancient Medicine, On the Art of Medicine*), Aristotle, and Galen. But nautical almanacs seem not to have been produced in the quantity of, nor to have circulated as widely as, medical texts. It may have been the high esteem in which medicine was held that prompted doctors to become literate so early.[43] But given the nature of Hippocratic medicine, why would doctors ever have regarded the medical treatises as useful?

---

[38] *Definitiones* 19.347 Kühn; cf. Craik 1998: 3. These treatises may have been in Doric (Craik 1998: 9). Note in this regard that the charlatan doctors of New Comedy are depicted as speaking in Doric (Jacques 1998: xxxviii–xl).

[39] R. Thomas 2000: 24.

[40] Jouanna 1974; Craik 1998; Grensemann 1975. Hanson 1997: 305 states that one of the prescriptions from *Diseases of Women* Book II "achieved written form outside the *Corpus*" in approximately 600 B.C.E.

[41] By the first century C.E., even midwives were expected to be literate (Soranus 1.3).

[42] The *Nautical Star Guide* attributed to Phocus of Samos and the *Astrologia* of Cleostratus of Tenedos (Kirk, Raven, and Schofield 1983: 87). On the earliest technical literature in Greece, see Kahn, this volume: 147–52.

[43] Lonie 1983: 148, arguing that the high morale of doctors may have made them more progressive.

A characteristic of many of the early Hippocratic treatises is the inclusion of lists.[44] It is suggested that these were originally written down by a student as an aide-mémoire of all the things he must take into consideration when attending a patient, without detailing the significance of each item on the list. The list could serve the same function for a teacher. In either case, the lists seem to be useful primarily in the context of an orderly supervised perusal of the texts in which they appear – texts that would be augmented orally by the teacher and inwardly digested by the student so the knowledge could be used when needed. That is to say, even the exiguous information the texts enshrine could not be readily accessed from the texts themselves in a clinical situation. Certainly, such a text as the *Aphorisms* (often referred to as a vade mecum of medicine) could not originally have been of much use if it were not ultimately intended to be memorized. Although statements on similar topics are often grouped together, there is no systematic organization of the material that would enable it to be used as a ready reference on any occasion that might arise.

Another common characteristic of early medical material is that it seems to be amassed and compiled in a diachronic process.[45] The ancient Greek view of medicine as a human skill discovered and developed over time could encourage one to add one's own discoveries to the store of existing medical knowledge. The treatises speak of a dialogue carried on by physicians through books (*Regimen* 1.1):[46]

> If I thought that any one of my predecessors to write on human regimen in its relation to health had throughout written with correct knowledge everything that the human mind can comprehend about the subject, it would have been enough for me to learn what had been correctly worked out by the labor of others, and to make use of these results in so far as they severally appeared to be of use. As a matter of fact, while many have already written on this subject, nobody yet has rightly understood how he ought to treat it. . . . Most men, when they have already heard one person expounding a subject refuse to listen to those who discuss it after him. . . . I shall accept correct statements and set forth the truth about those things which have been incorrectly stated. I shall explain also the nature of these things which none of my predecessors has ever attempted to set forth.

[44] Lonie 1983: 150. [45] Craik 1998: 94–5.
[46] Cf. also *Regimen in Acute Diseases* 3.

At least one Hippocratic author thought the process was still ongoing in his day at the end of the fifth century, and he projects the dialogue into the future (*On Ancient Medicine* 2): "But medicine has long had all its means to hand and has discovered both a principle and a method, through which the discoveries made during a long period are many and excellent, while full discovery will be made, if the inquirer be competent, conduct his researches with knowledge of the discoveries already made, and make them his starting point."[47] Committing discoveries to writing, therefore, was one way of making manifest the accretive achievement of the *technē* of medicine and ensuring the author's place within it.

Medicine, therefore, was one of the earliest *technai* to employ technical treatises to disseminate its knowledge, though as we have seen they would be of little value without some medical expertise extrinsic to the texts themselves. Plato says that one cannot become a doctor from books but can only learn the preliminaries (*Phaedrus* 268a–c, 269a). Aristotle asserts that medical treatises are of use to nobody but a trained doctor (*Nicomachean Ethics* 1181b1–12):

> We do not see men becoming expert physicians from a study of medical handbooks. Yet medical writers attempt to describe not only general courses of treatment, but also methods of cure and modes of treatment for particular sorts of patients, classified according to their habits of body; and their treatments appear to be of value for men who have had practical experience, though they are useless for the novice.[48]

Useless, that is, without the guidance of a trained physician.

But other treatises were written for a wider public, notably *On Ancient Medicine*, *On the Sacred Disease*, and *On the Nature of Man*. All of these begin as polemics, the first against users of hypotheses, the second against magical healers and soothsayers, the third against monists. However, although they begin as polemics, they quickly move on to describing a specific physiological theory that supports their brand of therapy (balancing humors in *On Ancient Medicine*, applying hot and

---

[47] Cf. Lonie 1983: 157–8. *Places in Man* 46, *On the Art of Medicine* 8 hold that all of medicine has been discovered.

[48] Cf. Aristotle, *Politics* 1286a9: "It is foolish in any *technē* whatever to proceed strictly by the book."

cold in *On the Sacred Disease*, venesection in *On the Nature of Man*) and then briefly cover related topics that could seem to challenge their theories (diseased organs in *On Ancient Medicine*, nonphlegmatic mental illness in *On the Sacred Disease*, peccant material not obviously humoral in *On the Nature of Man*). All three treatises end with a remark on treatment of the most general nature:

> If a man can in this way conduct with success inquiries outside the human body, he will always be able to select the very best treatment. And the best is always that which is farthest removed from the unsuitable. (*On Ancient Medicine* 24)

> Whoever knows how to cause in men by regimen moist or dry, hot or cold, he can cure this disease also, if he distinguish the seasons for useful treatment, without having recourse to purifications and magic. (*On the Sacred Disease* 21)

> Diseases which arise soon after their origin, and whose cause is clearly known, are those the history of which can be foretold with the greatest certainty. They must be cured by combating the cause of the disease, for in this way will be removed that which caused the disease in the body. (*On the Nature of Man* 13)[49]

All three treatises share a structure that suggests they were intended for more than a general defense of medicine. This is indicated at the beginning of *On the Nature of Man*: "He who is accustomed to hear speakers discuss the nature of man beyond its relations to medicine will not find the present account of any interest." That is, the treatise is intended for those with a specifically medical interest. Since Galen, it has been argued that *On the Nature of Man* is a conflation of two treatises, the first intended for a general audience and the second, where the material becomes more technical, for a more experienced audience. But a comparison of the overall structure of the treatise with *On Ancient Medicine* and *On the Sacred Disease* shows that the description of general physiology is given to support the primary method of treatment advocated by the author. A recent paper, analyzing the language of *On the Nature of Man*, concluded that it was written as a unity for protreptic

---

49 Two chapters follow Chapter 13 in the traditional ordering, but they are misplaced. The Loeb translation of this passage has been adapted to follow the text of the *Corpus Medicorum Graecorum*.

purposes.[50] Similarly, *On Ancient Medicine* and *On the Sacred Disease* were written not simply to defend medicine's good name but to attract pupils.

Although it had always been possible for a nonfamily member to become apprenticed to a doctor, before the fifth century the profession, like other *technai*, seems largely to have been handed down from father to son. In the fifth century, however, the number of individuals from nonmedical families seeking training in medicine increased to the point where *iatroi* from famous families or centers of medicine could expect to make a living simply by teaching medicine. This could be a result either of the increasing status of medicine (*Precepts* 7 says that those who portray themselves as physicians without real knowledge find themselves "suddenly exalted"), the deliberate opening of the ranks by the traditional medical families (Galen says Hippocrates decided to make medical training available to strangers owing to an insufficient number of family members willing to become doctors),[51] or a combination of the two.

Treatises written for public consumption, therefore, were competitive not solely, or even primarily, for patients. Competition between practicing physicians would more likely be played out at a local level on the basis of personality and efficacy. It is generally believed that many doctors were itinerant, and after completing an apprenticeship in an area where there was a concentration of doctors, a doctor would presumably try to set himself up in a new area (perhaps his original city) where there was less competition.[52] A treatise such as *Airs, Waters, Places*, which seems aimed at readers with considerable medical expertise, would thus be appropriate at the end of a period of study before the students left for new regions – perhaps as a handbook from a lecture or course aimed at the newly minted doctor. But the fact that the author of *Airs, Waters, Places* describes many different types of region does not mean he expects any one doctor to visit them all. A phrase in *Law* 4, "traveling through the cities,"[53] is commonly taken

---

[50] Price 1999. On the convention of using the language of oral lecture and debate in written treatises, see Thomas, this volume.

[51] *Commentary on the Oath*; cf. *Bulletin of the History of Medicine* 30 (1956): 52–87, cited by Jouanna 1999: 47.

[52] An inscription from Metapontum ca. 250 B.C.E. shows seventeen doctors for a population of no more than 7,000 (*SEG* 30.1175, Nutton 1995: 14–15 n. 64).

[53] ἀνὰ τὰς πόλιας φοιτεῦντας.

to refer to itinerancy, but it could just as well refer to doctors who go, severally, from one place of origin to another city. We know from *The Physician* and *Decorum* that a lot was entailed in setting up a surgery. Herodotus (3.131) remarks that Democedes was successful on arriving in Aegina despite not having any equipment with him. And a doctor who took on apprentices would have these problems multiplied. It seems counterintuitive that a doctor who had an established, successful practice in one region would become itinerant on principle. Hippocrates' move to Thessaly and the attempts to lure Democedes to Athens and Samos at an ever increasing salary do not strike me as true itinerancy. *Decorum* focuses on how a doctor should build up a good reputation by his continued presence in a city, and Chapter 2 implies that moving round from city to city is characteristic of frauds.[54] A doctor may travel around outlying areas for a short period of time, but he would normally return to his surgery as a base.

If the authors of the medical treatises were itinerant and published their works in order to win patients in an unfamiliar town, what would be the chance of being on hand when any given individual fell sick of the illnesses he claimed to be able to treat? If the treatises were only meant to be delivered orally upon arrival at a new town, it seems intuitively unlikely that patients would want to put themselves in the hands of an unknown doctor who was avowedly following his own newly developed theories, however well founded. Under the assumption that the authors of these treatises were competing primarily for patients, Lloyd remarks on the surprising willingness of patients in the ancient world to submit to newfangled treatments: "We might expect a reasonably deep-seated caution, if not conservatism, to prevail."[55] In fact, Plato has Gorgias remark that his brother, a practicing physician, and other doctors sometimes had to call on his rhetorical skill to persuade patients to submit to certain therapies (*Gorgias* 456b). There might be less caution if the doctor's reputation had preceded him, but there is no evidence that any famous doctor was itinerant in this way,

---

[54] Though the latter remark may refer to philosophers only, and not to doctors at all, since the author talks of young men rather than the general populace falling in with these itinerants and of crowds gathering around them, rather than individual sick people visiting them.

[55] Lloyd 1987: 68–9, though he does not ignore the fact that authors of the treatises would also hope to attract students.

and if he were he would not need his arguments to win him patients, unless, coincidentally, another medical authority of comparable stature happened to be in the vicinity at the same time. Such arguments as the treatises offer, however, are useful for enticing would-be medical students away from established authorities. Then, at a later date, when the students were physicians trying to attract a clientele, they could claim the authority of their teacher to validate any new treatment to their more conservative patients.[56]

Physicians new to an area and relying on efficacious treatment to build up a reputation and a practice would not always win the day simply by citing the authority of their teachers. Sometimes, they would find it necessary to persuade a patient of the efficacy of certain treatments, as the case of Gorgias' brother shows, or to defend their particular theory against opponents.[57] *Places in Man* 28 implies that doctors sometimes took over another doctor's patients. In *Epidemics* 5.14, several physicians are said to be in attendance at one bedside. *Prorrhetic* 2.1 remarks that rival doctors try to steal patients from one another; *Diseases* 1.1 gives advice on eristic. But most practicing doctors would not be accomplished rhetoricians or authors, even, according to Gorgias, his own brother.

Conversely, those who wrote on medicine were not always doctors. Thucydides seems to refer to medical writers both lay and professional in his discussion of the plague (2.48.3).[58] This has led to the claim that not only was there no difference between self-avowed physicians and those they called charlatans, and very little between *iatroi* and the educated layman, but also that in some cases it was difficult to distinguish between the professional physician and the professional sophist.[59] However, Gorgias' anecdote about his ability to persuade patients is told to show how much power rhetoric can have over nonspecialists, the point being that he is *not* a physician and is not confused about the

---

[56] The problem of the anonymity of the treatises of the Hippocratic Corpus is complex, but given their rampant egotism it seems inherently unlikely that they were originally meant to circulate anonymously.

[57] Modern physicians do the same, though their rhetoric usually centers on statistics.

[58] Epicharmus the comic dramatist also wrote on medicine. Plato was numbered among medical writers by the author of *Anonymus Londinensis* by virtue of the *Timaeus*. See Craik 1998: 2.

[59] Lloyd 1979: 86–98.

matter at all. Plato obviously intends his readers to be surprised and perturbed at the possibility that somebody with only Gorgias' knowledge of medicine could win the post of public physician over a true doctor. The acknowledged overlap in the ancient world would be those trained physicians who had also obtained some rhetorical skill.[60]

Aristotle lists three types of doctor (*Politics* 1282a3): (1) the ordinary practitioner (*dēmiourgos*), (2) the master craftsman (*architektonikos*), and (3) the informed layman (*pepaideumenos peri tēn technēn*, contrasted later with "the experts," *tois eidosin*). Elsewhere, Aristotle says that the defining characteristic of a master craftsman is not that he is better at his craft (or at least not simply that – there is presumably a gradation of ability within the category *dēmiourgos* itself), but that he is able to teach and explain it to others (*Metaphysics* 981b7). It is this group of doctors that produced the medical treatises, frequently in order to attract and instruct students.[61]

The use of advertising to attract pupils was characteristic of another group who made a living from teaching in the ancient Greek world – the sophists. Gorgias' *On Not-Being*, *Helen*, and *Palamedes* are not simply attempts to argue a position, nor produced for entertainment alone, but rather display what an individual would be able to accomplish after studying with him. Prodicus is said to have enticed students into his fifty-drachma course by offering a one-drachma lecture as a teaser (Plato, *Cratylus* 384b). Given the lack of copyright laws in the ancient world, why would anybody who wanted to make a living on the basis of teaching their technical expertise ever commit anything to writing if not as an enticement to paying pupils? Medical teachers needed more far-flung advertising than sophists because they expected their students to travel to them rather than vice versa. This might be expected, since medicine was a more established *technē* than rhetoric and needed a more extended course of study and more equipment.[62] This is not

---

[60] For arguments that medical authors did present parts of their written works orally, see Kollesch 1992.

[61] I disagree with the claim of Kahn 1996: 213, that although doctors were included in the word *sophistēs*, they took refuge behind their technical specialties and that Protagoras was the first to present himself openly as an educator.

[62] Of course, once schools such as the Academy and the Lyceum were established, students did travel to Athens to study. Plato's emphasis in his published dialogues on writing as a second best way to study philosophy would have been excellent advertising.

to say that there were not also traditional practicing physicians who took on apprentices locally. Rather, it was the aristocrats of the medical world, established in the traditional medical centers, who could expect to attract students who could afford to travel further and pay more. On returning to his hometown or settling in a foreign one, a physician could say, "I studied with so-and-so," and have it carry significance even if his teacher was not local.

Once they had attracted students from outside the traditional medical families (that is, students who had not been schooled in medicine since childhood), teachers found the need to produce more detailed handbooks. *Epidemics* 3.16 states, "The power, too, to study correctly what has been written I consider to be an important part of the art of medicine." *Epidemics* 6.3.12 says that the method of medicine consists in studying large numbers of accounts, still emphasizing the accrual of detail as important, but from written sources as much as from firsthand experience.

Certain passages in the Corpus suggest that some doctors began to feel that medical knowledge was beginning to circulate too widely. *The Oath* states, "I will hand on precepts, lectures, and all other learning to my sons, to those of my master, and to those pupils duly apprenticed and sworn, and to none other," while *Law* declares, "Holy things are revealed only to holy men. Such things must not be made known to the profane until they are initiated into the mysteries of science." The dissemination of medical knowledge would be easier to control as long as it was contained only in oral teaching.[63] The early and widespread use of writing among doctors broke this monopoly.[64]

By the fourth century, doctors felt threatened by the unregulated circulation of medical ideas in a way that did not occur before written texts were used. *Decorum* 4 comments that those who think they know

---

[63] Craik 1998: 9 argues that one of the reasons so little is known about dosages in the ancient world is that herbalists deliberately kept their knowledge secret, in part by not committing them to writing.

[64] Cf. Bowman and Woolf 1994: 8: "The exercise of power through texts makes it essential to regulate their use, but literacy is not easy to control and texts have therefore often been at the heart of struggles for power." R. Thomas 1994: 37 contests this view: "Books as such were not seen as a threat by the Greeks partly because they were only one way amongst many of circulating ideas." On the Hippocratics' comfort with writing to interact with colleagues, see K. Usener 1990.

medicine from words (*logoisi*) rather than from education (*mathēsios*) "show themselves up like gold proved by the fire to be dross." *Places in Man* and *Breaths* also emphasize the need for learning from experts.[65] These texts are not produced by practicing physicians to encourage the profession into voluntary self-policing of its reputation, but by teachers of medicine to discourage anybody from thinking they could learn from books all there was to know about being a doctor. Although *Law* is often cited as evidence for the low opinion of medicine in the fifth and fourth centuries and is seen as an attempt to improve its status, the advice it gives is simply that physicians should be properly trained. Those who are, as the author says, doctors "in reality" (*ergōi*), the ones who would be giving the training, do not need to be told this. The treatise can achieve its purpose only if it can persuade those who want to be doctors and do not want to be shown up as charlatans that training from a true professional is a necessity. This raises an interesting question: could it be possible that the figure of the charlatan shows up earlier in the medical texts than elsewhere because the authors found the threat of exposure helpful as a recruiting tool even before the figure began to be more widely lampooned in society as a whole?

[65] See Craik 1998: 234.

6

Literacy in Greek and Chinese Science

Some Comparative Issues

Geoffrey Lloyd

W ork done in the wake of the pioneering studies of Goody and Watt, Havelock, and others has put on the agenda a series of evidently crucial, if highly obscure, questions. If we can all agree that the existence of written records and other types of texts makes a difference, the issue is: what difference? The key questions include: who is in control; who makes the texts; who has access to them; who uses them; and for what purposes? How are those who do the writing recruited and trained? How and by whom is the ability to read them acquired? Who is responsible for the transmission and dissemination of texts or for deciding which texts are for more general, which for only restricted, circulation? What, indeed, did "circulation" consist of, and what, more generally, were the occasions on which the texts were used or their contents performed? We shall certainly not be in a position to appreciate the differences literacy makes in a given society at a given period until we have some idea about the answers to questions like those – not that that list is meant to be exhaustive. To get a sense of those differences, we need, ideally, to take a range of different societies and periods into account: we need, in fact, a comparative approach.

Let me explain my agenda. What were the different effects, on ancient Chinese and Greek science, of the modes of literacy for which we have evidence? I use the term *science* as a conventional placeholder for what passed as the study of the heavens and that of the human body, and I shall include also the study of health and disease – medicine, in other words – and, indeed, also mathematics.[1] In this chapter, I want to explore one aspect of those differences, namely, what they owed to literacy and, more generally, to what I call the contexts of communicative exchange.

I shall divide my discussion into two parts. The second will tackle the specific question of what the very different styles of mathematics cultivated in China and in Greece owed to the different technologies of communication that were available and that were used. But to get to grips with that I need first, in the more extensive first part of the chapter, to set the scene with a general discussion of those technologies. Let me emphasize, however, that I do not aim at a comprehensive coverage of the issues in the second, specifically mathematical, part of my analysis, let alone in the first scene-setting section. Moreover, even my more limited conclusions are subject to an important general reservation. Neither for China nor for Greece can we be confident that our extant sources provide an entirely reliable database on which to propose valid generalizations. Those sources, in each case, are both biased and incomplete. I shall underline particular concerns over particular points in due course. But the problem is a general one and needs to be borne in mind throughout.

TECHNOLOGIES OF COMMUNICATION IN CHINA AND GREECE

Let me begin with China. By the time of the Eastern Han dynasty (ca. 23–220 C.E.), certain classic texts had acquired canonical status and their transmission and use are comparatively well documented. The canons (*jing*) in question included not just the so-called Confucian classics[2] but also medical and mathematical texts. The medical classic *Huangdi neijing* (*Inner Canon of the Yellow Emperor*) exists in three different recensions (*lingshu, suwen, taisu*), thought to have been compiled around

---

[1]   On the differences between the "science" produced in China and in Greece, see Lloyd and Sivin (forthcoming), and on the influence of technologies of communication on early Chinese thought, compare Lewis 1999.

[2]   The five generally recognized Confucian classics were the *Yijing* (*Book of Changes*), *Liji* (*Rites*, or *Records of Ceremony*), *Shijing* (*Odes*, or *Songs*), *Shujing* (*Documents*), and *Chunqiu* (*Spring and Autumn Annals*). These became the standard education for intending officials by edict of the emperor in 136 B.C.E.

the middle of the first century B.C.E. The two chief early mathematical classics, the *Zhoubi suanjing* (*Arithmetic Classic of the Zhou Gnomon*) and the *Jiuzhang suanshu* (*Nine Chapters of the Mathematical Art*) – which I shall be concentrating on below – date from a century either side of the Common Era.

By Eastern Han times, we hear of fictive "lineages" (*jia*) whose primary responsibility was the preservation and transmission of the canonical texts. The classification of philosophical and other groups was sometimes achieved by reference to these lineages – the term *jia* is often translated as "schools." Those in turn served as the basis for the cataloguing of the books in the imperial and other libraries.[3] We hear, too, of schools in the sense of teaching establishments where the study of the canons was carried on. Nor should we think of those schools as serving just the purely disinterested function of promulgating learning. Entry to the imperial civil service depended, generally, on knowledge of the primary canons. The schools themselves came to be judged by how successful their pupils were in gaining the top jobs in the imperial bureaucracy. The study of the key texts was crucial not just for gaining a reputation for learning, but for a career.

However, if those are among the clearly defined features of the organization of learning in the Eastern Han dynasty, how far do they apply also to earlier periods? Recent scholarship has served to highlight the dangers of reading too much of the Eastern Han picture backward, even to the earlier, Western Han dynasty, or to the Qin, let alone to the preunification situation of the Warring States period. One of the first classifications of six prominent *jia* comes in the final chapter of the *Shiji*, which contains Sima Tan's ideas, recorded by his son Sima Qian. But that chapter does not mention texts as such in any prominent role in that context. Those six *jia* are differentiated in the first instance by the way they set about giving advice on government.[4] They represent Sima Tan's ideas on *that* subject, not his thoughts on the structure of philosophical lineages. Although on the basis of scattered references in the *Shiji* and

---

[3] The earliest extant comprehensive bibliographical survey is in Chapter 30 of the *Hanshu* by Ban Gu (ca. 90 C.E.), drawing on the work, now lost, of the imperial librarians Liu Xiang (died 8 B.C.E.) and Liu Xin (died 23 C.E.). Cf. Lewis 1999: Chapter 7.

[4] *Shiji* 130, 3288–9. See Petersen 1995; Smith (forthcoming); Csikszentmihalyi and Nylan (forthcoming).

elsewhere it used to be held that in the fourth century B.C.E. there was already an important prototype of an imperial Academy founded by King Xuan at the Ji gate of his capital city Qi, that idea has now been exploded as another case of reading back later institutions into an earlier period.[5] Like many kings and powerful ministers of the Warring States period, King Xuan aimed to collect around him as many brilliant "guests" as he could. They included several prominent thinkers, such as Zou Yan, but there is nothing in the earlier, more reliable evidence that suggests that these "guests" formed a school or had any kind of teaching function.

We have, then, to be on our guard. Some of the conventional accounts, accepted until quite recently, of the early Chinese philosophical "schools" need to be reexamined more critically. The primary sources on which they are based cannot be accepted at face value as historical accounts, but come from authors with their own definite, often polemical, agenda. This applies not just to Sima Tan's account, preserved in the *Shiji*, but also to the groupings found in *Zhuangzi* 33.[6] There too, as in *Shiji* 130, other philosophers are criticized for having appreciated only part of the truth, or the Way. That chapter is thought to date from some time in the second century B.C.E., but even earlier, Xunzi, at the end of the third century, attacks twelve thinkers not so much on purely intellectual grounds as for the disastrous advice they offered on government and social relations.[7] Among those criticized is no less a figure than Mencius (Mengzi) – one of the most famous and respected of the interpreters of Confucius' thought in the fourth century. Yet, according to the conventional view, Xunzi himself was a "Confucian."

Such a term as *ru* ("literati"), used of those who are often labeled Confucian, indicates sometimes no particular allegiance to the teachings of Confucius (Kong Fuzi) himself, but rather a reputation as a figure of learning. Where the conventional view sees the legendary Lao Dan as the founder of "Daoism," we must be clear that following the Way was an ideal that was far from the exclusive characteristic of those who admired such canonical texts as the *Daodejing*. On the contrary, it was

---

[5] Sivin 1995b: Chapter 4, 19–28.

[6] On *Zhuangzi* 33, see Graham 1989: 376. The chapter in question does not belong to the earliest stratum of *Zhuangzi* (the so-called Inner Chapters), but dates perhaps from the second century B.C.E.; see Graham 1981.

[7] *Xunzi* 6, on which see Knoblock 1988–94: 1.212–29.

a goal shared by philosophers of widely differing views, even though they disagreed on precisely what following it entailed. The term *Mohists* is slightly more determinate, referring to the followers of Mo Di, often thought of as the chief fifth-century rival to Confucius himself. Yet both *Zhuangzi* 33 and *Hanfeizi* 50 report factionalism within their ranks and disagreements on the interpretation of the Mohist canon.

If we should be cautious about accepting the classificatory framework within which early Chinese philosophy is generally discussed, what, positively, can be said about the way in which texts were used, and about the conduct of philosophical inquiry and the ambitions of philosophers more generally? Due allowance must be made for the variety of texts that have come down to us or that are reported or described in our sources. Beyond the medical and mathematical classics that I shall discuss below, the so-called Confucian classics include, for instance, the *Book of Odes* and the *Spring and Autumn Annals*, the former a collection of poetry, the latter a record (attributed to Confucius himself) of events in the state of Lu from 722 to 491 B.C.E.

However, to tackle the questions raised in the last paragraph, we may take the evidence that the *Lunyu* (*Analects*) – also ascribed to Confucius – provides. This, like so many of the early texts that are extant, is nowadays thought of as a compilation, put together over an extended period, maybe from early in the fifth century to the middle of the third B.C.E.[8] This text represents Confucius in conversation with his pupils – Zilu, Zigong, Zixia, and so on – and other interlocutors. We have, then, what purport to be dialogues, or at least exchanges, and one lesson we are to learn is that Confucius tailors his replies to the situation and to his interlocutor's progress in understanding.

As written representations of what purport to be live conversations, the analogies with Plato are obvious. Yet two points of dissimilarity stand out immediately. First, the *Lunyu* itself became a text that the pupil had to master, indeed to memorize, as part of his induction into the group. It is clear from other sources that it was only after the text had been committed to memory that the pupil began to turn to its interpretation.[9] Learning the text by heart was a kind of rite of passage,

---

[8] Brooks and Brooks 1998 date the various strata that they postulate between 479 and 249 B.C.E.

[9] See, for example, Sivin 1995a.

testimony to the seriousness and dedication of the student. The pupil's admission to the lineage depended as much on his character and moral probity as on any intellectual attainments he might display. The duty of members of a lineage, *jia*, in Eastern Han times at least, was to hand on and preserve the canonical text, the *jing*. Second, Confucius was not just interested in teaching disciples. His ambition was to find a ruler who would accept his advice about government. His primary preoccupation, throughout, was with human behavior and social relations. But this was not (as we say) an academic interest. He desperately wanted to see his ideas implemented, desperately indeed, since in the event he never did find a ruler who would implement them.

At this point, one might think of Plato's equally desperate attempts to influence Dionysius II, tyrant of Syracuse. Certainly, those attempts were also driven by Plato's sense that he needed at least to *try* to find someone to carry out some of his political program. Yet after his disastrous third visit to Sicily, Plato's sphere of operations was Athens. The Academy he founded was, indeed, to be a training ground for statesmen. But the personal goal of its members was leading the philosophical life – an end in itself.

More important, Confucius' ambition to influence rulers was shared by many, maybe even most, early Chinese philosophers. The list of those who sought to act, and indeed acted, as advisers to rulers includes Mencius, the Mohists, Hui Shi, Gongsun Long, and Han Fei. The *Daodejing* has a lot to say about the cultivation of the self, but the policy of *wu wei*, "no ado," is one that rulers are advised to follow. In parts of the *Zhuangzi* compilation, too, the issue of good government comes to the fore even while other sections promulgate an ideal of other-worldly disengagement. At the end of the Warring States period and the start of the imperial period inaugurated by the Qin and carried on by the Han, we have a series of works that provide comprehensive summaries of knowledge and cover a diverse array of subjects, including the calendar, music and ritual, agriculture, and not least government itself: the *Lüshi chunqiu*, put together around 239 B.C.E. by Lü Buwei (prime minister to the man who later unified the empire); the *Huainanzi*, compiled under the direction of Liu An, king of Huainan, before 139 B.C.E.; and the *Chunqiu fanlu*, the work, in part, of the prominent statesman Dong Zhongshu, around 134 B.C.E. But in each case these were compiled by or under the direction of statesmen; their principal aim was to set out the knowledge the ruler will need for good government, not just a matter of what we might call political theory, to be sure, but everything required for a correct understanding of the world as a whole.

The target at which much Chinese philosophical writing is aimed is the ruler, to whom advice was often offered in the form of the "memorial to the throne." Such "memorials" had to be written to be presented. No one would dream of just speechifying in front of the emperor if they had an important proposal to put to him, nor would they have been allowed to do so. Dong Zhongshu is the author of some remarkable examples,[10] and before him, Li Si, prime minister to the first Qin emperor, produced in 213 B.C.E. a famous "memorial" advocating the burning of philosophical texts in private hands. The latter example shows that collections of such texts were common enough to be seen as a threat by authorities who saw their contents as subversive.[11] But the ruler was the target, not just because he was in a position to implement policy; he was also the prime source of patronage. Even before the civil service expanded as it did, exponentially, under the Han dynasty, the courts of rulers were an important source of support for intellectuals of different types.

The teaching function is thus often subordinated to the task of persuading the ruler or his ministers. Of course, Chinese intellectuals also sought to impress other intellectuals, and they criticized other groups of individuals often enough (though more often the dead than their still living contemporaries). Yet the main type of occasion on which debates or discussions were held was in the presence of the ruler, and more often than not on matters of state policy (one example is the discussion represented in the *Yantielun*, the discourses on salt and iron).[12] Dialogues between master and pupil appear, as I remarked, in the *Lunyu*, and the *Zhuangzi* produces some striking exchanges where Confucius is worsted, including one, for instance, at the hands of the notorious robber Zhi.[13] But in every discipline pupils were expected to adopt a deferential, even reverential, tone toward their masters. They were certainly not expected to challenge or contradict them.

[10] See, for example, *Hanshu* 56, discussed by Queen 1996: 249–54.
[11] Two slightly different versions of Li Si's "memorial" are given in the *Shiji* 6, 254–6 and 87, 2546.
[12] See Nylan 1994 for an analysis of the evidence on the courtly conferences and debates down to the second century C.E.
[13] See, for example, *Zhuangzi* 29.

This leads to concrete evidence for the role of texts in the transmission of medical learning in particular. Li Si's "memorial" excluded technical treatises from his ban, which helps to confirm their existence and importance. Works on medicine and agriculture were specifically excepted.[14] We find, indeed, many examples of medical texts alongside philosophical and literary ones, in the tombs that have been excavated from the late Warring States and early Han periods. We also have some evidence as to their role. In the biography of the doctor Chunyu Yi contained in *Shiji* 105, Chunyu Yi describes how he came to learn medicine. He was apprenticed first to a doctor called Gongsun Guang, who teaches him a number of "formulas" (these appear to include both written texts and oral teaching). Chunyu Yi swears, in return, not to divulge these inappropriately to anyone else ("I would die sooner than transmit them wrongly to anyone"). But when Gongsun Guang has taught him all he knows, he recommends another doctor, Yangqing: "His formulas are exceptional, not the sort that the uninitiated know about." Gongsun Guang provides him with a letter of introduction, and we are given an account of Chunyu Yi's first encounter with his new teacher. When it became clear that he was accepted for instruction, he not only expressed his delight but "left his mat and made repeated obeisances."[15]

The evidence from Chapter 48 in the *lingshu* recension of the *Huangdi neijing* enables us to go a step further. This chapter gives a fictional account of the Thunder Duke receiving a text from the Yellow Emperor himself. This is preceded by the Thunder Duke undergoing purification for three days and then sealing his oath with a ritual in which he cuts his arm and smears the blood. Thereupon, the Yellow Emperor "grasped his hand with his left hand and with his right conferred the book on him, saying 'Take care. Take care. I will now explain it to you.'"[16]

We shall be returning to mathematics at the end, but for now let me summarize the chief points that have emerged so far from this rapid survey. First, we must be wary of the diachronic dimension to the problems. In the Eastern Han dynasty, there were academies training people in the classics partly as a means of gaining access to posts in the imperial civil service. By then, the term *jia* was used of the fictive lineages that

---

[14] Exceptions were also made for technical treatises on divination, as well as of the official histories of the state of Qin itself.

[15] This text is analyzed in Sivin 1995a: 178–84; also cf. Hsu forthcoming.

[16] See Sivin 1995a: 184–8.

had responsibility for the preservation and transmission of the canons (*jing*). There are continuities, but also discontinuities, with earlier practices. Pupil–teacher entourages go back to the fifth century, but they were less formal than the Han academies. More continuity can be seen in the manner in which texts were transmitted. Even though the use of the term *jia* to describe the fictive lineages involved is mainly an Eastern Han development, the medical evidence especially suggests that much earlier the transmission of the text *could* be a solemn affair, with the pupil granted access subject to a ritual initiation.

Let me turn now, even more rapidly, to the Greek evidence, to bring out the chief general points of similarity and dissimilarity with the Chinese data. In this case, too, there are important discontinuities and transitions that have to be borne in mind in evaluating the relative roles of the written and oral modes of communication at different periods and for different genres. I shall concentrate, at this stage, on philosophy and medicine.

While written texts are attested from Anaximander onward, it is well-known that when they were consulted, they were more often read out and discussed than studied privately and in silence.[17] This is what Plato describes as happening in the case of the book Zeno is said to have brought to Athens (*Parmenides* 127cd). Although Plato does not spell out what the book contained, it undoubtedly included technical philosophical argumentation. What was the nature of the discussion that followed such a reading? Plato's dialogues purport to represent some such, though they are, of course, fictional accounts of considerable artistry. When he stresses that Socrates will follow wherever the argument leads, he wants to underscore the contrast with the persuasive arts of sophists whose sole concern (Plato would have us believe) is to please the crowd. Yet even if we should discount the rhetoric of Plato's appeal to the truth as arbiter, it is still obvious that the contexts of these exchanges are rather different from those normally encountered in China, even those of Confucius' exchanges with his pupils, let alone that characteristic Chinese situation, the presentation to the throne. The key point of difference is the assumed equality of the interlocutors in Plato's dialogues.

---

[17] See Thomas, this volume, on public reading of written texts; see S. Usener 1994 on reading in the fourth century.

Some of our early medical evidence, from the Hippocratic Corpus, serves to throw more light on what were apparently common contexts of oral communicative exchange. *On Diseases* I offers advice on how the doctor should deal with the question-and-answer sessions he can expect to have not just with patients, their relatives, and their friends, but also with other doctors, who are present at the case and keen to debate the diagnosis and treatment.[18] We recall from Plato that Hippias, Gorgias, and others prided themselves on their ability in analogous sessions, even though they were no match for Socrates (Plato implies) in that department.[19] We hear, indeed, of several sophists who publicized themselves at the Panhellenic games by giving lectures and offering to answer questions afterward.[20]

Some of the Hippocratic works represent, or at least originated in, such lectures (*epideixeis*).[21] One such is the treatise *On the Nature of Man*, which opens by addressing those who are accustomed to *hearing* a different approach to medicine. That work describes lectures given by rival speakers – on the subject of the constitution of the human being, no less – where the aim was evidently victory as decided by the crowd of bystanders.[22] That was just the kind of situation that Plato contrasted with true philosophical debate (though there is no need to agree with his condemnation). Such occasions were, to be sure, partly entertainment, but they also served to raise the public's interest in a wide range of questions.

The model that such debates bring to mind is, of course, that of the law courts and the political assemblies, where Greek citizens of the classical period acquired considerable experience in evaluating arguments for and against various propositions, on guilt and innocence, and on

---

[18] *On Diseases* 1.1, discussed in Lloyd 1979: 91–2. The advice on question-and-answer sessions contained in this treatise would have no point if it did not correspond to a possible real-life situation. Other treatises, discussed in Lloyd 1979: 90, confirm that doctors had good reason to be concerned lest a consultation be turned into a public lecture.

[19] For Hippias, see Plato, *Lesser Hippias* 363c–d; for Gorgias, *Meno* 70c, *Gorgias* 449b–c; for Protagoras, *Protagoras* 318b, 329b, 336b–d.

[20] See Plato, *Lesser Hippias* 368b–e; Aristotle, *Rhetoric* 1414b29–34, discussed in Lloyd 1987: 91–2.

[21] See Thomas, this volume.

[22] *On the Nature of Man* 1, discussed in Lloyd 1979: 92–4, quoted and discussed by Dean-Jones, this volume: 115–16.

matters of state, including the constitution itself. The decision rested with them in their role as jurors or members of the assembly. It is not at all surprising that no Chinese philosophical or medical debate follows that pattern, since there is simply no Chinese parallel for the Greek experience of a citizen acting as both judge and juror in lawsuits, or of citizens gathering to make decisions in an assembly that was plenipotentiary.[23] I shall have more to say about the influence of this model elsewhere on Greek intellectual life when I come to mathematics.

Of course, unless qualifications and exceptions are noted, my Greek picture will seem quite unbalanced. The Hippocratic works I have mentioned, like Plato's dialogues, are themselves all written productions, artful ones at that, and the fact of their being committed to writing serves to make them available, as Goody argued, for a different type of ruminative critical scrutiny than any that can be given to an oral performance – the original lectures themselves.[24] Moreover, some works in the Hippocratic Corpus are very different from the type of demonstration lecture (*epideixis*) I have spoken of. Some treatises record detailed case histories, deal with problems to do with surgical procedures, or set out lists of drug recipes.[25] While many insist on open exchanges between doctor and patient – and on the doctor being intelligible to lay people – some suggest that medicine is not to be taught to just anyone. *Oath* 1 limits that instruction to family and to those who have sworn the oath. *Law* 5 puts it that "holy things are revealed only to holy people. Such things must not be made known to the profane until they are initiated into the mysteries of knowledge." The Thunder Duke would have approved.

Going further afield, we know that by the end of the fifth century a fair body of technical literature had already been produced in such fields as agriculture, architecture, astronomy, and harmonics. Private

---

[23] The Chinese political ideal, accepted in all our extant classical Chinese sources, is that of the benevolent rule of a wise monarch. The differences between Greek rhetoric, envisaging, primarily, Greek law courts or political debates in the councils or assemblies, and Chinese rhetoric, directed principally at persuading the ruler or his ministers, are examined in Lloyd 1996: Chapter 4.

[24] Goody 1977: Chapter 3. See Yunis, this volume, on differences in attending an oral performance and reading a written text.

[25] See Lonie 1983 on the interplay between oral and literate communication techniques in the Hippocratic Corpus.

collections of this material were beginning to be made, though Euthydemus' library, reported in Xenophon, was clearly exceptional.[26] If we go further afield in time and allow for the diachronic dimension, one increasingly important new genre is the commentary.[27] Homeric scholarship and exegesis were well established in the fifth century, and by the end of the fourth Hippocratic scholarship flourished in Alexandria. Apollonius of Citium writes a commentary on the work *On Joints* in the first century B.C.E., and by Galen's day, three centuries later, Hippocratic commentaries were not just a vehicle for philological analysis but a battleground where rival claims to appropriate the authority of the model physician were debated.

Even when these and many other reservations are added, there are still important differences between some Greek and some Chinese communicative situations. Both societies used oral and written modes, to be sure. But there is no Greco-Roman parallel to the Chinese use of their canonical texts as the basis for examinations to enter the imperial civil service. Again, Chinese debates are less often face-to-face and never (as far as I know) judged by a lay audience. Greek intellectuals, philosophers, and doctors did not generally think of the ruler as the person to persuade, but sought to impress their peer group or even the general public. With fewer opportunities for patronage or state support, the Greeks relied more heavily on teaching to make a living, and there your reputation and livelihood depended on your performance in lectures and face-to-face debates.

STYLES OF MATHEMATICS IN CHINA AND GREECE

Now that the scene has been set, I want to turn more briefly to the particular evidence for the development of mathematics, a useful test case since it is an area where we might expect the importance of the written mode to be particularly pronounced. Although we have only paltry fragments of Greek mathematics before Euclid, the corpus of work

---

[26] Xenophon, *Memorabilia* 4.2.8. See Jacob 1998 for an excellent comparative study of the rise of Greek and Chinese book collecting and libraries.

[27] The rise of the commentary as a genre in the Greco-Roman world and in China is now the subject of a considerable secondary literature. On the Greco-Roman side, see Cambiano 2001; on the Chinese side, see Lewis 1999: Chapter 6; Sivin in Lloyd and Sivin (forthcoming): Chapter 2.

ascribed to him offers an excellent example of the types of technical treatises that came to be produced in increasing numbers in the Hellenistic period. On the Chinese side, there are two important classics that I mentioned before, the *Zhoubi suanjing* and the *Jiuzhang suanshu*, which provide the basis for a close comparison and contrast between these two traditions. The questions on which we can thereby hope to shed light are (1) what Greek and Chinese mathematics owed to the written mode and (2) whether the differences between them reflect differences in the technology of writing in question.

The treatises in the Euclidean corpus, not least the *Elements* itself, represent one extreme end of the spectrum from the point of view of *impersonality*. Euclid himself does not just not obtrude: he is invisible, and his life and character are unknown quantities. Nothing, we might say, could be further from rhetoric and rhetorical self-advertisement than mathematics. Precisely. I shall come back to that.

Neither Euclid nor the Chinese mathematical classics are conceivable without writing. On both sides, however, we can detect the direct or indirect influence of oral modes of communicating, and maybe even more important general cultural influences. Where Euclid is concerned, Netz's fine recent analysis identifies an oral background (1) in the use of formulae, (2) in the structure of proofs, and (3) in the references to the immediately present visible object, the lettered diagram (the key element that secures the necessity and generality of the proofs).[28] At the same time, the *Elements* is inconceivable apart from the written mode. This emerges clearly as soon as we consider its architectonic structure.[29] The whole is a systematic presentation of most of the mathematics known to the Greeks at the time, and the systematic character of the presentation depends on the decisions Euclid (or his predecessors) made as to the logical sequences of theorems and problems – which of these are elementary, which derivative or dependent. Yet while we cannot

---

[28] See Netz 1999: 19, 297. The lettering of the points in the diagram serves as a convenient mnemonic aid. The situation of communication that the mathematical reasoning presupposes can be envisaged as, initially, an oral one, with the discussion of the problems of proof and construction presented by the diagram. But writing evidently becomes necessary when highly complex chains of interconnected arguments are assembled in systematic and comprehensive wholes such as the *Elements* as we have it.

[29] See especially Mueller 1981.

reconstruct the processes whereby those decisions were taken, it is sufficiently clear that the whole structure of the discussion, in thirteen books, would not have been possible without written notes.

While neither the *Nine Chapters* nor the *Zhoubi* has that kind of structure (in particular, neither attempts a sequence of deductive proofs from a given, limited axiom set), both are comprehensive discussions of a wide range of problems. While both are written compositions of considerable complexity, the oral mode influences each of them directly. Both take the form of dialogues, even though in the *Nine Chapters* the speakers are not named. There is an anonymous questioner, and an answer is introduced by the expression "the Art (or Method) says." But in these dialogues, Chinese teacher–pupil relations are very much in evidence. In the *Zhoubi*, the pupil Rong Fang asks the Master, Chenzi, about what his Way can do; for example, has he heard that it can comprehend (or calculate) the height and size of the sun? Chenzi replies that indeed all the things Rong Fang mentioned can be attained by "mathematics," *suan shu*, the art of numbers. "Your ability ... is sufficient to understand such matters if you sincerely give reiterated thought to them." In practice, however, Rong Fang, having gone away to try to solve the problems on his own, has to admit defeat, and it is only after a succession of humiliations that Chenzi concedes to explain his method.[30] Even in the *Nine Chapters*, the opening of each section takes the form of questions on particular examples, with their solutions given in the answers. But quite *how* the solutions are arrived at is delayed and, indeed, sometimes emerges only from the accompanying commentaries.

Not just the style, but also the content and aims of the Chinese works reflect Chinese patterns. The overall aim is not (as in Euclid) the axiomatic-deductive proof of the totality of mathematics, but (as the commentator Liu Hui says) to find the guiding principles, the *gangji*, that unify different areas of mathematics.[31] The parallels between the principles useful in different types of problems are the overriding concern – unity, then, rather than deductive structure. Once he becomes a master of such guiding principles, the pupil can be expected to

---

[30] See Cullen 1996: 176–81 on *Zhoubi suanjing* 23.

[31] Liu Hui's commentary is included in Qian Baocong's edition of the *Jiuzhang suanshu*. He refers to the *gangji* of mathematics in, for example, his commentary to Chapter 1 at 96.4.

practice the Way on his own, and it is not just the pupil in the dialogue, but the reader of the text, who can expect to have to serve a lengthy apprenticeship to master that Way.

If Chinese mathematics reflects Chinese views about the teacher–pupil relationship and the acquisition and internalization of knowledge more generally, Euclid too reflects Greek cultural values in his very different way. Euclid's chief concern, as I said, was with proof in the axiomatic-deductive mode, proceeding from indemonstrable premises to incontrovertible conclusions. The premises themselves are meant to be self-evident. The definitions, common opinions, and postulates are introduced without comment, and only when we reflect on competing views (alternative definitions or challenges to the status of the parallel postulate as a postulate) do we see the prior decisions that the presentation of the primary indemonstrables involved. But the solutions of problems and the proofs of theorems thereupon proceed in a very different way from the Chinese practices I have described. The proof often consists in, or at least crucially depends on, the construction of the diagram (*graphō* means both "draw" and "prove").[32] But here everything is transparent, as the lettered diagram is built up in a sequence that follows the order of the Greek alphabet. Here, the idea is *not* to get pupils to work it all out on their own, but to take the pupils/readers through a sequence of unchallengeable steps to see that the conclusion *must* follow. The pupils/readers are to be overwhelmed by the conclusiveness of the demonstration: "which was what was to be proved,"[33] as the proofs end. Who can fail to agree? The reasoning is claimed to be universally valid. It does not depend on the assent of individuals, for such assent can only be given by anyone who can understand the argument. Objections that appeal to some particular viewpoint are irrelevant. The impersonal nature of the reasoning thus secures its objectivity.

Yet that style of demonstration itself owes something to the political and legal settings of Greek adversarial culture previously mentioned.[34] One stimulus to the development of that mode of deductive proof comes, I suggest, from the negative models that rhetorical debates provided; mere persuasion, the philosophers argued, as practiced in the law courts

[32] Netz 1999: Chapter 1.
[33] ὅπερ ἔδει δεῖξαι, quod erat demonstrandum.
[34] Lloyd 1996.

and political assemblies, was not enough. To secure the truth, you must have incontrovertibility, to be attained by a combination of self-evident premises and valid deductive argument. Of course, Aristotle was the first to define strict demonstration as depending on those two requirements. But it was chiefly the mathematicians who exemplified it in practice. We might think that that is an obvious, even inevitable, goal for mathematics to set itself. Yet the fact is that neither Chinese nor Indian nor Babylonian nor Egyptian mathematics shared that aim. The Chinese were concerned not with axiomatisation, but with the general unifying principles of mathematics. But those differences between the different mathematical traditions are less surprising once we take into account the influence of those negative models in the Greek case – and the *absence* of such a stimulus in the Chinese one. Axiomatic-deductive demonstration was the ultimate weapon in Greek battles in persuasion.

To sum up on mathematics: in both Greece and China the mathematics practiced (as evidenced in our extant texts) depends, in certain crucial and distinctive ways, on the written mode. The most important aspects of this relate first to the role of writing in the transmission of canonical texts and second to the part that writing necessarily played in the construction of complex interconnected reasoning. However, the distinctiveness of the mathematics produced in either society depended neither on the mere use of the written mode nor on the particular modes of writing employed. Rather, it reflected general cultural and political factors, the different ideals and aims of learning, and the different conceptions of how learning should be transmitted.

CONCLUSION

In both ancient Greece and China, due attention must be paid to the diversity of communication situations and to the varied uses to which written texts of different types were put. We should guard against attempts to generalize from what is true of poetry, or poetic performance, or of the use of official records, all the way to philosophy and mathematics and medicine. Where those last two fields are concerned, there appear to be differences in how texts were used and in the balance between orality and literacy. In China, the role of texts treated as canonical is greater than in classical Greece, though in both societies the importance of canonical texts increases in time if we compare the Han with the Warring States or the Hellenistic with the classical period. But even Confucius looked back to what he thought of as the learning of the Sage Kings: a figure such as Theseus just does not rate beside the Yellow Emperor or the Duke of Zhou.

The intense Chinese respect for the canonical texts of past wisdom did not preclude disagreement, but the sense of loyalty within the lineage was, in general, far greater than what obtained in Greek philosophical groups such as the Academy or medical groups such as the Herophilean school.[35] (Perhaps the Epicureans were an exception.) Brought up in a culture of debate and probably owing more of their instruction to the oral mode, Greek pupils were not above challenging, and even refuting, their teachers in ways that cannot be paralleled in our Chinese evidence whether from the Warring States or from the Han periods.[36]

In both ancient societies, the literate formed a privileged elite, and in both the importance of written texts for many different purposes grew over time. But the nature of that importance and the trajectory of that growth were not the same. Yet the features that make for the differences, as described here, are not those that relate to the specific technology of the written word. None can be said to derive from, or even to be influenced by, the specific alphabetic or logographic modes of writing used in Greece or China. Rather, they all relate to wider political, social, or cultural values. No doubt, we have much more to learn about the specificities of the uses of literacy both in China and in Greece throughout their varied histories, but it is salutary also to attempt to use each of those two ancient societies as the contrast set for the other.

[35] See von Staden 1989 on Herophilus.
[36] On the broader issues relating to the divergent cultural ideals of learning that can be found in ancient Greece and China, see Lloyd and Sivin (forthcoming).

7

Writing Philosophy

Prose and Poetry from Thales to Plato

Charles H. Kahn

Philosophy is a talkative subject, and it must have begun in conversation. Unfortunately, all we have from the early period is texts, and these are not abundant. But if evidence for the use of writing in philosophy before Plato is fragmentary, evidence for oral performance in this period is almost nonexistent. What little we know is generally derived from Plato, like the picture of Zeno reading his arguments before a small audience in the *Parmenides*. But how well informed was Plato about practices a century earlier? Was Heraclitus' book designed to be read aloud before such an audience? Or does the report that Heraclitus deposited his book in the temple of Artemis mean that he wanted to keep it out of circulation? Did Parmenides and Empedocles compose their verses for public performance, or only for easier memorization? We do not have answers to such questions, and I will have little to say about conditions of performance or publication.

My topic, then, is the written use of prose and poetry in the development of Greek philosophy in its first two centuries, from Thales to Plato. I am using *philosophy* here as an abbreviation for "philosophy and science." The distinction is not always a useful one to draw in the Presocratic period. It is characteristic of Greek philosophy in its formative period – as again of European philosophy in the seventeenth century – that it develops in close conjunction with mathematics and natural science.

Let me begin by briefly recalling the scope and magnitude of what takes place in these two centuries. We are dealing with the origin and rapid rise to maturity of Western science and philosophy in their earliest recognizable form.[1] The first moments of this development are located in Miletus and then in nearby Greek cities: Samos, Ephesus, Klazomenai. But the movement soon spreads to Sicily and southern Italy, and eventually to Periclean Athens, with the arrival of Anaxagoras followed by Protagoras and the younger sophists. This rapid geographical diffusion reflects the broad contagion of a novel intellectual enterprise. The core of the new project is designated by the term *natural philosophy*, which includes everything from cosmology to biology. The boundaries of natural philosophy are faithfully marked by the series of Aristotle's physical treatises, beginning with first principles (in the *Physics*) and concluding with embryology (in the *Generation of Animals*). But the scope of this new Ionian *historiē*, or "scientific inquiry," is even wider than Aristotelian *physikē*. Neither geometry nor mathematical astronomy is included in natural philosophy, but both of them belong to the project that originates in Miletus. Furthermore, as the term *historiē* itself reminds us, the Milesian project was destined to include the investigation of the past that we call history; the first beginnings can be traced back to Hecataeus of Miletus and his *Genealogies*.

So it is a new intellectual world, a new stage of human thought, that begins in Ionia in the middle of the sixth century B.C.E. and quickly spreads throughout the entire Greek world. The question before us then is: what role did writing play in this development?

When posed in general terms, this question goes far beyond my competence, but I would like to take for granted some minimal assumptions. First of all, we can reject the simplistic dichotomy between oral culture and literate culture for the period in question, the sixth and fifth centuries B.C.E. Writing had been available in Greece since the eighth century, and it is difficult to believe that either Greek mathematics or

---

[1] I am assuming that the much earlier development of Mesopotamian science is an essentially different story. I believe that what took place in Ionia in the sixth century is in part stimulated by some acquaintance with Eastern models, as one aspect of the general "orientalizing" influence on archaic Greece. Traces of this influence are marked by Herodotus' report (2.109) that the gnomon comes from Babylon and by Greek familiarity with the zodiac and, later, with the names for the planets. But the details of the contact escape us.

Greek natural philosophy could have appeared in a preliterate society. Some level of literacy was needed for the development of the sciences in Greece in the sixth and fifth centuries, just as literacy was presupposed in the much earlier development of mathematics and astronomy in Mesopotamia. But if writing was a sine qua non, it does not follow that Greek science and philosophy are consequences of literacy in any further sense. We have only to look at the sequels of literacy in Mesopotamia, India, or China to see how diverse the uses of writing can be. It may be that the invention of the Greek alphabet and the development of Greek philosophy and science are in some sense products of the same critical inventiveness that is typical of archaic Greek society, but it would seem ludicrous to claim a relation of cause and effect between the alphabet and the science. Alphabetic literacy may have been a facilitator, but this concept is no more explanatory of the rise of Greek rationalism than it is able to explain the extraordinary power of Greek poetry and drama.

What role literacy played in the spread of the new science is another matter. Here it is a question of our ignorance. We do not know how many people could read and write in the sixth century, or how well. It is necessary to suppose that the creative participants in the new science were literate (as Anaximander and Hecataeus certainly were), but we do not know how texts were used or exactly what role writing played in the diffusion of what we may call the Greek Enlightenment. We can be reasonably sure that the new ideas were brought to the West by Ionian emigrants who were already initiates, as was Xenophanes and probably Pythagoras as well. When Anaxagoras arrived in Athens, his book presumably came too (unless it was composed there), but his personal influence must have been much wider than his reading audience.[2] In the *Phaedo*, Plato's Socrates claims to have first heard Anaxagoras' ideas from someone reading the book aloud (like Zeno reading his texts to a small circle in the *Parmenides*). These practices must be older, but we do not know when they began or when philosophers began composing works intended for public reading. We can only recognize our profound ignorance of the modalities of interaction between written texts and oral communication in the sixth century B.C.E.

[2]   See Thomas, this volume.

Before discussing the use of prose and poetry, I must say what I mean by *prose*, for the term is not quite self-explanatory. I prefer to rely on a default notion of prose, so that any lengthy piece of writing that is not in metrical form automatically counts as prose. But even the restriction to writing might seem arbitrary, as in Molière's joke about the *bourgeois gentilhomme* who discovered that he had been speaking prose all his life without knowing it. The *Oxford English Dictionary* actually gives as the definition of *prose* "the ordinary form of written *or spoken* language, without metrical structure" (emphasis added), but it adds: "especially as a division of literature." This addition introduces a third sense of "prose" – as discourse that is not only written but aspires to be literary. It is in this third sense that the work of Pherecydes can be safely counted as the oldest Greek book in prose. As a theogony, it deliberately sets out to rival Hesiod. The treatise of Anaximander, on the other hand, regardless of whether it is older or younger than Pherecydes,[3] does not fit into any established literary genre and hence does not aspire to represent prose "as a division of literature." (I am using *literary* in a broader sense than does Andrew Ford in this volume, so that for me Homer and Hesiod count as literature.)

Nevertheless, Greek prose in the default sense, as the written form of the spoken language, must be as old as writing in Greece. This is true even though two of the earliest preserved examples of Greek writing are actually in verse.[4] Rosalind Thomas has shown how diverse are the uses made of writing in the graffiti of the eighth and seventh centuries: curses, dedications, claims of ownership, grave markers; one of the early examples is a potter's signature.[5] These are all private uses. But in the seventh century writing emerges into the public domain with the inscription of laws in stone. The earliest known example comes from Dreros in Crete in the second half of the seventh century.[6] Athens got its first written lawcode from Draco in about 620 B.C.E., and there is an important constitutional inscription from Chios dated ca. 600 B.C.E. The nonliterary use of written prose was thus established as a major civic reality by the end of the seventh century.

---

[3] "It was and is a matter of opinion whether the contemporary of the Seven Wise Men [viz. Pherecydes] was not earlier than the philosopher of Miletus" (Jacoby 1947: 21).

[4] But not the very earliest one, which is a simple ownership claim dated ca. 740 B.C.E. See R. Thomas 1992.

[5] R. Thomas 1992: 57–61.   [6] R. Thomas 1992: 66.

The use of prose for literary purposes is a different story. Accepting the ancient view that Pherecydes' theogonical work is the oldest Greek prose book, we can say that the tradition of prose as a form of literature begins around 550 B.C.E.[7] It is no accident that this date coincides with our starting point for the documented history of Greek philosophy. It is true that Aristotle and others begin their account one generation earlier, since they name Thales as the first natural philosopher. But Thales in the first half of the sixth century is a borderline case for the history of philosophy, precisely because (as far as we know) he did not leave behind a prose treatise. Our information for Pythagoras, at the end of the sixth century, is similarly unreliable, since the alleged Pythagorean vow of silence apparently had as its counterpart a ban on writing. Thus there is no Pythagorean treatise before Philolaus in the second half of the fifth century. By then written prose had been the established instrument for philosophy and science for over one hundred years.

On the other hand, we recall that three major figures in the Presocratic tradition – Xenophanes, Parmenides, and Empedocles – made use of the older medium of verse. I want to reflect here on the origin and development of the prose treatise as a vehicle for philosophic and scientific thought, but also on the option just mentioned – the pursuit of the new science in the old genre of didactic epic verse. Finally, we will consider the radical break with both traditions in the dialogues of Plato.

PHERECYDES OF SYROS

We have seen why, and in what sense, despite our ignorance of the precise date, Pherecydes can reasonably be regarded as the author of the first prose book. But why did Pherecydes decide to write in prose rather than in verse? We can only guess, but my guess is that he chose prose in order to distance himself from the model of Hesiod's *Theogony*, with which he is competing, and probably also from the Orphic poem in hexameter verse that we know from the Derveni papyrus.[8] One way

---

[7]   The best ancient tradition puts Pherecydes' *floruit* at 544–541 B.C.E., which would make him younger than Anaximander; see Schibli 1990: 2. For Anaximander's date, see p. 145.

[8]   The date of the Orphic poem is unknown. West 1983: 110 dates it to ca. 500 B.C.E., but I have the impression that it is earlier than Pherecydes. On the Derveni papyrus, see Yunis, this volume: 195 with note 21.

of understanding the avoidance of meter is to see it as a challenge to the poetic tradition. Perhaps there is an implicit claim to greater truth: verse would be suited for fiction, prose for facts. (This contrast may be implicit in Hecataeus' opening sentence, quoted below, pages 153–4.) Of course, Pherecydes' theogony is a fantastic story of his own invention, but presenting it in prose seems to give it a kind of veridical claim. At any rate, in later times prose was regarded as *pezos logos*, "pedestrian discourse," less given to flights of fancy.[9]

We cannot be sure of Pherecydes' motivation, but we do know that a work in literary prose is something new in the middle of the sixth century. In this and other respects, Pherecydes' work belongs to the new age that is dawning in Ionian speculation. Although Pherecydes is certainly no *physikos* in the tradition of natural philosophy developing in contemporary Miletus, he is nevertheless responding to new modes of thought. His cosmogony is much more allegorical and symbolical than Hesiod's. Thus, his opening sentence runs: "Zas and Chronos were forever and Chthonie."[10] All three names play on traditional divinities (Zeus, Kronos, and Gaia), but they also contain etymological and symbolical overtones: Zas suggests life; *chronos* means time; *chthoniē* alludes to the underworld. Pherecydes' claim that these first gods were not born (as in Hesiod's poem) but always existed may well reflect the influence of Milesian philosophy, as does the similar insistence by Xenophanes a generation later that it is impious to speak of gods coming into existence.[11] But even if Pherecydes is entirely independent of the new natural philosophy, and whether or not he is relying on Orphic or Near Eastern models, his deliberate deviations from Hesiod show a fundamentally new way of thinking about how the world began.[12] And the enterprise of rationalizing mythology, which Pherecydes is pursuing, will also provide one of the subjects for Milesian *historiē*, as we can see from the *Genealogies* of Hecataeus in the next generation.

---

[9] Compare the suggestion of Laks 2001: 147 that Pherecydes' prose, by avoiding an appeal to the Muses as source, amounts to a "secularization" of the genre by contrast with Hesiod. I have learned a good deal from Laks' article, which he kindly allowed me to see in advance of its publication.

[10] Ζὰς μὲν καὶ Χρόνος ἦσαν ἀεὶ καὶ Χθονίη (DK 7 B1).

[11] Xenophanes, DK 21 A11, B14. Cf. also Anaximander DK 12 A5.

[12] Schibli 1990: 133–4.

It is natural to ask what earlier uses of prose (other than law codes and inscriptions) Pherecydes might have been familiar with. Before speculating on origins, however, let us consider the well-attested scientific tradition that begins in Miletus.

ANAXIMANDER OF MILETUS

On the authority of Apollodorus, Diogenes Laertius reports that Anaximander was sixty-four years old in 547 B.C.E. "and died soon after."[13] If this is correct, Anaximander's dates would be approximately between 611 and 545 B.C.E. His book, of which only one sentence has survived but whose outlines we know from the Theophrastean doxography, is the first specimen of a new genre, the treatise *peri physeōs*, "on the nature of things."[14] The success of the new genre is evident from its continued use by Anaximenes, Anaxagoras, Diogenes, and others in the Ionian tradition, and by Alcmaeon and Philolaus in Doric prose. The genre *peri physeōs* is also illustrated by the physical poem of Empedocles and the cosmological section (the so-called *Doxa*) of the work of Parmenides, and it is paralleled by those fragments of Xenophanes that deal with natural philosophy. As we can see from both the doxography and the extant fragments, these treatises and poems often deal with a standard set of topics in an established order, beginning with first principles and the origin of heaven and earth and ending with the formation of human beings. (There is a partial precedent for this order in Hesiod's *Theogony*.) We have a clear parallel, for both these topics and this ordering, in Plato's *Timaeus*. As I have mentioned, the same traditional pattern is preserved in Aristotle's physical writings, beginning with *Physics* and *De Caelo* and ending with *De Anima*, *Parva Naturalia*, and the biological works. This set of topics, and probably this ordering

---

[13] Diogenes Laertius 2.3 = *FGrH* 244 F 29. Diogenes also claims (2.2) that Anaximander "made a summary exposition of his doctrines" (τῶν ἀρεσκόντων αὐτῷ πεποίηται κεφαλαιώδη τὴν ἔκθεσιν), which Apollodorus had access to.

[14] I do not mean to beg the question of when the title περὶ φύσεως came into use. But there is some evidence that Plato and Aristotle knew Empedocles' poem under this title; see Kahn 1960: 6 n. 2. I assume that the term was already in use in the fifth century. It is hard to believe that Gorgias' witty title περὶ τοῦ μὴ ὄντος ἢ περὶ φύσεως was not his own invention. And compare φύσεως in Euripides frag. 910 Nauck (cited at DK 59 A30 in connection with Anaxagoras).

as well, goes back to Milesian times and ultimately to the book of Anaximander; the genre *peri physeōs* is extraordinarily conservative.[15]

We have a later rearrangement of the old pattern in Lucretius' poem *On the Nature of Things*, where the order of topics has been altered because of doctrinal priorities: for Epicurean reasons, psychology and perception are treated by Lucretius in Books 3 and 4, before cosmogony and meteorology, which are postponed to Book 5. But Lucretius Book 5 includes an important extension of the cosmological narrative, an extension that finds a Hellenistic parallel in Diodorus Siculus. After the formation of the world and living creatures, both Lucretius and Diodorus offer a history of human culture, from primitive man in the state of nature to the creation of the city and the arts. Here, Lucretius is following Epicurus, who follows Democritus, but this addition of a *Kulturentstehungslehre* to the *peri physeōs* tradition is probably older than the atomists. It must go back at least to Anaxagoras and perhaps even to his Milesian predecessors, since human history in this perspective is simply a continuation of cosmogony. As von Fritz pointed out long ago, we can identify the common origin of natural philosophy and history in Milesian *historiē*. Hecataeus, too, was a Milesian.[16]

Anaximander's book, then, is the prototype for a long-lived literary genre, the prose treatise *peri physeōs*. But this same little book is also our first partially preserved example of a wider, almost certainly older tradition – the tradition of technical prose, which perhaps surfaces first in Miletus but which appears elsewhere in Ionia almost at the same moment in the architectural works to be mentioned later. (I am here using "prose" in the default sense, leaving aside the question of literary aspirations.) By technical prose I mean memoranda and notes used in practicing, improving, and teaching a technical specialty. In

---

[15] Some scholars have suggested that the order of topics in the doxography depends on Plato's *Timaeus* and Aristotle rather than on the original order of the lost treatises. However, I think we can be sure that the general sequence is older than the *Timaeus*, because (1) the order is determined by the logic of cosmogony, which, replacing theogony, starts "in the beginning" and works down to the present; (2) this order is confirmed in part by the extant fragments of Parmenides and Anaxagoras; and (3) it is repeated in the origin-of-culture texts from Lucretius and Diodorus, both of which derive from pre-Socratic sources. Hence it is clear that the *Timaeus* and Aristotle are generally following (rather than creating) a traditional order of topics.

[16] von Fritz 1953.

the late sixth and early fifth centuries, such prose is well attested both in Ionic and in Doric Greek before it appears in Athens in the middle or late fifth century. The works of Hecataeus provide two early examples of prose treatises that do not belong to the genre *peri physeōs*: the quasi-historical *Genealogies* and a geographical work, *gēs periodos*, or "Travels Around the World." Scylax of Caryanda, who explored the Indus for Darius, apparently produced a *Periplous* (a "voyage around") known to Hecataeus and Herodotus, even though the treatise preserved under his name is a later reworking.[17] Fifth-century examples of technical prose treatises in history, science, and the arts are well documented. The best preserved are those older Hippocratic writings that are relatively free of rhetorical elaboration.[18]

THE ORIGINS OF THE PROSE TREATISE IN GREECE

I want to look now for the origins of this phenomenon, the appearance of the prose treatise in the sixth century B.C.E. A good place to start is with the book of Heraclitus (*floruit* ca. 500), the first prose work from which we have substantial remains. We can learn something of the intellectual environment at the end of the sixth century from two fragments in which Heraclitus refers polemically to his predecessors. Heraclitus attacks Hesiod, Pythagoras, Xenophanes, and Hecataeus for their *polymathiē* ("much learning"), which did not teach them understanding.[19] Since Pythagoras (and his associates) did not set down their thoughts in writing, he can be known to Heraclitus only by reputation via the oral tradition, but Heraclitus knows the other three from their literary work. We notice that in this text a prose author, Hecataeus, has joined the company of two poets, Hesiod and Xenophanes. If prose literature was new with Pherecydes in the middle of the sixth century, it is at home by the end of that century, as Heraclitus' own work will show.

Even more revealing for the early history of prose is another text in which Heraclitus singles out Pythagoras for special attention (DK 22 B129): Pythagoras "practiced *historiē* more than all other men, and

---

[17] *FGrH* IIIC.709; Hecataeus, *FGrH* 1 F 295, 296; *RE* III.A.1.619–46; Herodotus 4.44.

[18] See Dean-Jones, this volume: 112.

[19] πολυμαθίη νόον ἔχειν οὐ διδάσκει· Ἡσίοδον γὰρ ἂν ἐδίδαξε καὶ Πυθαγόρην αὖτίς τε Ξενοφάνεά τε καὶ Ἑκαταῖον (DK 22 B40).

selecting from these compositions (*eklexamenos tautas tas syngraphas*) he made his own brand of wisdom, much learning, artful knavery."[20] Since *syngraphē* is the normal term for a prose treatise, fragment B129 implies that such writings were available in some abundance in the second half of the sixth century.[21] Not all scholars have been persuaded of the authenticity of the curious phrase *eklexamenos tautas tas syngraphas*, "selecting from these compositions," but the consensus of editors of Heraclitus (except for Diels) has accepted these words as genuine.[22] So we must ask ourselves: if this wording is authentic, what sixth-century *syngraphai* could Heraclitus be referring to?

In an earlier paper, I collected references to texts that might qualify as Pythagoras' alleged sources.[23] The only obvious cases are the two early prose authors already mentioned, Pherecydes and Anaximander. Perhaps we might add Anaximenes, but Hecataeus would certainly be too late to count as a source for Pythagoras. Besides the works of Pherecydes and the two Milesian cosmologists, what *syngraphai* could Heraclitus be referring to?

There are two archaic traditions that deserve our attention in this regard. The first is a set of didactic poems of a strictly practical nature.[24] These may be thought of as a continuation of the genre created by the agricultural manual contained in Hesiod's *Works and Days*. (Perhaps hexameter poetry was used for this purpose before Hesiod, but it is simpler to assume Hesiod's originality here.) We do not know when other authors began to imitate Hesiod in composing didactic epic poems, but Nilsson argued for the antiquity (though not the authenticity) of the following:

1. A *gēs periodos*, a geographical description of the world, ascribed to Hesiod, that would be the precedent for Hecataeus' work of that genre.

---

[20] Πυθαγόρης Μνησάρχου ἱστορίην ἤσκησεν ἀνθρώπων μάλιστα πάντων καὶ ἐκλεξάμενος ταύτας τὰς συγγραφὰς ἐποιήσατο ἑαυτοῦ σοφίην, πολυμαθίην, κακοτεχνίην.

[21] For the restriction of *syngraphē* to works in prose, see Dover 1997: 183–4. Herodotus uses the term only once (1.93.1) for his own activity of recording things worthy of wonder (θώματα).

[22] The authenticity of fragment B129 is reinforced by the parallel uses of ἐκλέγεσθαι cited by Mansfeld 1990: 444.

[23] Kahn 1983.   [24] See Nilsson 1905.

2. An *Astronomy* concerned with star settings, likewise ascribed to Hesiod.

3. The famous *Nautical Astronomy* handed down under Thales' name but also attributed to Phocus of Samos.

4. An astronomical poem of Cleostratus of Tenedos, containing the first Greek mention of the signs of the zodiac.

5. Less well attested is a *Kataplous*, or versified description of harbors.

These lost archaic poems would not be works of speculation but practical handbooks for use in agriculture and navigation. One motive for the use of verse would be ease of memorization. Such sixth-century verse handbooks would be the direct ancestors of the technical literature in prose that is attested by the books of the Milesians.

Since the term *syngraphē* in Heraclitus fragment B129 is normally used only to refer to works in prose, the early verse handbooks do not properly qualify as references for Heraclitus' charge of plagiarism against Pythagoras. At what point were prose handbooks first produced for the same practical purposes, such as the *Periplous*, attributed to Scylax in the time of Darius? In this connection, we must consider another technical tradition from an even earlier period that almost certainly made use of prose. In his preface to Book 7 of *On Architecture*, Vitruvius lists a number of temples whose architects left behind a description of their buildings. Among these are two works that belong to the middle of the sixth century B.C.E. and hence to the time of Pythagoras. One is a description of the Heraion at Samos by the famous Samian sculptor and architect Theodorus, and the other is an account of the second colossal Ionian construction, the Croesus temple of Artemis at Ephesus by Chersiphron and Metagenes.[25] These two major architectural achievements marked the birth of monumental temple building in Ionian Greece. The Samian Heraion was the first Greek temple entirely in stone on this monumental scale, and its rival in Ephesus was even larger and built in heavier marble rather than in local stone. It is reasonable to suppose that the treatises composed by the architects in each case were designed to publicize the glory of their constructions,

---

[25] The books are mentioned only by Vitruvius 7, preface 10, but they are assumed to be the source of the other information on these early temples in Vitruvius and Pliny. See, e.g., on Chersiphron in *RE* III.2.2241–2.

but these writings would inevitably have included some technical detail.[26] Recently, Robert Hahn has argued that Thales, Anaximander, and the Ionian architects (Theodorus, Chersiphron, Metagenes, and also Eupalinus, the builder of the Samian tunnel in the next generation) should all be considered together as "practical men with broad interests and competence in matters pertaining to applied geometry."[27] The two colossal temples are dated in the middle of the sixth century, and the corresponding books must have appeared in the same period. Recalling that Anaximander is said to have died shortly after 548/7 B.C.E., we see that he and the temple architects are exact contemporaries as well as close neighbors.

So we have three technical treatises in prose from the middle of the sixth century (the *peri physeōs* by Anaximander and the two temple descriptions, one by Theodorus, the other by Chersiphron and Metagenes), at approximately the same time as the book of Pherecydes. Were there more prose treatises in this period, and is it only a matter of chance survival that we have no similar evidence for early writings in geometry, music, and sculpture? The earliest treatise on music is ascribed to Lasus of Hermione, at the end of the sixth century.[28] We do know of a number of fifth-century treatises, such as the *Canon* of Polyclitus and the work of Hippodamus of Miletus, the urban planner, whose lost book must have formed the basis for Aristotle's very detailed discussion of it in *Politics* 2.8. We might think of Hippodamus as the last representative of the Milesian school. His work seems to have included natural philosophy and political theory as well as city planning. No quotations from Hippodamus have been preserved, but his book must have been in prose, in the technical tradition attested for the earlier Milesians and for the Samian and Ephesian architects.

To return to the conditions for the emergence of prose in the sixth century: This event is surrounded by large stretches of the unknown, but it would not be wise to confuse the unknown with the nonexistent.

---

[26] "Although these architectural works are lost, it seems likely that the detailed information about the two temples preserved in later authors is derived from them. If so, we can be sure they were not preliminary specifications for the buildings, as sometimes has been argued, for we learn of the problems that arose during the construction. The emphasis seems to have been on the technical problems involved." (J. J. Coulton, cited by Hahn 2001: 260–1).

[27] Hahn 2001: 83.   [28] *OCD* s.v. Lasus.

Our task is not only to mark carefully the limits of what is attested, but also to take into account the importance of what happens not to have been preserved.[29] The little cluster of treatises from the middle of the sixth century – the works of Pherecydes, Anaximander, and the architects – suggests that the use of prose had suddenly become a recognized form of communication for a semiliterate or quasi-literate audience, an audience with access to books even if the texts were normally read aloud. (By quasi-literate I mean people like Lysis' parents in Plato's dialogue [*Lysis* 209ab], who may be interested in books but expect to be read to.) It seems plausible to assume that there were other prose writings in the sixth century and that it is simply an accident that so few books are attested for this period. We would then have a natural explanation for the phrase "these compositions" (*tautas tas syngraphas*) in Heraclitus fragment B129. My concern here is not to defend the authenticity of this phrase but rather, assuming authenticity, to ask what writings there were for Heraclitus to refer to as available in the time of Pythagoras. My hypothesis is to suggest the existence, by the middle of the sixth century (and perhaps much earlier), of a fairly widespread use of written prose for largely practical purposes, including technical notes or memoranda and other devices for recording and accumulating information, produced by and designed for specialists in astronomy, geometry, architecture, sculpture, and music. Much of this written material would be unintelligible except to readers trained in the corresponding *technē*. Such technical documents would include "the purely practical canons of proportions long employed by Greek artists,"[30] as well as the applied mathematics of the building trades, which permitted such sixth-century achievements as the colossal temples and the tunnel of Eupalinus. It is precisely this "technical," narrowly pragmatic use of writing that is in question when we say that the rise of Greek science is unthinkable in a preliterate society.

Yet we must distinguish between this essentially technical and utilitarian use of writing, which we can assume as an internal instrument

---

[29] Compare Dover 1997: 60 on Greek rhetoric before Antiphon: "For the historian, the fact that data of the highest importance are irrecoverably hidden in darkness is extremely unsatisfactory; but we must never allow that patch of darkness to slip out of our field of vision, never treat what cannot be investigated as if for that reason it did not matter."

[30] Pollitt 1974: 258.

for training and progress within a particular discipline, and the new literary use that is attested by the cluster of treatises known from the middle of the sixth century. Certainly for Pherecydes, and perhaps for the other early authors as well, the composition of an extended text is designed not to train experts in some field but to make the material available to a larger audience, probably by way of a public reading.[31] A similar function may have been served earlier by metrical composition in the verse manuals ascribed to Hesiod and Thales. I suggest that our cluster of titles from the middle of the sixth century signals the moment when the prose treatise begins to take over the role previously served by didactic hexameter verse, the moment when technical material begins to be presented in the form of literary prose.

To return now to Heraclitus fragment B129. When Heraclitus accuses Pythagoras of selecting his ideas from "these compositions" (*tautas tas syngraphas*), is he referring only to these newer, more literary compositions or to older, more specialized notes and memoranda? Perhaps we do not need to choose; the transition from the latter to the former must have been a gradual one. And since we have no quotations from the architects' writings and only one short quotation from Anaximander, we cannot really say how far these early "treatises" had moved away from technical handbooks, designed for use by specialists, in the direction of a literary work for a broader audience (as represented by the book of Pherecydes). We may suppose that it is to all sorts of *syngraphai*, or "writings down," of astronomical lore, physical speculation, and applied mathematics that Heraclitus is referring when he accuses Pythagoras of deriving his system of cosmic harmony from an extensive practice of *historiē*, that is, from the study of mathematical proportions in astronomy and the arts.[32] One of the most likely referents would be the *syngraphē* of Anaximander, with its numerical ratios for the dimensions of the earth and the celestial rings.

FROM PROSE TREATISE TO PROSE LITERATURE

To sum up our results so far: The Ionian prose treatise emerges in the middle and late sixth century from an assumed tradition of technical

---

[31] This argument is pursued further in the chapters by Thomas and Yunis.

[32] For this view of Pythagoras as a pupil of the Milesians and for the source of the Pythagorean tradition in cosmology, see Kahn 2001.

memoranda that must go back almost to the invention of writing both in Greece and earlier in the East. On this view, the writings of Anaximander, Anaximenes, and the Samian and Ephesian architects, which happen to be recorded for the middle or late sixth century, might be regarded simply as the tip of the iceberg. Most of the earlier technical handbooks would soon go out of date and disappear without a trace. Given the extent of our ignorance, it is difficult to say how far the titles that have been preserved were more literary in form, designed for a wider audience, and how far their survival is due to external advantages. Thus, the architectural writings remained of interest to Vitruvius (or to his sources) because they were composed by famous artists and associated with the two colossal temples. The book of Pherecydes was preserved into late Roman times, presumably because of Pherecydes' association with Pythagoras, as well as his bizarre style and imaginative allegory, all of which appealed to later Platonists and Neoplatonists. For quite different reasons, because of their cosmological content and their role as ancestors of the *peri physeōs* tradition, the treatises of Anaximander and Anaximenes lasted long enough to be studied and excerpted by Theophrastus in the middle of the fourth century, after which they practically seem to disappear.[33] The books of Hecataeus and the fifth-century natural philosophers (*physikoi*) were of more durable interest and more frequently quoted by later writers. Thus, we have a collection of the first sentences from these books, probably cited as titles in the Alexandrian library and preserved by Diogenes Laertius (or, in the case of Hecataeus, preserved by Demetrius, *On Style*). The opening sentence of Hecataeus' *Genealogies* is quite striking: "Hecataeus of Miletus says as follows: I write these things as they seem to me to be

---

[33] The later doxography for Anaximander and Anaximenes seems almost wholly dependent upon Theophrastus. An exception is the possible citation of a single word from Anaximenes by Plutarch (DK 13 B1). Diogenes Laertius (2.2) remarks with surprise that "Apollodorus of Athens somehow encountered" Anaximander's book. And we now have epigraphical evidence that a copy of this book was also present in the second century B.C.E. library at Tauromenium. See Blanck 1997, who speculates that the Tauromenium copy may have come from Alexandria, where Apollodorus presumably found the book. The remark in Diogenes Laertius (2.3) that Anaximenes "used an Ionic style that was simple and unadorned" may come either from Apollodorus or from Theophrastus. It is apparently the latter who is quoted by Simplicius for the comment on the poetic expressions in the passage cited from Anaximander.

true. In my opinion the *logoi* of the Greeks are many and ridiculous."[34] Hecataeus' self-identification as Milesian confirms the impression that he is writing for a broader audience, not limited to his native city.

Perhaps we can recognize in Hecataeus' words the spirit of the new science, which insists on a confrontation with the older, essentially poetic tradition in the interest of truth. But if so, this attitude is not the prerogative of the prose treatise. The most explicit statement of such confrontation, and the first shot in the ancient quarrel between philosophy and poetry, comes in the attack on Homer and Hesiod in the work of the philosopher–poet Xenophanes, a contemporary of Hecataeus.

Both the attack on erroneous *logoi* and the fierce self-assertion in the first person show that Hecataeus, like Xenophanes, intends his work for a larger public: this is no technical handbook. My guess is that the Milesian cosmologists were writing in a less personal and less polemical style; there is no parallel in the prose of Anaxagoras, who seems to have begun in a businesslike way: "All things were together."[35] Working not in the specialized fields of astronomy and cosmology but in proto-history and geography, Hecataeus aims his writing at a popular audience – the audience that was actually captured two generations later by the larger talent of Herodotus. We might think of Hecataeus' book as an unsuccessful attempt to transform the Ionian prose treatise into a work of literary art. As we have seen, an earlier, more successful attempt to do just this – to produce a work of prose literature – had been made by Pherecydes. But the real achievement in this line is the work of the two great masters of Ionic prose: Heraclitus and Herodotus.

There is no need to expand here on Herodotus' achievement as the creator of narrative history, or on his power as a storyteller and a stylist. Writing in the age of the Athenian tragedians, he aims like Homer to produce a work that will guarantee to the great deeds of the Greeks and barbarians "their due meed of glory."[36] In the writings of Herodotus and then of Thucydides, the Ionian prose treatise has finally achieved the status of a major literary genre. The etymology of the term *history* reminds us of the continuity of this enterprise with its sixth-century beginnings. Like the Milesians before him, Herodotus presents to the

---

[34] Ἑκαταῖος Μιλήσιος ὧδε μυθεῖται· τάδε γράφω, ὥς μοι δοκεῖ ἀληθέα εἶναι· οἱ γὰρ Ἑλλήνων λόγοι πολλοί τε καὶ γελοῖοι, ὡς ἐμοὶ φαίνονται, εἰσίν (*FGrH* 1 F 1).

[35] ὁμοῦ πάντα χρήματα ἦν (DK 59 B1).

[36] Rawlinson's phrase from Herodotus' proem.

world the product of his "research": the first sentence of his work opens with the words "this is the demonstration of my *historiē*."[37]

In Hecataeus, and above all in Herodotus, Milesian science has become history. In the case of the other great Ionic stylist, Heraclitus, it has become something else: our first philosophical classic. Heraclitus' book contained enough references to natural phenomena and cosmology for Aristotle and Theophrastus to classify him among the *physikoi*. But if his sentences are so memorable even today, that is not only because of their poetic power. Heraclitus has succeeded in a task that the *physikoi* proper seem not even to have undertaken, namely, to project a vision of the cosmos that provides a meaningful interpretation of human life and death. Thus, the alternating or simultaneous kindling and going out of ever living Fire mark the measures of the up-and-down path of the deep *logos* of the human soul. And like Herodotus, perhaps like all great writers, Heraclitus has achieved his result by drawing on the resources of different genres and traditions. By choosing the medium of the prose treatise, as well as by the cosmological content of his *logos*, Heraclitus has identified himself with the new science. But his conception of the *psychē* draws on a different source, the Pythagorean tradition, which seems to have been exclusively oral.[38] And his characteristic style derives in part from the aphoristic manner that is typical of another oral tradition, the wisdom of the Seven Sages. It has often been noted that Heraclitus' book preserves the convention of an oral *logos*: his "hearers" fail to understand him, and he speaks of his own "hearing the *logoi*" of others (DK 22 B1, 108). Was his book composed for reading aloud? I will return to this question of performance.

THREE POETIC EXCEPTIONS

We have seen that from Anaximander to Anaxagoras, Diogenes, and Democritus – roughly, from 550 to 400 B.C.E. – the standard vehicle of Greek natural philosophy was the Ionian prose treatise (turned into Doric with Alcmaeon and Philolaus). Why then did three major thinkers from this same period choose to write in verse?

---

[37] Ἡροδότου Ἁλικαρνησσέος ἱστορίης ἀπόδεχις ἥδε.

[38] We should take note, however, of the ancient report that some Orphic writings were composed by Pythagoras or by Pythagoreans; see Linforth 1941: 110–14; West 1983: 7–20; Kahn 2001: 20.

The question calls for a different answer for each of the three exemplars: Xenophanes, Parmenides, and Empedocles. For Xenophanes, the question need scarcely be raised. As an elegiac poet, he was a typical figure of his age, composing in a form designed for oral performance, for example, at a symposium. The appropriate parallel is not to Anaximander or Thales but to the Athenian sage, Solon. Like Solon, Xenophanes was an original thinker who used the popular medium of the day in an effort to shape public opinion on highly controversial matters. In the sixth century, elegiac verse was used for the pamphleteering function that was served by the funeral oration in Plato's day.[39] In Xenophanes' case, the burning issues were not so much political as theological. And behind his new, more austere conception of the gods[40] lies a new view of the natural world that derives from Milesian cosmology. Colophon, like Samos, is no great distance from Miletus, and Xenophanes was, like Pythagoras, one of those Ionians who carried the new science with them westward to southern Italy. Xenophanes is a poet whose world view was decisively shaped by the new natural philosophy. That he should also count as the teacher of Parmenides (as Aristotle reports) seems to me much more dubious.[41] I want to emphasize my scepticism on this point, because I think there is no good reason to suppose that Parmenides' choice of hexameter verse was significantly influenced by the precedent of Xenophanes. The didactic epic had been created long ago by Hesiod, by "Orpheus," and by others, and this option was equally available for all three of our philosophic poets.

[39] See Kahn 1963 on the funeral oration. There is no reason to insult Xenophanes by calling him a rhapsode on the basis of an overinterpretation of DK 21 A1: αὐτὸς ἐρραψῴδει τὰ ἑαυτοῦ. Of course he recited his own poems, but so did Solon.

[40] In the plural – Xenophanes is no monotheist. Like any Greek, Xenophanes makes systematic use of the plural θεοί; see Lesher 1992: 98–9.

[41] In the *Sophist*, Plato jokingly referred to "the Eleatic tribe, beginning with Xenophanes and even earlier" (242d). Since Plato likes to describe Parmenides as defending "the thesis of the One," we can see how, abstractly considered, the "one greatest god" of Xenophanes B23 could be thought of as the ancestor of the Parmenidean One. Furthermore, Plato may be alluding to the fact that Xenophanes had composed a poem on the colonization of Elea, but there is no evidence that he had settled there. I take it that the conception of Xenophanes as a proto-Eleatic is a distortion of the doxographic tradition, beginning with Aristotle, who here (as often) seems to have taken Plato's lighthearted remarks too literally.

Parmenides' choice of verse is the most problematic, since he is the least naturally gifted as a poet. His use of the epic form must hang together with his extraordinary proem, in which an unnamed *kouros* ("young man") reports a supernatural chariot ride that transports him from the halls of Night to the precinct of the goddess. This presentation of Parmenides' doctrine as a divine revelation could scarcely fit into the customary frame of an Ionian prose treatise. But this natural explanation of the poetic form only relocates the question: why does Parmenides choose to present his accounts of Truth and Opinion, *Alētheia* and *Doxa*, as the content of a supernatural revelation?

The parallel with Hesiod's inspiration by the Muses in the *Theogony* is certainly apt, but does not touch the deeper question of why a rigorous argument should be represented as the utterance of a goddess. There may have been other, more esoteric literary antecedents that are now lost, involving divine revelation, that would make Parmenides' proem seem less of a singularity.[42] And there is also the possibility, endorsed by several commentators, that Parmenides' allegorical journey should be read as the expression of a deep personal experience of enlightenment. But such biographical hypotheses must remain pure speculation. What is clear is that Parmenides' choice of this genre and this inspiration serves to emphasize the immense disparity between his own conception of Being and the world view of Ionian physics formulated in the prose treatises. Furthermore, perhaps the most important philosophical consequence of Parmenides' presenting his doctrine as a divine revelation is that it provides a neat device for avoiding the logical incoherence that would attach to any *human* claim to denounce the specieswide error of a mortal point of view.[43] Parmenides' poetic framework thus allows him to assume the position to which all philosophy seems to aspire: to see the world from a god's-eye point of view.

There are other, more technical advantages of the poetic form. Verse is easier to memorize, of course, and the force of Parmenides' argument would be easier to appreciate for someone who had committed it to memory and could review it at will. Furthermore, in the archaic Greek

---

[42] Suggested by Hermann Diels, cited in Coxon 1986: 17, and developed by Bowra 1953. The new material on Empedocles (below, note 44) points in the same direction.

[43] Similarly Most 1999: 354.

world, poetry still seems better adapted for public reading. All three poetic authors give the impression that they are targeting a wider audience than their more prosaic colleagues. And in the case of Parmenides and Empedocles, the two Western authors, we have the suspicion, difficult to confirm, that there is a strong influence of quasi-Pythagorean proselytizing in their background.

Empedocles' choice of epic verse is easier to explain, since he has the precedent of Parmenides immediately before him. We can see, both from Empedocles' vision of the divine Sphere and from his rejection of the usual notions of coming-to-be and passing-away, that he has been profoundly influenced by Parmenides' argument. In addition, Empedocles is a considerable poet with a difficult, baroque style. If we knew more of the religious poetry of this period, we might understand Empedocles much better. The new Empedocles material from the Strasbourg papyrus indicates that his poem *peri physeōs* contained much religious material (including an emphasis on reincarnation and an acknowledgment of prenatal pollution) that had previously been assigned to the poem entitled *Katharmoi* (*Purifications*). The new material does not, however, show that the two titles refer to a single work, as some scholars had suggested.[44] It seems rather that, just as Parmenides had included a *peri physeōs* as a section of his larger poem (namely, as the *Doxa*, following on the *Alētheia* and the allegorical proem), so Empedocles has enclosed his poem *peri physeōs* within a larger, more apocalyptic framework, perhaps inspired by a tradition of religious poetry that has largely disappeared from our view.

PLATO

No poet of the classical period – and perhaps no poet before Lucretius – followed in the footsteps of Parmenides and Empedocles. There seem to be no more didactic epics by philosophers. (There is only a partial parallel in Cleanthes' *Hymn to Zeus*; for science, but not for philosophy, there is a kind of continuation in Aratus' *Phainomena*.) The Ionian prose treatise is continued or replaced, first by the writings of the sophists, such as Protagoras' work entitled *Truth* and Gorgias' parody of a treatise "On the Nature of Things," and then by the handbooks on rhetoric, the technical prose of the fourth century, the school treatises of Aristotle

---

[44] See the new texts in Martin and Primavesi 1999, with discussion on 114–19.

and Theophrastus, the writings of Epicurus (including the new episto-
lary form, made popular by Isocrates), and so on into Hellenistic times.
But the major formal innovation – not only for philosophy, but for literature generally – is the Platonic dialogue.

The dialogue form has been so long established in the history of philosophy that it is easy to overlook the unique historical circumstances of
its creation. Plato did not invent his new art form *ex nihilo*. He found
in existence a minor prose genre, the *logos Sōkratikos*, or "Conversations with Socrates," apparently based on the mime and practiced on a
small scale by writers such as Antisthenes and Aeschines. In my view,
Plato's three shortest works (*Crito, Ion, Lesser Hippias*) can be thought
of as continuing this common practice of the minor Socratics, but with
the *Gorgias* and *Protagoras*, *Symposium* and *Phaedo*, we have something
new: a major literary form rivaling comparison with the masterpieces
of Attic drama.

The availability of the Socratic dialogue form was a godsend for Plato,
and not only for literary reasons. We must bear in mind that Plato's primary contact with philosophy in the person of Socrates was exclusively
oral. Of course, Socrates and Plato were also acquainted with the work
of the Presocratics in the written mode. But Socrates, Plato's paradigm
philosopher, did not write. His practice of philosophy was entirely conversational, "dialectical," as Plato will say. The existence of the Socratic
dialogue genre permitted Plato to make use of his extraordinary dramatic talent without betraying the Socratic conception of philosophy
as a form of life rather than a form of literature. Plato was thus able
to depict in writing the Socratic practice of philosophy by the spoken
word.[45] And we can see from Plato's own comments on writing, both
in the *Phaedrus* and in the *Seventh Epistle*, that he was himself acutely
aware of this tension.

It would be pointless for me to try to summarize here what I have said
in a recent book on Plato's "philosophical use of a literary form."[46] Let
me make only one point in connection with the technical prose treatise.

With an allowable degree of oversimplification, we can divide Plato's
dialogues into two groups. (I think of this division as chronological,
but the chronology is not essential.) The first group begins with the
Apology and the shorter dialogues and ends with the *Republic* and the

---

[45] See Yunis, this volume.   [46] Kahn 1996.

Phaedrus. The second group begins with the *Parmenides* and *Theaetetus* and includes *Sophist, Statesman, Philebus,* and *Timaeus.* (The *Laws* does not really fit into my second group. That is one of the simplifications.) I want to suggest that this division into two groups corresponds to two different audiences – exoteric and esoteric. The shorter dialogues and the great literary works are directed to a wider circle of educated readers (or hearers, perhaps). Of course there is plenty of philosophical content, but one does not need to be a philosopher to read these works with pleasure. And, in fact, they are often read today in courses in literature or humanities or classics-in-translation, as well as in introductory courses in philosophy. This is the group of dialogues I am calling exoteric or dramatic.

The other group, from *Parmenides* and *Theaetetus* to *Sophist* and *Timaeus*, I call esoteric or technical. These are works of philosophy written for philosophers. Of course the author of these more technical dialogues is still a great writer, and the contrast is above all one of tendency. But I suggest that Plato wrote the dialogues of the first group in what we might call a protreptic stance: these are works designed to attract a wider audience and draw the readers into philosophy. Their literary charm is an essential element in their effect upon the audience. The works of the second group are directed toward readers who are already committed to philosophy. The dialogue form is preserved, but the conversational frame becomes more mechanical, the tone is increasingly didactic, and the content approaches more and more to the condition of a technical treatise – until at last, in the long, unbroken monologue of Timaeus, we actually have a treatise *peri physeōs*. After the brilliant diversion of the Platonic dialogue, the Ionian prose treatise has thus returned to reclaim its place as the natural vehicle for philosophy and science.

One closing remark about the role of oral performance in the story I have told about the development of literary forms. Werner Jaeger once cited the passage from Plato's *Parmenides*, where Zeno reads his paradoxes before a small audience as a model for understanding the role of the extant treatises as read in Aristotle's school. So in the proem to the *Theaetetus*, Euclides has a slave read the philosophical dialogue aloud to himself and Terpsion.[47] But these oral performances of a written

---

[47] Jaeger 1912: 138–40; *Parmenides* 127c–d; *Theaetetus* 143a–c.

work are never conceived as standing alone. A fuller picture is given in the *Phaedo*, where Socrates reports his contact with the book of Anaxagoras: first he heard someone reading from it, then he read it for himself (97b–8b). Copies of the book were easily available, as Socrates tells us in the *Apology* (26d). Even if (as I assume) Socrates' narrative in the *Phaedo* is entirely fictitious, it will still represent the normal form of exposure to the earlier tradition, as conceived by Plato at the end of the fifth century. Both for poetry and for prose, oral performance plays a major role, but it is no longer indispensable. Behind the oral reading lies the text.[48] Philosophy, like history, has become a form of written literature.

[48] Compare Xenophon, *Memorabilia* 1.6.14, where Socrates reports "unrolling" the books of wise men of old with his friends. Since this is described as a group activity, we must imagine someone reading the text aloud. However, I agree with Burnyeat 1997 that when Socrates in the *Phaedo* reads the book of Anaxagoras for himself, of course he reads silently.

8

Prose Performance Texts

Epideixis and Written Publication in the Late Fifth and Early Fourth Centuries

Rosalind Thomas

I n the early fourth century, Alcidamas wrote a piece attacking the trend toward writing speeches rather than speaking spontaneously, *On the Writers of Written Speeches or On Sophists*, yet he admitted that it was ironic that he, too, had written his piece because it would bring him fame. Written publication and oral performance jostled side by side in the late fifth and early fourth centuries. The very attack by Alcidamas, not to mention Plato's critique of written texts, imply a cultural shift. But what exactly is shifting, and where? The period offers a particularly arresting combination of prose texts and performances. Oral performance and display are still important. Indeed, the techniques are elaborated and refined, but at the same time written texts are being made that have some relation to these performances, and there are more and more documents in Athenian public and private life. The very nature of publication, written or oral, seems precarious. How did texts manage to survive at all in the late fifth and early fourth centuries? The diversification from poetry to prose as the main medium for serious reflection and the appearance of new genres make the relation of written texts to oral performances even more interesting. The period gives us numerous descriptions of oral performances, especially in Plato and Xenophon, and texts that seem in various degrees to belong to that performance milieu, from early oratory to sophistic *epideixeis* to medical display lectures. Many of these texts are now anonymous, and much of this rich evidence indicates texts or performance pieces that lie at interstitial points between what later became established genres.

This chapter concentrates on the display performance, or *epideixis*, and the oral performances of pieces that already were or later became written texts. It examines the evidence for publication, whether oral or written, and asks what the relation is between oral performances and written versions. It asks whether any particular group was associated with written publication of literary texts, and whether in fact some of the texts we still have, regarded as "pamphlets," might originally have been epideictic oral performances. Following from this, it asks whether there are implications or explanations here for the appearance of new genres and for the increase of written literary texts in this period.

Written texts certainly increased in number in the late fifth and early fourth centuries, but why? Perhaps because the written text was perceived to give authority. Yet it cannot be only that, since documentary evidence, even in fourth-century Athens, is not regarded as highly in the courts as oral testimony.[1] Thucydides sought to give authority to his *History* not through documents, but through a careful sifting of evidence and search for proof as a sign of his superior research. Was writing increasingly resorted to in order to ensure long-lasting fame? It is sometimes said that Thucydides stressed his writing (1.1.1) to signal that his work would last forever – as if Herodotus was not also writing a work to last.[2] Or that Thucydides' style was only suited to reading (in private or silently), not to performance, another stage in the transition toward the dominance of the written word.[3] Yet the most difficult texts could be communicated by reading them aloud: when in Plato's *Parmenides* Socrates came across something he did not understand, he simply asked Zeno to read it aloud again (127d–e). There are evidently difficulties in assuming a neat division between written texts and oral performances, between a style suited to writing and one suited to performance, which is precisely why the lectures and display performances

---

[1] See R. Thomas 1989: 40–3; Cohen, this volume.

[2] I take it that Thucydides' disdain for "[rhetorical] competition" (1.22.4) was not exclusively targeting Herodotus (if at all; see R. Thomas 2000: 267) and that the scale and range of Herodotus' work were aiming at lasting reputation.

[3] Gribble 1998: 45–6; cf. Hornblower 1991: 19–20.

of the period are so interesting.[4] What is central here is the nature of cultural and intellectual activity in the period: are we missing large areas of cultural life by having to concentrate on the (few) written texts we have? What do we imagine lies between and behind the written texts that are our main surviving evidence from this period of rapid cultural and political change?

WRITTEN TEXTS AND PUBLICATION IN THE LATTER HALF OF THE FIFTH CENTURY B.C.E.

If we are looking for steps in the growth of written texts and in their perceived importance, much revolves around the late fifth-century sophists. (Since the word *sophist* in the late fifth century may still denote a wise man or philosopher, untainted by Plato's hostile interpretation, I use it merely as shorthand for the famous fifth-century sophists such as Protagoras.)[5] They left written texts; perhaps, then, they were particularly associated with the book,[6] popularized it, and used texts to confer authority and prestige on their work. Support for this comes from Prodicus' interest in the exact use of words (*orthoepeia*), which Protagoras shared: perhaps this concentration on exact meaning was made more necessary, or possible, the theory goes, by the supposed exactness of the written word – though Plato portrays discussions of *orthoepeia* as totally oral. Prodicus is mocked by Aristophanes as virtually equivalent to a book: "A book has ruined this man, or Prodicus has or at any rate one of the idle chatterers" (*PCG* frag. 506). Yet while the sophists produced written texts, they were mainly known from lectures and performances.

The trouble is that our evidence of their actual writings naturally emphasizes the written side of their activity; descriptions of these men's discussions, lectures, and display performances are therefore

4   See Gagarin 1999: 165: Plato's *Parmenides* warns against an easy acceptance of the division between "oral style," which Gagarin defines as a style of speech intended primarily for oral performance, and "written style," in speeches intended for reading. Some distinction is useful, but ancient reading was usually aloud; see Johnson 2000.

5   For problems with seeing the sophists as a unified group, see Lloyd 1979: 87, 1987: 92–5; Wallace 1998; R. Thomas 2000: 283–5.

6   O'Sullivan 1996. Pfeiffer 1968: 30–2 takes Plato's attack on writing as mainly directed at the sophists.

particularly useful, and Plato gives us the most vivid evocations. He does not single out the famous sophists for producing books or indeed for being particularly represented by books. In the *Protagoras*, Plato mocks Prodicus for staying in bed and in the *Cratylus* for his expensive lectures. In the *Theaetetus*, Socrates and Theaetetus mention Protagoras' written work a few times, but elsewhere in the dialogue it is Protagoras' spontaneous speech and theories that are prominent. Most sophists are present in person to be attacked. It seems profitable to ask what relation to writing the individual famous sophists actually had, and how far the pejorative term *sophist* (as used by Plato) is associated with written texts, but also to spread the net more widely to other thinkers.

In Plato, we hear about the written versions of the doctrines of Zeno, Anaxagoras, and Parmenides. The *Parmenides* begins with Zeno reading aloud a "written piece" (*ta grammata*), which is then discussed. He has brought the piece to Athens and everyone gathers specially to hear it. The written text is not a substitute for the writer himself, as with Protagoras in *Theaetetus*, for the dialogue is an elaborate retelling by Antiphon of what he had heard from Pythodorus, a conversation that took place over a generation before – all the characters taking part in the original conversation are dead. Yet Zeno is there in person in that conversation reading aloud something he wrote.

Perhaps the concision of Zeno's arguments meant that his theories were presented in the form of a written text that had to be read aloud: Socrates mentions the length of the proofs (*Parmenides* 128b) and makes the point that Parmenides in his own poems had produced fine enough proofs already. The "genre" of the piece was probably also relevant. It was simply a defense of Parmenides, as Zeno called it, and not the kind of piece suited to a performance. At any rate, Zeno backed off rapidly in the discussion and defended his written work on the grounds that it was not attempting anything new: his defense was a youthful composition (*to gramma*), written in a spirit of rivalry (*philonikia*), which was stolen once it had been written, and so he was not able to decide whether it was ready to be "brought into the light" (128b–e). This may be Plato's way of denigrating Zeno's theories, since Zeno's youthful writing beautifully illustrated Plato's strictures about written texts in the *Phaedrus*. But it is also an interesting reminder that once written, texts might get distributed unofficially – that is, without the consent of the author. As we know from later authors, the written notes of a great man might get circulated without his knowledge.[7]

The "books" of Anaxagoras also figure prominently in Plato. They occur in the famous passage of the *Apology* that gives evidence of a book trade in Athens (26d–e): Socrates suggests that Meletus is willfully confusing him, Socrates, with Anaxagoras, yet the jurors are not "so ignorant of writing" as not to know that these doctrines are in Anaxagoras' book, "and can be bought for as little as a drachma in the market." This is quite a circumlocution if Socrates was really trying to say that they had all read the book. Surely, it is either a general hint that they should know something about Anaxagoras, or, more likely, an attempt to bring the audience politely into the discussion of Meletus' inexcusable confusion.[8] At any rate, Socrates describes in the *Phaedo* how he came across Anaxagoras' doctrines: when he was still interested in the inquiry into nature, he first heard Anaxagoras' book in a gathering where someone was reading it aloud. Inspired, he then read the books as fast as possible but decided that Anaxagoras' explanations for the natural world were unsatisfying (98b).

This, too, is suggestive. These passages are usually mentioned to show the early presence of a book trade, but the *Phaedo* also suggests how books really get circulated: books may lie in the agora for a single drachma (the daily wage of a skilled workman), but a single text may be read aloud to a gathering of people and discussed. This sounds close to the "readings" we hear of in the early modern period, where one book could suffice for circulation to many people.[9] Perhaps we are also glimpsing the peculiarly communal way in which ideas were presented in classical Athens, which meant that reading to a group was quite natural.

It seems significant that it is the written work of natural philosophers, rather than sophists, that Plato portrays as being read aloud from a written text. Even in the *Theaetetus*, where Protagoras' written work is mentioned, there is an amusing attempt to bring Protagoras into the discussion in person though he was long since dead – so even here, Protagoras is not simply represented by his book. Socrates produces

---

[7]   See Quintilian, *Institutio Oratoria* 1.prooemium.7; Alexander 1990: 235.
[8]   See Woodbury 1976 on a similar remark about Athenian audiences in Aristophanes, *Frogs* 1114.
[9]   See K. Thomas 1986.

a clever parody of a speech by Protagoras and continues to address him for some paragraphs; at one point he even imagines him popping up from the earth, his head just visible (*Theaetetus* 171d). If anything, then, it is the dense, bare prose of the natural philosophers that is presented in written form,[10] the sophists being more prominent as speakers and performers. We might have expected, given Plato's strictures about writing and the sophists, that he would have paired them more closely if he could. Yet in Plato, the famous sophists are no more associated with the written word, or more book minded, than others.

Plato's *Phaedrus* deserves a close look.[11] The main concern is with the art of rhetoric rather than the sophists per se, and the entire discussion is prompted by Phaedrus' enthusiastic arrival with a written text of Lysias' *epideixis*. So even in the *Phaedrus*, the criticisms of writing (274b–8e) are raised as a pendant to the criticism of Lysias and of rhetoric. Before this, Socrates and Phaedrus discussed the nature of rhetoric, concluding that none of those who profess to teach or write about the art of speaking have said much of worth, and *true* rhetoric, as defined by Socrates, needs philosophy. To start the discussion, Phaedrus says there is a great deal on rhetoric "in the books written about the art of speaking" (266d), and they go through a list of rhetorical rules and theories that presumably come from these books (271b).[12] Several famous sophists are mentioned by name but so are others, including teachers of rhetoric, and this section is more about theories of rhetoric than sophists as such. While the art of speaking was important to many of the new sophists, this section of the *Phaedrus* does not pointedly identify sophists with written publication. The attack is on fatuous or pedantic rules on the art of speaking.

In the main critique of writing (274b–8e), the aim is also wider. Plato objects to writing as "a recipe for recollection, not for memory: your pupils will have the reputation for wisdom without the reality: they will receive a quantity of information (*polyēkooi*) without proper teaching, and will seem very knowledgeable when they are for the most part quite ignorant" (275a–b). Socrates claims that one cannot acquire a true

[10] See Kahn, this volume.
[11] Plato's criticism of writing also surfaces at *Protagoras* 329a; *Sophist* 231d–3b (especially 232d).
[12] Note the slide from writing to hearing lectures (271c): "Those who nowadays write manuals of speaking, whom you have heard [ὧν σὺ ἀκήκοας], are rogues."

knowledge of an art just through writing; writing can only remind the reader of what he already knows on the subject (275c–d, 278a). One cannot question a piece of writing – it can only say the same thing over and over again (275d). In short, writing is useful for storing up things for the forgetfulness of old age (276d), but it is not the path to true wisdom: for that one needs dialectic and the Socratic method (276e–7a). This objection would include any sophists who wrote speeches or other pieces, but Socrates also criticizes Lysias "or anyone who has written or will write, either in private or public, laying down laws, writing a political piece, who thinks that any great permanence or clearness resides in it" (277d). In conclusion, he sends his message "to Lysias, or anyone else who composes *logoi*, to Homer and other poets ... and thirdly to Solon and anyone who has written treatises in the form of political utterances, calling them laws" (278c). This sweeping condemnation, then, includes the revered figures of Solon and Homer, as well as, by implication, sophists and others, like the natural philosophers, who left writings. Similarly, Socrates exhorted Phaedrus to believe that "Nothing serious has ever been written in prose or poetry – or spoken for that matter, if by speaking one means the kind of recitation that aims merely at creating belief, without examination and instruction" (277e). A sophist who engaged in rhetoric would be doubly condemned, but so would anyone who did not engage in dialectic.

If the prominent sophists were most often seen and heard in performance, they produced written texts too. What kind of texts? Some of the evidence is ambiguous and may imply either a written text or an oral discussion, and it is useful to outline the kind of evidence we have for a few sophists. For instance, *On Truth* and other unspecified works of Protagoras were available in writing; Theaetetus and Socrates talk of having often read his "Man is the measure" theory (Plato, *Theaetetus* 151e, 161c, 166d). When the Stranger in the *Sophist* declares that the sophists write down and publish (*dedēmiosiōmena*) arguments in every art so that anyone who wants can learn, Theaetetus immediately takes this to refer to "the Protagorean works about wrestling and the other arts" (232de). Protagoras is mentioned along with many other writers in the section of the *Phaedrus* criticizing "books written on the art of speaking" (266d). In addition to his works *On the Gods* and *On Being*, Diogenes Laertius (9.55) gives a series of other titles of "surviving books," which include neither of these.

Prodicus' piece, "The Choice of Heracles," was both performed numerous times and written down. Xenophon recorded Socrates mentioning "the written piece about Heracles"; Socrates then proceeded to relay the content from memory, while admitting that Prodicus "displayed" it "in grander words than I did just now" (*Memorabilia* 2.1.21). A written version is implied in Plato's *Symposium* (177b), mentioned with irony alongside a *biblion* in praise of salt; it appeared in a work called *Horai* (DK 84 B1). Prodicus' views were later cited in connection with the art of speaking; he is mentioned in the *Phaedrus* passage along with Hippias (267b), but there is no clear indication of specific written texts on rhetoric here or elsewhere. By contrast, his work on the meaning of words (*orthoepeia*) is cited frequently; a text clearly survived.[13] And Galen included Prodicus among a host of men who wrote "on nature," or perhaps "on the nature of man" (DK 24 A2, 84 B4).

As for Hippias, for all his numerous skills and polymathy, he seems to have been known to posterity almost entirely through Plato and Xenophon. His "Trojan Dialogue" is known only from Plato and Philostratus. He is described in the *Lesser Hippias* as bringing with him various pieces, poems and prose *logoi*, that is, presumably in writing (368c–d), but perhaps most were merely prepared lectures. Specific titles have been preserved, including the list of Olympic victors, and it is striking that apart from the *Elegies*, these titles do not imply pieces appropriate for performances – unless we are to envisage bravura catalogue recitations. A work known as the *Collection* (*synagōgē*) contained apparently miscellaneous information, probably including things said by Homer and other poets, and "prose writings (*syngraphai*) both Greek and barbarian."[14] It is a fascinating early example of the production of a written collection from written texts, illustrating Hippias' polymathy and also his attempt to make something new and varied out of a textual world.

Some of Gorgias' *epideixeis*, of course, survived in writing, the *Helen* and the *Palamedes* being the most impressive among the paltry remains of sophistic texts to survive. His work *On Not Being or On Nature*

---

[13] Aristotle, *Rhetoric* 1415b, on Prodicus' fifty-drachma lecture, is ambiguous. Radermacher 1951 collects the painfully slight evidence for rhetorical manuals (*technai*) before Aristotle; on Prodicus, see pp. 66–9 (nos. 6–12 on *orthoepeia*).

[14] DK 86 B6. Other titles listed in DK 86. Philostratus (*Lives of the Sophists* 1.11) mentions lectures, *dialexeis*, and the "Trojan Dialogue."

survived to later generations (DK 82 B1–5), as did his Funeral and Olympian orations. So too did a work on the art of speaking, for in the *Phaedrus* (266d), Socrates mentioned the "books written on the art of speaking" by the sophists and included Gorgias. Further, individual speeches, or *epideixeis*, were written down and coexisted with "manuals," or *technai*, of the kind listed in the *Phaedrus*. Individual speeches in written form were also used as practical examples by pupils, as Phaedrus enacts in that dialogue and Aristotle states much later (*Sophistic Refutations* 183b).

Even in Plato, a few texts are made prominent that are not by the famous sophists (or even by sophists in Plato's sense), but by natural philosophers. When Xenophon recalls a conversation by Socrates on whether wisdom can really be learned from books alone, Socrates is talking to the recalcitrant and hermetic Euthydemus, who has a large collection of books "of poets and the most illustrious wise men (*sophistai*)." The ensuing conversation implies that Euthydemus is hoarding written works on medicine and architecture as well as the whole of Homer (*Memorabilia* 4.2). Again and again, when written texts are mentioned as problematic in any way, they are by a wider collection of writers than just sophists. Written texts were evidently available in increasing numbers by all kinds of intellectuals, poets, sophists, and philosophers. We should not exaggerate the famous sophists in this process because we happen to know more about them than we do about more shadowy figures in the late fifth century.

Different types of written text seem to have existed, but it is difficult to decide whether they simply replicate what was heard in performance. There is particular ambiguity over whether a given text might be private and meant for the author's own use or published in some formal way for public consumption. It is useful to stand aside here and consider the ambiguity of the term *publication*. The printing press makes it obvious what is formally published: the stamp of approval of a publisher, the formal binding, the neat appearance of the text. A definitive version of a text is produced with a date of publication and subsequent dates of later editions, though it is interesting that the sophisticated appearance of computer manuscripts (not to mention the Internet) means that the visual distinction between a manuscript and a publication is now blurred. The importance of samizdat texts in the former Soviet Union underlines the rather precarious authority of official publishers.

Manuscripts in the Greek world may have been produced in single or multiple copies, but we may at least ask whether a written text was for the author's own record only, for the author to use for revising, for the author to memorize and perform from, or for the author to send out into the wider world and allow to be replicated and sold. Several of these possibilities could be considered "publication." In the *Parmenides*, Plato portrays Zeno reading from a manuscript to a group of listeners, yet the manuscript was, Zeno claims, previously stolen and circulated. Zeno uses the phrase "bring out into the light" (128de).[15] In this case, "publication" seems to arise from a mixture of Zeno's own readings and the "samizdat" text that was stolen and circulated.

Manuscripts could be in circulation either without the author's consent, which presumably meant they were "unpublished," or as a record of something taught or performed by a prominent man. For instance, in the *Phaedrus*, Phaedrus has come hot foot from hearing a speech by Lysias, an *epideixis*, or display performance, on the subject of love. Teased by Socrates, Phaedrus protests that his memory could not do justice to it. Nonsense, says Socrates, I'm sure you've got Lysias to repeat it several times and got the text too so as to learn it by heart (228a–c). Phaedrus protests, to be precise, that he did not learn every single word (228d) but got the general notion (*dianoia*) of almost everything, and so can give a summary of the main points.[16] But it turns out that Phaedrus borrowed the text anyway (perhaps the only text),[17] and he reads it out. So this is a text of an epideictic performance, and the written text is regarded as a vehicle for memorization, and thence for the attainment of skill in speaking. The written text is a verbatim record of what Lysias was publishing as an oral performance, and it was for Phaedrus or anyone to learn by heart, just as schoolchildren, in Protagoras' description of Greek schooling, had texts of poems in order to memorize them (*Protagoras* 325e).[18] The texts are servants to the performance.

An example of someone turning something into a text that was not meant to be one occurs in the *Theaetetus*. Unlike the *Parmenides*,

---

[15] ἐκφέρειν εἰς τὸ φῶς.

[16] An indication of Greek expectations that fairly accurate learning by heart was possible in special circumstances (note *idiotēn*, 228a; cf. also Alcidamas, *Sophists* 18), *pace* Small 1997: 202–23, who downplays the possibility of accurate recall.

[17] παραλαβών (228b) may imply that this is the only text.

[18] See Ford, this volume: 24–30 on texts used in schooling.

which is supposedly retold from memory, the *Theaetetus* is presented as a record of a conversation between Socrates and Theaetetus held just before Socrates' death, which Socrates remembered and relayed to Eucleides (142d). Eucleides made notes (*hypomnēmata*) from the conversation, wrote down what he remembered at leisure, and consulted Socrates later to fill in gaps, so all was written down (143a). Presented as a dialogue to avoid "the tedium of narration," it is read aloud to Terpsion by a slave (143b–c). This elaborate scaffolding gives veracity to the following conversation between Socrates, now dead, and Theaetetus, and, in imagination, with the even older Protagoras.

We should not underestimate another kind of publication for which we have already seen evidence (*Parmenides*, *Theaetetus*), namely, private readings from written texts in private houses. Such readings gave an opportunity for small and congenial audiences, as well as for further revision.[19] Private readings to like-minded friends would lie quite outside the realm of commercial publication. Perhaps we should compare "the private gatherings" where sophists tended to argue, mentioned in the *Sophist* (232c), though these seem to be conversations rather than readings, or the numerous hints in Plato's dialogues that people gathered in private houses to meet a famous sophist hosted by a wealthy Athenian. The fragmentation of the forums of literary performance in fourth-century Athens[20] may have begun in the late fifth century. Private activity in private houses may be as important as publication in the grand public spaces.

It seems likely that this kind of text production was just as crucial in the increasing circulation of texts as any book trade. Quantification is impossible; clearly, there was a book trade, but texts could be produced by authors for their own use and then lent, or unofficial texts could be produced by others. Our explicit evidence shows texts made for authors to learn by heart for oral performance and texts that are notes made by someone else – neither exactly authorized for publication in a commercial sense. These are all in some sense unpublished texts (Lysias in *Phaedrus*) or unofficial texts that were not made by the author (Eucleides in *Theaetetus*). That made no difference to the excitement such texts caused, but the implications are striking: some such texts

---

[19]   See Kelly 1996; cf. also Hudson-Williams 1949; S. Usener 1994.
[20]   Emphasized by Wallace 1995.

may have survived to become our (now) anonymous texts, unofficial pieces that effectively became deprived of any known authorship at all. Demand for written texts may also have been fed by the novelty of the display performance, the *epideixis* – to which we now turn.

THE DISPLAY PERFORMANCE

The word *epideixis* literally means "display," but it came to denote a formal display piece, a showy lecture, as distinct from a speech given to the courts or assembly. Whatever private readings there were, the most popular method of conveying new theories and advertising skill was by some kind of oral exposition, particularly the *epideixis*. People went along to the new teachers, as Strepsiades and Pheidippides do in the *Clouds*, and took in their oral teachings. So fashionable and exciting were the oral performances of the time that Thucydides chose to express his superior claims to truth by saying that he was *not* going to present merely what is pleasant to the ear (1.20–2): his work was not a mere "competition piece for immediate listening" (1.22.4). The very term *competition piece* (*agōnisma*) suggests a public performance, not simply hearing a text read aloud, and perhaps other fifth-century historians performed their work to an audience.[21] We hear of Hippias lecturing to enthusiastic Spartan audiences on genealogies and ancient stories (*archaiologia*), and his Trojan *logos* was to be delivered in a school in Athens as well as in Sparta (Plato, *Greater Hippias* 285b–6b). Other sophists gave formal performances to large audiences at Olympia and in the theater and Lyceum in Athens.[22]

What form, or forms, does the display performance actually take? And what is the relation of oral performance to written text? We should not assume that the *epideixis* of the late fifth and early fourth centuries corresponded simply to Aristotle's epideictic genre of speeches (*genos epideiktikon*).[23] Aristotle's definition belonged to a later, more text-oriented period, when genres had crystallized and oral delivery had slightly different connotations. In the *Rhetoric* (3.12), he distinguished

---

[21] See Hornblower 1991: 61–2 on Thucydides 1.22.4; R. Thomas 2000: 257–67 on Herodotus.

[22] Plato, *Greater Hippias* 286a–b; Philostratus, *Lives of the Sophists* 1.1; Rutherford 1995: 110; Demont 1993: 192–201.

[23] See Demont 1993.

the "agonistic style," which is for oral delivery, from the "written style"; the agonistic style encompassed speeches for the assembly and for the courts, whereas the written style was epideictic: "The epideictic style is most like writing for its objective is to be read" (*Rhetoric* 3.12.5). But the *epideixis* began in a far wider context, as Demont has argued, in which there was more emphasis on the primary meaning of *epideixis*, "show" or "display," and it was essentially a presentation and proof of some form of excellence or ability. The public demonstration of knowledge of a *technē* was a specific form of *epideixis*. The early evidence (given later) implies that epideictic activity covers a wide range of methods and types of oral discussions, presentations, and speeches, as well as subjects, for in the late fifth century it is virtually impossible to separate the epideictic from the agonistic, or the *epideixis* from oral performance.

This helps immensely in distancing the rigid categories of later rhetorical theory and reminding one of the greater fluidity and only slow development of genres. But under the wider category of *epideixis* may be drawn together some excellent recent analyses that purport to deal with slightly different things. Gagarin, for instance, has analyzed what he designates "oral style" in the sense appropriate to a piece meant for oral delivery, not for reading aloud or silently, and uses Gorgias' *Helen* as an example, which Gagarin finds more comparable to Antiphon's delivered speeches (1, 5, 6) than to the *Tetralogies*. This similarity between an ornamental *epideixis* and some early court speeches confirms the suspicion that the two were initially developing together. From a different angle, Jouanna examined some early Hippocratic works as either *epideixeis* or didactic lectures, and in an extended comparison of *Helen* with the Hippocratic treatise *On Breaths* showed striking similarities in style and presentation of argument.[24] Whether we call this oral style or epideictic style, or even simply early rhetoric, we seem to be dealing with an identical phenomenon – a style suitable for oral delivery to a live audience, lively, clear, argumentative, demonstrative, syntactically uncomplicated, possibly even rhyming, with a strong first-person presence. When someone gives a display performance, that *epideixis* may have several types of relationship to a written text, sometimes rather

---

[24] Gagarin 1999 (though for Gagarin, reading must involve reading aloud); less elaborately, Jouanna 1984, 1988: 10–24, 167–74.

confused in modern discussion.[25] Such stylistic analyses give one a very different image of the early *epideixis* from Aristotle's later image, and they enrich our picture of Greek cultural life.

The Gorgianic *Palamedes* and *Helen* are the best known of such display pieces, but the extravagances, rhyming, and repetition of Gorgias' style perhaps distract from other examples that were delivered by less famous men and on more serious subjects. Some of the early medical texts preserved under Hippocrates' name, for instance, are evidently *epideixeis*. *Breaths* and *On the Art* are so sophistic (i.e., rhetorical) in style, and so untechnical, that historians of medicine have traditionally thought them to be merely by "sophists" in Plato's hostile sense, rather than by doctors. It is now emphasized that the late fifth-century doctor needed the art of persuasion, that the medical art could and did use some of the techniques of the public performance, and indeed that there might be considerable blurring between doctors and other intellectuals.[26] For our purposes, it is interesting that, although their subjects are medical (concerning the existence of an art of medicine and the centrality of "breaths"), they stand as neglected examples of early *epideixeis*, which is what they call themselves, using the language of display.[27] They also show features suitable for performance: insistence that the author is right and all others wrong, first-person style, rhetorical questions, sophistic tricks, awareness of a live audience, and a polemical stance.

Other early Hippocratic essays, though less obviously "sophistic" in style, share some of these features. *On Ancient Medicine* 2.2 uses the language of display and is probably an *epideixis* on more technical material. *On Regimen* markedly partakes of a more textual world: the author opens (1.1) with an explicit opposition to the *writings* of predecessors and speaks of his own *written* piece.[28] Most vividly, the opening section of *On the Nature of Man* sets the author quite consciously in a context

---

[25] E.g., Demont 1993: 194–6, 201–9; cf. Hudson-Williams 1949; Schloemann 2000: 56–8.

[26] See especially Lloyd 1979; Jouanna 1984, 1999; Dean-Jones, this volume.

[27] E.g., *Breaths* 5.2, 15.1, 15.2; cf. *Art* 1.1, 3.1, 13. For details, R. Thomas 2000: 250–4; Jouanna 1988: 167–74.

[28] Using the verb *syngraphō*. See further Demont 1993: 196–7; Ducatillon 1969 on the double audience of this work; cf. Jouanna 1999 on the date, Jouanna 1988 on "didactic lectures."

where display performances are common and then distances him from epideictic contests.[29] The author scornfully describes verbal contests where one speaker gives one theory, another opposes it, and a third may present yet another, which shows the emptiness of their pretensions to the truth: the winner is simply the one who has "the most fluent tongue" to persuade the crowd (*On the Nature of Man* 1). These contests sound similar to the kind of *epideixeis* that are typically mentioned in the introduction to a Platonic dialogue between Socrates and some famous and self-satisfied sophist. It is the debate, spectacle, and oral performance that cause the stir and create excitement and anticipation; the debate itself might concern medicine, science, or the nature of man.

What is particularly significant about these medical lectures is that they overturn the idea that the typical *epideixis* is a mock defense of some legendary figure (Helen, for instance) and remind us that display lectures existed on more serious subjects – precisely the kind of lectures that tend to be lost for the major sophists. They serve as an antidote to Plato's scornful picture of the *epideixis*. Likewise with claims reminiscent of the treatise *On the Nature of Man*, Gorgias' *Helen* (13) argues for the power of persuasion by citing the "astronomers" (*meteōrologoi*), "compulsory debates of words," and the philosophers' "contests of arguments," in which persuasion and skill win over "truth." These contests evidently concerned philosophy, natural philosophy, or medicine, and constituted relatively technical subjects. The feverish search for novelty is criticized equally by Xenophon's Socrates, who mocks Hippias' facile claim that he can say something new on anything (*Memorabilia* 4.4.6), and by Thucydides' Cleon in his rebuke of the Athenian Assembly (3.38.5). It may be premature to judge a piece as too technical for a general educated audience just from its "scientific" contents.

We tend to think of the famous sophists giving formal lectures, and our surviving texts give an impression of finished pieces, but much more is implied about display performances in Plato's portrayals. It is there that we find the most vivid, evocative picture of a ceaseless toing-and-froing of prominent, famous, or pompous individuals performing and

---

[29] Jouanna 1975: 19–38.

ready to perform to audiences of any size.[30] Plato's brilliant evocations of the cultural and social background to the philosophical discussions give a glimpse of the complexity of activities that can never be conveyed simply by the surviving text of any one display piece or, for that matter, by Plato's criticisms of them.

There are hints, for instance, of several degrees of formality: an *epideixis* is not necessarily a formal lecture or oral performance to a large audience. At the beginning of the *Euthydemus*, Euthydemus and Dionysodorus have been "displaying" wisdom, and a fearful Socrates hopes they will put off the rest of the *epideixis* until later (275a). This *epideixis* is not necessarily a set piece. Sometimes an *epideixis* is on the shelf, ever ready for performance: it is prepared, known by heart, and comes out, at least in Socrates' jaundiced eyes, as a kind of set piece. This is the danger with Hippias, who is portrayed, perhaps unfairly, as ready to launch into a display at any moment (*Protagoras* 347a–b). At the start of *Lesser Hippias*, Hippias has been giving an *epideixis* to a small group who were not enjoying it, and he boasts of giving his prepared *epideixis* to the Greeks at Olympia (363d). Socrates is dying to interrupt and ask questions about the content, but, as he says with irony, he did not dare interrupt the *epideixis* (364b). Hippias' display pieces have their own momentum and are unstoppable.

Prodicus is portrayed as giving notoriously expensive lectures, and here again the word is *epideixis*: Socrates mentions the fifty-drachma *epideixis* (a formal lecture with controlled entry and audience) that Prodicus gave on the correctness of names, but Socrates could not afford the fee, and, sadly, the one-drachma lecture was less helpful (*Cratylus* 384b). The *Greater Hippias* (282c) mentions that Prodicus gave *epideixeis* for young men alongside his diplomatic activities, and his piece on the "Choice of Heracles" is referred to by Xenophon as an *epideixis* (*Memorabilia* 2.1.21). Prodicus' image tends to be bookish and reclusive – he is wrapped up in bed at the beginning of the *Protagoras* – yet he, too, is connected with display performances. Perhaps the lectures deal with themes that he also treats in writing, but his stress on the correctness of words does not disassociate him from the art of extempore speaking.

---

[30] Some of the following examples are discussed in R. Thomas 2000: 249–69; cf. von Reden and Goldhill 1999 on performance within the Socratic dialogue.

Exactly what Gorgias is "displaying" and the nature of his rhetorical art are under scrutiny in the *Gorgias*, but Gorgias too seems ready at the slightest encouragement to launch into a display (as indeed is Polus). He is said to have been "displaying fine things," but Chairephon's suggestion that he give another exhibition to the assembled group is squashed by Socrates, who wants him simply to answer some questions and defer his *epideixis* to another time (447b–c). A little later, Socrates suggests curtly that Gorgias should make "a display of the shorter method now, the longer one at some other time" (449c). From this portrayal, Gorgias' *epideixeis* seem to be varied in form and extempore, not the labored and prepared pieces of Hippias.

Protagoras is regarded as brilliant in performance. In the *Greater Hippias*, he is said to have made a lot of money from giving *epideixeis* to "all sorts of people" (282c–d). At the beginning and the end of his long speech in the *Protagoras*, the verb *epideiknumi* ("display") implies that his speech is an *epideixis* (320c, 328d) and that it could equally take the form of a story (*mythos*) or a *logos*. There is also an interesting interchange between Protagoras and Socrates. Socrates comments that Protagoras is able to answer questions, unlike so many others, and how desirable it is to combine speaking at length (*makrologia*) and briefer question-and-answer (*brachylogia*). Socrates also makes clear that "he cannot manage these long speeches" (329b, 334e–5c), but when he tries to persuade Protagoras to turn to the question-and-answer method, Protagoras retorts, "I have had verbal contests with a great many people, and if I had done as you tell me to do, and spoken according to the instructions of my antagonist, I should never have got the better of anyone, nor would the name of Protagoras have become known in Greece" (335a). As the argument continues, Alcibiades points out that Protagoras is better at the long speeches (*makrologiai*), Socrates at discussion (*dialegesthai*), and that Protagoras' habit of answering a question with a long speech only manages to elude arguments and spin the whole thing out till "his hearers" have forgotten the question (336b–d). The whole exchange is itself an *agōn* on how best to conduct an intellectual discussion.

Indeed, Protagoras clearly has the facility to extemporize and produce long and eloquent speeches. The whole discussion shows that even "speaking at length" means speaking at length impromptu, not just giving a previously prepared speech. Some critics have been unwilling to accept this, perhaps because they assume a sharp division between delivering a public performance and creating a written piece. Nor is there reason to doubt that Protagoras' known written works could have been performed as long speeches or *epideixeis*.[31] The "verbal contest" (*agōn logōn*) mentioned by Protagoras in the dialogue is a central part of this world.[32]

A wide spectrum of types of prose performance emerges: the display performance (*epideixis*) that people pay for (Prodicus); other kinds of *epideixis*, whether off the cuff or repeating a previously performed piece (Hippias, Gorgias), and where the audience is fluid (as portrayed in Plato). There are also formal or semiformal "contests of words" (*agōn logōn, antilogiai*), which Protagoras is said to have initiated (Diogenes Laertius 9.52) and of which the contest in the *Symposium* is an example. There are also what Plato called *makrologiai* and *brachylogiai*, speeches long and short, the latter much preferred. Indeed, *brachylogiai* seem simply to be short expositions of a speaker's position or theory. And then there are winners and losers, as *On the Nature of Man* and Protagoras' retort to Socrates imply.[33] These elements might also be combined, with a more fluid and wider range of possibilities than allowed by the later epideictic genre.[34]

The techniques of display and persuasion were also adaptable for a mass audience and for the different subjects of political debate in the assembly, the tricks of the *epideixis* developing hand in hand with the growing sophistication in mass democratic rhetoric. Even specialists might have to prove their capability to a mass audience; a public doctor was expected to display his worth to the citizen body in public.[35] Plato implies that the Assembly heard advice from architects, ship builders, and other experts (*Protagoras* 319bc). The ability to speak well in the relatively privileged or protected sphere of the *epideixis* would

---

[31] Nestle 1942: 282 suggests that Protagoras' work *On the Original State of Things* was at some point a public lecture.

[32] For Socrates' own use of the vocabulary of *epideixis*, see R. Thomas 2000: 256 n. 24.

[33] Cf. also *Protagoras* 338a–b (an umpire to ensure brevity); *Lesser Hippias* 363c–4a (contests at Olympia); Alcidamas, *Sophists* 18 (*agōnes*).

[34] Demont 1993: 184, 205 also connects the early *epideixis* with visual spectacle and other forms of demonstration, perhaps accompanied by a speech (e.g., on horsemanship).

[35] Aristophanes, *Acharnians* 1030–2; Lloyd 1979: 86–98; Dean-Jones, this volume.

flow over into larger democratic arenas, as Thucydides' Cleon attests in reprimanding the Athenians for listening to political speeches as if they were spectators at a public debate of sophists (3.38.7). It is unlikely that the delights of the *epideixis* were confined to a thin wedge of highly educated and sophisticated Athenians.

SPEECH AND WRITING: PERFORMANCE, WRITTEN TEXT, AND GENRE

What relation do these display performances have to texts, and what relation do our texts have to display performances? We can see at least three types of relationship. First, the oral performance may be a verbatim (or nearly verbatim) repetition, orally and from memory, of words that are recorded in writing – this would fit the repeated and repeatable lectures such as those of Prodicus. But we also see indications that a display piece may be a spontaneous performance that is not replicating anything in writing. A third possibility, which fits many Platonic instances, is that a "display" may be a spontaneous performance, that is, it is improvised, but it offers ideas which are – or will eventually be or have been – developed in a written text. Protagoras' myth might be one such example. We like to think that the texts we have were texts (and identical to ours) from the start, but this is surely a fallacy.[36] Even in the far more text-oriented modern world, many writers compose partly in their head before committing the words to writing – Gibbon and Mark Twain spring to mind, and even Henry James dictated his voluminous works.[37]

As for our surviving written texts, there is little indication that the written and spoken versions of performances might differ fundamentally in style (apart from the dramatic and nonverbal aspects of the performance, which inevitably are lost; they may have been most striking in law court speeches).[38] An epideictic style is often visible in excessive claims to have proved points, use of the first person, rhyming, rhetorical questions, and a lively awareness of the audience. It would seem that the written version was an aide-mémoire rather than an artifact on its

---

[36] So Demont 1993: 196 on medical texts, Pfeiffer 1968: 31 on Hippias' Trojan lecture.

[37] For James' remarkable method of composition, see L. Edel, *Life of Henry James* (Harmondsworth, 1977), Vol. 2, 458–61, 731–2.

[38] See Hall 1995.

own, and as Alcidamas states (*Sophists* 13), even those who compose in writing attempt the impromptu style, since it is more convincing. For the fifth-century lectures, the texts seem roughly to replicate oral delivery. Written versions of existing *epideixeis* show characteristics suitable for delivery before an audience. The early medical texts confirm that there could be textual differentiation between *epideixeis* and other pieces, with dramatic differences in style and argument between, at one extreme, pieces like *Breaths* and *On the Art*, and *On Regimen* at the other, which is conscious throughout that it is being written, or the *Epidemics*, which include tight lists of data.

It is striking that Plato's portrayals of *epideixis* seem mostly uninterested in the existence of written text. Even if a written version may lie in the background, the strong implication is that a speaker should be capable of speaking knowledgeably about a wide range of topics, eloquently and probably impromptu; Hippias' penchant for repeating set pieces is disappointing. The reputation of speakers rests both on the quality of their ideas (or knowledge) and how they express them to a live audience in public. Their presence was dramatic and apparently modeled in part on that of the poet.[39] Verbal facility is initially admired by Socrates and then mocked. Even in the *Sophist*, where the Eleatic Stranger outlines all the subjects discussed by sophists, where he remarks on the fact that they are "made public (*dedēmiosiōmena*) and laid down in writing for anyone who wishes to learn" (232d), the distaste seems focused on making this knowledge so public. The phrase "anyone who wishes" (*ho boulomenos*) was a standard democratic expression signifying the openness of various activities to the *dēmos*.

As Socrates' barbed comments about various sophists' displays indicate, they are objectionable for reasons similar to those that apply to written texts. Someone like Hippias, who can only speak in formal set pieces, does not think about what he says; Protagoras' favored method of debate, via a longish speech, is good for winning contests, but Socrates' preferred method of question-and-answer is better for getting to the heart of a problem. In short, for the Platonic Socrates, the display piece has inadequacies similar to those of written text: it inhibits dialectic and therefore the pursuit of true philosophy.

---

[39] It is reported that Hippias and Gorgias wore purple robes (Aelian, *Varia Historia* 12.32).

If, then, we may envisage different kinds of written texts, there are curious implications. If a sophist goes around demonstrating his theories in more or less impromptu *epideixeis*, there is a danger that no written versions will survive at all. Or what if his much-repeated lecture on a certain topic is written down in a text that remains an aide-mémoire for the author but is not properly circulated or published? Much of what two generations of intellectuals said and thought in the fifth century could have been circulated by word of mouth, which might be highly effective in Athens, but the long-term prospects for survival would be quite low. Most writings by the famous sophists have surely been lost because of Plato's criticisms and the intellectual advances of the next generations. But it is tempting to suggest that a further reason is the form in which they produced their work. If so much of their output was in the form of speeches or display pieces (or even more loosely, discussions), then the main publication might indeed be in the form of the public lecture, or *epideixis*. Add to that the possibility that there might be only a single written version, or very few copies, and it seems even less likely that much would survive. Hippias is an extreme case: by all accounts he had a vast range of knowledge and claimed expertise in subjects from genealogy to astronomy to making clothes. Yet virtually none of this is mentioned in the ancient testimonies in such a way as to suggest that he produced written texts on most of these subjects. We do not even have the impressive array of titles for Hippias that we do for Democritus and Protagoras. Ironically, most of our information about Hippias comes from Plato.

It is perilous to speculate on why literary texts may or may not have survived when so many factors are involved, but we may ask whether written texts were even known to later generations. The oral performance of short pieces would, on the face of it, seem a powerful method of publication to contemporaries, but more risky if they wanted later generations to know their thoughts as well. This is precisely the joke that Alcidamas (*Sophists* 32) makes against himself when he points out that, though he supports impromptu speaking, he has written out his piece because, among other things, he wishes for future fame. Even if an *epideixis* were written down, it might have a perilous chance of survival. It is significant that Prodicus' much delivered piece on the "Choice of Heracles," which *was* written down, is preserved in the ancient testimony only in the purportedly oral version of Socrates as reported by Xenophon.

One begins to wonder if the large number of anonymous texts we have from this period is partly a by-product of this situation: there is an explosion in the number of texts, as it were, but not of authors. The texts collected in the Hippocratic Corpus are of varied authorship, and though there has been debate since antiquity about which were genuinely by Hippocrates, many are effectively anonymous. The so-called *Dissoi Logoi* ("Double Arguments") and Anonymus Iamblichi, of sophistic provenance, could be compared in their uncertain authorship to many of the speeches in the corpus of the orator Lysias. The best chance of survival for a floating text was to be attached to the corpus of a well-known author, as the "Old Oligarch" became attached to Xenophon.

The very form of a written text of a display piece meant for oral delivery might contribute to later anonymity. An *epideixis*, after all, does not need to name the author of the piece, because the author is there proclaiming it. *Epideixeis* are generally uninhibited about stressing the personality and views of the author; indeed, egocentrism, so to speak, is one of the main features of this proto-genre. Yet there is obviously no call for the author's name to be fixed into the first line, as it is in the massive works by Herodotus or Thucydides, which could not simply rely on the author's presence and declamation for their publication.

The work *Dissoi Logoi* is perhaps a case in point. Written in Doric, this curious piece takes the form of an *epideixis* and must be the written version of what was once a performance. The author speaks frequently in the first person and is insistent and argumentative in a manner reminiscent of *Helen, On the Art,* or *Breaths,* though he is more wooden. The structure of sentences is relatively straightforward, and within the text (e.g., 1.12–14), there is plenty of repetition, rhyming, and mini-conversations or dialogues signposting the stages of argument and what "others say" as opposed to what he declares – all features seen by Gagarin and Jouanna as suitable for oral delivery.[40] There is no mention of writing, and though this is not conclusive by itself, the author consistently talks in terms of saying and speaking, rather than writing.

[40] See note 24.

The work does not call itself an *epideixis* explicitly, but it does mention *apodeixis* ("proof") several times (2.20, 6.1, 6.13).[41] More significant is the author's insistence throughout on considering other people's arguments, how he will show them to be inadequate, and the way he emphasizes in the first person that he has reached such and such a point, and has proved that he is right. For example (2.20):

> What, then, have I accomplished? I said I would show that the same things are proper and shameful, and I have shown this in all cases.

While not so rhetorical as *Breaths*, there is thus ample evidence that the *Dissoi Logoi* was in the style appropriate for oral delivery and for a display piece;[42] it could be an *epideixis* of some unknown sophist or philosopher that the author wrote down but that was preserved somehow without the author's name. Or was it preserved by a student? We do not know.

Similarly with the piece on Athens' democratic constitution attributed to the "Old Oligarch." Though it is often called a pamphlet, that term seems more reminiscent of the religious and political controversies waged by printed pamphlet in the sixteenth and seventeenth centuries and in the early era of printing. The Old Oligarch's work has the form of a display piece of the fifth century B.C.E., an exercise in controversial argument, a defense of the democracy parallel in form to Gorgias' defense of Helen. It begins in a way that suggests it was a display piece (1.1): "But since they have decided to have it so, I will show (*apodeixō*) how well they preserve their constitution and accomplish those other things for which the other Greeks criticize them." It abounds in claims to have proved the case, first-person insistence, and rhetorical questions, which can also be found in other *epideixeis*. It is a curious piece, as all agree, but such bafflement may be related to a modern unease with *epideixeis* and anonymous authors.[43]

---

[41] See R. Thomas 2000: 250, 252 on the close association between *epideixis* and *apodeixis*.

[42] Cf. *Dissoi Logoi* 5.13, 5.15. Note also expressions like φέρε ἄλλο δή · αἴ κτλ. (3.14; cf. 1.14) and first-person expressions of opinion (passim, e.g., 3.1, 3.7, 6.7).

[43] See, most recently, Hornblower 2000. Leduc 1976 sees this work as a sophistic *agōn*.

Could a similar fate have overtaken the Hippocratic *Breaths* or *On the Art*? People might flock to the lectures of a spectacular performer who either wrote out a later version of his *epideixis* or recorded the single version he knew by heart. This is even more likely for more didactic pieces like *Airs, Waters, Places*. Why put your name on a lecture, especially if the copy is only for your own use? Besides, if the main vehicle for intellectual discussion and activity is the public lecture, as it was increasingly becoming in the late fifth century, it is unlikely that everything the teacher teaches will end up published in written form. On the other hand, why go to the fifty-drachma lecture if you can get hold of a text? There may have been a tension between the pupils' desire to get hold of a text of a lecture or a speech – thus the urgency of Plato's Phaedrus – and the interest of the teacher not to disseminate everything in written form.[44] Some recent debate about written *technai* seems to assume too readily that the new teachers would blandly distribute copies of all their speeches or other teachings.[45]

The range of topics covered by these performances is enormous, and finally, we may wonder if these display pieces were the germs of many later genres. We find mythical fables such as Protagoras' created to present political theory in a more pleasing form, moral discussions in the form of fictional conversations between mythical figures (Prodicus, Hippias);[46] learned discussions of Homer or technical subjects such as medicine or agriculture (Xenophon, *Oeconomicus* 16.1), and formal contests on any subject a sophist or natural philosopher claimed to know about (*On the Nature of Man* 1), from the nature of man to the definition of justice. So important was the performance mode that much of what got written down and preserved was put in the form of a speech or *epideixis*, and kept relatively short. It might also explain why some pieces we have are disappointing or unsophisticated: what worked well in the excitement and novelty of performance is less impressive read silently in a modern study. And it helps explain why we have so little left in written form. It was the performances and visual presences that made their mark.

[44] See Dean-Jones, this volume: 120–1.
[45] Demont 1993: 202–3 suggests some difficulties arising from the existence of written texts.
[46] K. Morgan 2000: 105–30.

So why the growing number of written texts produced by sophists, doctors, and others? Some are private copies, some go out into the wider world, some are written versions of what was really meant to be performed. It is likely that the great sophists have left so little written work not only because of Plato's hostility, but also because so much of their activity was more or less in public performance. Their reputation and prestige did not primarily rely on the authority of a written text. However, they and others did produce written texts on a wide variety of topics – from moralizing tales to lists of victors or philosophical problems – and many of these seem to represent or repeat in essence what was also published orally. The proliferation of new genres by the early fourth century, many of which seek to reproduce the appearance of live discussion or performance, may also be related to this explosion of lectures and display pieces on so many different subjects, crystallized in later written form perhaps from the all-embracing *epideixis*.

In our sources, there are suggestions of a thirst for the new skills and ideas – if necessary in written form – that could well encourage the creation of more written versions (e.g., Lysias' display piece in the *Phaedrus*). Any written version of a performance or new theory would have further and longer-lasting circulation, as Alcidamas admits wryly of his own written piece – hence "unofficial" texts as well as authorized ones. If larger numbers of Athenians or other Greeks were now anxious to hear the new theories or techniques, that would also generate a demand for texts. What is more, the late fifth century seems to see a loosening of the traditions surrounding where and when one would hear performances.[47] Poetry tends to have specific occasions for performance, often religious, often rather formal, but in the "new education," nonpoetic performance is far more possible anywhere – in private houses, public areas, schools.

Texts are a shortcut if you miss the performance; they can also avoid the awkwardness of a massive or public performance. Certainly, there are private performances and private readings, but how convenient, too, to circulate a text if, like Isocrates, you are peddling antidemocratic views in Athens.[48] Isocrates, who may offer a retrospective commentary on what we have been discussing, is often seen as symptomatic

---

[47] Wallace 1995. [48] Yunis 1998, Ober 1998: 46–7.

of a growing reliance on careful written composition in oratory. Yet we should be careful of taking him as representative of a trend in any simplistic way, for his various remarks on this matter are strikingly defensive, self-consciously going against the norm. This reactionary writer had a double problem in the open-performance culture of democracy: not simply that his *logoi* were carefully composed in writing, but also that they were read aloud from a text by a second person – neither recited from memory like an *epideixis*, nor received by an audience as if the author spoke spontaneously.[49] Written speeches were increasingly being composed in advance for clients to use as their own in the courts: this much distrusted habit, fed by democratic judicial pressures,[50] must surely have meant that Isocrates' defense of careful written composition (concerning, moreover, current political issues) may not have commanded much respect in the realities of Athenian political life. Minority views could be circulated in writing without the risk of public humiliation from a hostile live audience.

So, too, is there a wider context to Alcidamas' apparently backward glance at impromptu speaking. His defense of improvisation also implied an increasing reliance on written texts and written composition. His objections suggest that he is talking not so much of the fifth-century brand of speaker, but the next generation, particularly those of Isocrates' persuasion, who were parting company from the public performance culture of the fifth century and probably also writing fine speeches for others to perform. Alcidamas' highly practical points (*Sophists* 9–10, 22–6) about the advantages of being able to speak off the cuff perfectly fit the world of the display performance we have been discussing, but they also apply excellently to the needs of day-to-day political speaking in the fourth century – the need in a trial, for instance, to be able to respond rapidly, adapt to audience reaction, and exploit opponents' arguments. Perhaps Alcidamas' polemic was prompted partly by the fact that the pupils of fourth-century sophists thought this quite adequate, but we may also stress that the polemic was still tied to the demands of a live audience and to the needs of the fourth-century democracy.

---

[49] See Isocrates, *To Philip* 25–9; *Panegyricus* 8, 11–13, 14; *Philip* 11, 81 (on Isocrates' lack of courage and weak voice). Cf. Hudson-Williams 1949; S. Usener 1994.

[50] Hesk 2000: 209–15.

With more texts in the public domain, the live teacher was even more necessary to ensure proper understanding of his teachings, and the teacher had to do more than compose the written texts. This supported the eventual development of the philosophical, medical, and rhetorical schools and led to a reverence for the founder and the writings – sometimes also the oral teachings – that he left behind him. But all knew that short of such schools, written texts were necessary to perpetuate ideas.

9

Writing for Reading

Thucydides, Plato, and the Emergence of the Critical Reader

Harvey Yunis

Interpretation occurs when a person seeks to understand the meaning of discourse.[1] The factors that affect interpretation are practically countless. This chapter is concerned with one such factor as it arises in the texts of Thucydides and Plato: how does the author anticipate the reader's burden of interpretation and attempt to guide the reader's pursuit of meaning? For ease of reference, I will borrow from Plato and call this the problem of the absent author.

The problem of the absent author is potentially present whenever a written text is read: by their nature written texts circulate on their own and are read by people with no contact with the author.[2] Yet it is not the case that written texts necessarily present problems of interpretation. A text's meaning might be expressed so as to be immediately "read off" from the words, in which case the author's absence is irrelevant to understanding the text: the text is simply understood when it is read. Such is one aim of the plain style of prose writing. Such is the aim of written warnings like a stop sign, or the written message Nicias sent from Sicily in 414 B.C.E. to warn the Athenians of the army's dire straits (Thucydides 7.8). Moreover, the problem of the absent author is not restricted to written texts; it can arise in orally conveyed utterances, as

---

[1] Hirsch 1976 on interpretation generally.
[2] Olson 1994: 115–42 on interpreting written texts.

in cryptic messages from the gods. As Heraclitus noticed (DK 22 B93), the recipient of an oracle typically has to discern the god's intention amidst words that express it obscurely or ambiguously. Since the god is not available to make his meaning plain, the recipient faces a pressing interpretive problem, whence religious exegetes – interpreters – have occasion to offer their services.[3]

Historically, Thucydides and Plato reflect most clearly the explicit concern with hermeneutics – the systematic pursuit of understanding discourse – that arose around 400 B.C.E. in reaction to the changes then occurring in the way discourse was being composed and reaching its audience. The increased use of written texts, in addition to and alongside traditional modes of poetic and rhetorical performance, caused writers to consider how texts were and could be interpreted.[4] Thucydides and Plato recognized that interpreting a written text was, in certain respects, different from interpreting orally delivered discourse. For written texts that have subtle didactic aims and require the reader to exercise critical thinking, as is the case with the texts of Thucydides and Plato, the reader's interpretive problem becomes acute. Insofar as such texts were new, so too were the corresponding problems of interpretation.

This chapter considers, first, how textual interpretation was practiced and understood in late fifth- and early fourth-century Greece in contrast to poetic performance. I will then argue that Thucydides embraces the interpretive possibilities of written text in order to achieve his didactic ends. Plato, on the other hand, whose objections to textuality and textual interpretation are well-known, created, at least in some of his works, texts that encourage critical reading while avoiding the interpretive problem of the absent author.

PERFORMANCE AND THE POETIC EXPERIENCE

Plato's dialogue *Ion*, which depicts a Homeric rhapsode of the middle to late fifth century, considers the manner in which poetic texts are received. Plato's irony is conspicuous; his purpose is clearly not historical.

---

[3] See Kahn 1979: 123–4 on the hermeneutic implications of Heraclitus' obscure style, Manetti 1993: 14–35 on the hermeneutics of Greek divination.

[4] On the rise of hermeneutics and its connection with rhetoric and written texts, see Most 1984; Eden 1987, 1997. Isocrates was also aware of basic hermeneutical issues, but scarcely went beyond the basics; see Eden 1987: 60–3; Szlezák 1999: 34–5.

Rather, he puts two modes of poetic reception in sharp contrast in order to illustrate their essential characteristics.

When Ion performs Homer, he functions as the poet's surrogate, and his recitation of the text moves the audience to tears, terror, and amazement (*Ion* 535e). The audience's emotional reaction, which is pleasurable for them and wins the rhapsode admiration, enables them to experience vicariously the travails of Achilles, Odysseus, and the other characters. As if to signal the uncanny power of this performance, Plato ascribes it to divine inspiration (*Ion* 536b). This reaction to performed poetry was also described by the sophist Gorgias (*Helen* 9):

> Those who hear it [poetry, *poiēsis*] are overcome with fearful shuddering, tearful pity, and mournful yearning, and through the words [of the poetry] the soul experiences a feeling of its own over the good fortunes and ill-farings of other people and their affairs.
>
> (trans. McKirahan, adapted)

For the brief time of the performance, the audience experience the fictional events as if they were real and as if they themselves were undergoing them. As is clear from tragedy, a genre that offers the poetic experience while conceding little to realism, the effect of poetic performance does not depend on verisimilitude. Rather, it depends on the power of language to beguile.[5] So long as the audience are emotionally involved and undergoing the poetic experience, experiencing the events vicariously, they do not consciously seek to understand what the *poet* means by the text he composed. Even if, as may happen, any particular statement made during the performance is not transparent, the lack of transparency must be overlooked or ignored by the audience if the poetic experience is to be maintained.[6] For if the audience shifts their attention away from the performance and ponder instead what the poet means, their emotional intensity will dissipate and the poetic experience will be interrupted. In poetic performance (in the ideal case), neither

---

[5] See also Gorgias, DK 82 B23, and Verdenius 1981. The text known as *Dissoi Logoi* speaks of verisimilitude, but with no details (DK 90.3.10). Barthes 1986b discusses "the effect of the real" in modern literature based on a superabundance of connotative features, which is a fundamentally different effect from that which Gorgias and Plato have in mind. The modern sense of "the effect of the real" enters in Hellenistic poetry; see Hunter, this volume: 231–2.

[6] This point is implied in the treatment of Aeschylus in Aristophanes' contest between Aeschylus and Euripides (*Frogs* 905–1499).

the author nor his absence is even noticed; the performance conveys meaning on its own.

It would be false to assume that performed poetry does not give rise to interpretation at all. In a basic sense, the performers themselves are the primary interpreters of the poetic text.[7] And the audience may reflect on a performance afterward and interpret what they have seen and heard.[8] Further, a tragic poet may call attention to the conventions of his drama in such a way that he disrupts the dramatic illusion and the audience's poetic experience. This may well constitute an invitation to the audience to consider what the poet means by the words and actions on stage even as they are being performed. However, interpretation of this kind does not belong to the emotionally involved, nonreflective aspect of poetic performance described by Plato and Gorgias, but is, rather, distinct from it and disrupts it.[9] On the other hand, the poetic experience need not be restricted to performance. By suggesting that a catharsis of pity and fear is the goal of experiencing tragic poetry (*Poetics* 1449b27), Aristotle too values the emotional, nonreflective aspect of poetic experience. Yet Aristotle also argues that although the spectacle of the theater enhances the experience, fundamentally, the poetic experience can be conveyed just by reading a drama, provided that the story is told with sufficient art (*Poetics* 1453b1–11). Thus, in certain cases, the beguiling features of poetic performance can be carried over into reading texts.[10]

---

[7] G. Steiner 1989: 7–11.　　　　　[8] This is the argument of Meier 1993.

[9] Goldhill 1986: 244–64 on the *Verfremdungseffekt* in tragedy. Two examples are not discussed by Goldhill: Heracles' speech rejecting as mere poetic myth the events that brought about his own downfall in the play (Euripides, *Heracles* 1340–6); the question raised by the chorus of *Oedipus the King* whether the failure of Apollo's oracle means the end of their worship (Sophocles, *Oedipus the King* 883–910), on which see Henrichs 1995.

[10] See Ford, this volume, on Aristotle's interest in reading tragic poetry. A parallel situation occurs with rhetoric, which can be received either in performance or by reading; on the experience of reading Demosthenes as opposed to hearing a live performance, see Plutarch, *Demosthenes* 11.4, Hunter, this volume: 218–19. It is in accord with Aristotle that novels can be so entertaining as to provide individuals reading alone with a version of the nonreflective poetic experience. Cf. the distinction made by Barthes 1976: 22–3, and elaborated by Josipovici 1999: 15–16, between "consuming" the text, characteristic of "naive" readers, and "rereading" it, the critic's task, which goes against the grain of the text.

Writing for Reading

Plato ascribes to Ion a second role in addition to his spellbinding performance of Homer: Ion is also the interpreter (*hermēneus*) of Homer (*Ion* 530c, 535a), which is the main concern of the dialogue. In this role, though he wears the same rhapsodic garb and speaks from the same stage, Ion no longer performs the poetic text or speaks in the poet's voice, but plays himself and speaks in his own voice. He functions as the interpretive reader of the text even though the text, which he has memorized, is not there in a book or roll in front of him (*Ion* 537a). No example of Ion's Homeric interpretation is actually given, but Plato has Ion claim that he "embellishes Homer" (530d);[11] and Plato characterizes Ion's interpretive activity as entailing the distinction between the poet's words and the poet's meaning (530b–d):

> SOCRATES: You [Ion] have to understand [Homer's] meaning (*dianoia*) and not merely his words (*epē*). In fact, one could not be a good rhapsode unless one understood the things said by the poet. For a rhapsode must be an interpreter of the poet's meaning to the listeners.
>
> ION: ... No one else could pronounce so many and such fine meanings (*dianoiai*) of Homer as I.[12]

Continuing the ironic treatment, Plato has Ion boast that he surpasses Metrodorus of Lampsacus and Stesimbrotus of Thasos as an interpreter of Homer (530c–d).[13] The evidence for these figures and their work is meager, but it is clear that in the late fifth century they were prominent among those who began to interpret poetry in a way that had no

---

[11] εὖ κεκόσμηκα τὸν Ὅμηρον.

[12] καὶ τὴν τούτου διάνοιαν ἐκμανθάνειν, μὴ μόνον τὰ ἔπη, ζηλωτόν ἐστιν. οὐ γὰρ ἂν γένοιτό ποτε ἀγαθὸς ῥαψωιδός, εἰ μὴ συνείη τὰ λεγόμενα ὑπὸ τοῦ ποιητοῦ. τὸν γὰρ ῥαψωιδὸν ἑρμηνέα δεῖ τοῦ ποιητοῦ τῆς διανοίας γίγνεσθαι τοῖς ἀκούουσι.... οὔτε ἄλλος οὐδεὶς τῶν πώποτε γενομένων ἔσχεν εἰπεῖν οὕτω πολλὰς καὶ καλὰς διανοίας περὶ Ὁμήρου ὅσας ἐγώ. On Plato's use of *dianoia* to refer to the poet's meaning as opposed to his words, see Flashar 1958: 30–2.

[13] Ion's boast is also a snub against Metrodorus and Stesimbrotus, implying that Plato put them in the same category as Ion, that is, as incapable of authoritatively interpreting Homer as the fatuous Ion is. See also Xenophon, *Symposium* 3.6: Socrates and Antisthenes disparage the rhapsodes for their ignorance, especially their ignorance of "hidden meanings" (*hyponoiai*).

regard for the experience of performed poetry.[14] Metrodorus equated the Homeric gods and heroes with heavenly bodies and substances in an allegorical manner (DK 61.3–4). Stesimbrotus, a writer on contemporary fifth-century historical figures, also wrote about problems raised by the wording of Homer's text (*FGrH* 107 F 21–5). As the twenty-fifth chapter of Aristotle's *Poetics* shows, interpretation of textual problems became a major topic of fourth-century literary criticism; it was eventually incorporated into the Alexandrian scholarship on Homer.[15] Unlike Ion, Metrodorus and Stesimbrotus circulated their work in written texts.

It is necessary to distinguish poetic interpretation of this kind from another, earlier type of poetic criticism that was not hermeneutic and did not distinguish between words and meaning. Xenophanes and Heraclitus, the earliest critics of Homer, reject Homer because in their view he is wrong on certain moral or religious matters: Heraclitus objects to Homer as a source of wisdom; Xenophanes objects to Homer's view that the gods are anthropomorphic and engage in immoral activities.[16] Both Xenophanes and Heraclitus assume that Homer's text is a transparent, nonproblematic entity; its meaning is obvious and noncontrovertible. The only consideration is whether what is said by Homer is right or wrong. Nothing suggests that Xenophanes and Heraclitus were incapable of distinguishing between what Homer means and what he says. But since Homer's meaning was apparently not at issue for those to whom Xenophanes and Heraclitus directed their criticism,[17] to raise the question of what Homer meant would have added unwanted complications and distracted from their task. A similar phenomenon occurs when one archaic poet corrects another or corrects the vague, unspecified tradition.[18] This is not interpretation in the sense at issue in this chapter, but, like the Homeric criticisms of Heraclitus and Xenophanes, a dispute over right and wrong on some particular mythological "fact" or moral position. The so-called histories or genealogical writings of

[14] See Richardson 1975, 1992; Pfeiffer 1968: 32–42 on these figures. On early Homeric allegory in general, see Ford 1999.

[15] These problems concern the plain meaning of a text that is obscure because of archaic diction or odd grammar.

[16] Heraclitus DK 22 B40, 42, 56, 57; Xenophanes DK 21 B11, 12, 14–16.

[17] Cf. Xenophanes DK 21 B10.

[18] Beginning with Hesiod, *Theogony* 27–8. Cf. Solon frag. 29 West; Pindar *Nemean* 7.20–27; *Olympian* 1.37–58.

Hecataeus fall into the same category: Hecataeus aims to discard the tradition or to revise the facts as represented in the tradition, not to focus on some particular wording within the tradition and reinterpret what the words mean.[19]

Plato discusses fifth-century poetic interpretation in other works beyond the *Ion*. He represents the sophist Hippias as interpreting Homer in epideictic speeches delivered to great acclaim at the Olympic festival and elsewhere (*Lesser Hippias* 363a–e). Plato's Protagoras demonstrates his mastery of poetic interpretation by means of his speech on Simonides' ode to Scopas (*Protagoras* 339a–d). After eliciting Socrates' assurance that the poem is a fine one, Protagoras proceeds to uncover a logical contradiction lurking undetected within it, which, if true, would ruin it. He chooses two sentences in the poem, argues that they are logically inconsistent, claims that one poet cannot hold both statements at once, and concludes that the poet must be mistaken in one or the other.[20] Though Protagoras has, like Xenophanes and Heraclitus, concluded that the poet is wrong, he has done so only after distinguishing between words and meaning, evaluating what the words mean, and uncovering a meaning that previously was not apparent. (I will return later to Socrates' response, since it falls into a different category.) In Plato's representations of Hippias and Protagoras, like his representation of the rhapsode Ion, the interpreter stands as an expert before an audience and interprets poetry as a means of impressing the audience with his learning and intelligence. The audience may pose questions, which the expert fields with further displays of learning; the audience may even applaud if they are sufficiently impressed.

The best surviving extended example of poetic interpretation before Plato is the text preserved, imperfectly, on the Derveni papyrus.[21] The text stems from the middle to late fifth century. The author, who

---

[19] *FGrH* 1 F 1–35. On this confrontation of new thought versus older poetry, see Kahn, this volume.

[20] On Protagoras' treatment of the poem, see Hose 1998: 93–101; Most 1994.

[21] Because of the state of preservation, the papyrus, discovered in 1962, has yet to receive a definitive edition; see Janko 2001. For preliminary editions, see Anonymous 1982; Betegh (forthcoming). A thorough, but still preliminary text of columns 1–7 is presented by Tsantsanoglou 1997. The translation used here is based on Laks and Most 1997: 10–22. For the passages and issues under discussion, the translation of Janko 2001: 18–32 differs in minor points only. For the numeration of the columns and lines, see Laks and Most 1997: 9–10. The author of the papyrus text is unknown.

interprets not Homer but a cosmogonic poem ascribed to Orpheus, distinguishes between the poem's words and its meaning, as in this passage, which precedes his interpretations of particular verses and forms a general statement of his method (*Derveni papyrus* 7.3–7):[22]

> And the true [nature] of the words cannot be said even though they are spoken. The poem is a [strange] one and riddling for human beings. But [Orpheus] intended [by means of it] to say not [contentious] riddles, but rather great things in riddles.[23]
>
> (trans. Laks and Most, adapted)

From this point of the papyrus onward, the Derveni author uncovers the hidden meaning of several verses of the Orphic poem by arguments that isolate a meaning distinct from the words used in the poem. The word–meaning distinction is deployed, for instance, when the interpreter considers the poet's use of riddling language (9.10, 13.6, 17.13), synonyms (10.2–10, 11.5, 12.3–7), allegory (16.1), and etymology (22.7–13, 26.1–2).[24] At one point, the Derveni author parenthetically explains the fact that the poem's true meaning has not been grasped by people who have heard the poem (20.2–3):

> It is not possible to hear and at the same time to learn the meaning of the words.[25]   (trans. Laks and Most)

Stesimbrotus of Thasos is one among several possibilities; see Burkert 1986; Janko 1997.

[22] Column 7 is, according to its editor, "one of the most difficult columns to reconstruct" (Tsantsanoglou 1997: 117). What is presented as a coherent body of text is constituted out of several physical papyrus fragments, and the supplements are provisional; see Tsantsanoglou 1997: 117–28; Janko 2001: 21. If column 7 were reconstructed differently, that could conceivably alter or eliminate the Derveni author's statement of his interpretive principle in this passage. But the importance of the papyrus text for the current argument would hardly be diminished. The Derveni author's actual use of allegorical, analogical, and etymological interpretations is well established in the rest of the papyrus text, as indicated below.

[23] [κ]αὶ εἰπεῖν οὐχ οἶόν τ[ε τὴν τῶν ὀ]νομάτων [φύ]σιν καίτ[οι] ῥηθέντα. ἔστι δὲ ξ[ένη τις ἡ] πόησις [κ]αὶ ἀνθρώ[ποις] αἰνι[γμ]ατώδης. [ὁ δ]ὲ [Ὀρφεὺ]ς αὐτ[ῆι ἐ]ριστ' αἰν[ίγμα]τα οὐκ ἤθελε λέγειν, [ἐν αἰν]ίγμασ[ι]ν δὲ [μεγ]άλα.

[24] M. J. Edwards 1991 examines the interpretive moves in the text and argues that the author is "a critic, to whom no philosophical system has contributed more than was needed for the advocacy and exegesis of a recalcitrant text" (p. 204). See also Henry 1986; Most 1997.

[25] οὐ γὰρ οἶόν τε ἀκοῦσαι ὁμοῦ καὶ μαθεῖν τὰ λεγόμενα.

The context of this statement seems to be a dispute over the status of hieratic knowledge available to persons involved in initiation rites in different ways and at different levels.[26] But the statement also seems to entail the distinction between poetic experience and interpretation that was made evident by Plato in Ion's two roles of rhapsode and interpreter. Initiates who "hear" the things that are said during the rites – that is, those who experience the Orphic poem in performance – are as uncritical of and mesmerized by the poem as are those who, like Ion's rhapsodic audience, undergo the poetic experience of Homer. On the other hand, the expert interpreter of the Orphic poem, namely, the Derveni author himself, is, like Ion in his role as interpreter, capable of using the distinction between words and meaning to disrupt the poetic experience and to examine and enunciate the meaning of the words of the poem separately from the words. This critically derived interpretation of the poem constitutes what the Derveni author means by learning the meaning beyond mere hearing.

Poetic interpretation in the fifth century thus appears to be a reaction by experts to the public reception of poetry through performance, the original and primary means of reception. The interpreters dissolved the emotional, vicarious experience of performed poetry, applied the word–meaning distinction to the text, discovered semantic depth where none was apparent before, and revealed new meanings. As implied by the word *dianoia* ("thought," "intention"), the kind of meaning uncovered by these readers was specifically authorial intention. Further, the fifth-century interpreters of poetry constituted an expert elite vis-à-vis the public. This elite controlled the new poetic readings that they produced and fed them, so to speak, to a larger public either in epideictic speeches or in written texts, though the latter, by virtue of their abstruse subject matter, must have been of interest only or primarily to other members of the learned elite. The Derveni author conceives of his interpretations as possessing the aura of divine revelation vouchsafed to an elect few and denied to the many (*Derveni papyrus* 7.7–11):

> He (i.e., Orpheus) is uttering a holy discourse, and from the first [all] the way to the last word, as he [makes clear] in the [well-]chosen [verse] too: for having [bidden them] to put doors to their [ears]

---

[26] Obbink 1997.

he says that he is not [legislating] for the many, [but that he is addressing only] those who are pure in hearing.[27]

(trans. Laks and Most, adapted)

The notion that understanding is vouchsafed only to the few is echoed several times later in the papyrus (20, 23.1–8, 25.12–13). It has been noted that the manner in which the Derveni author claims privileged knowledge recalls two others kinds of privileged knowledge in Greece: knowledge available through initiation rites and the Heraclitean distinction between insight based on *logos* and the misapprehensions of the many.[28] The similarity between the cases is evident, but what separates the Derveni author from both of these other forms of privileged knowledge is that the knowledge of the Derveni author is acquired and displayed by interpretation of a written text.

The dynamic of reading and interpreting poetic texts that left traces in the record of the late fifth century and that can be directly observed in the Derveni papyrus had implications for any author seeking to influence readers in fourth-century Greece. Although the poetic texts clearly sustained interpretation, they were originally composed for performance in which the potential gap between words and meaning was not consciously exposed. But once that gap was exposed, there was, so to speak, no closing it. Any author who wrote for readers would now be aware that they were in a position to infer the author's meaning from his words, which made possible both interpretation and misinterpretation. Little information exists about who among contemporaries actually read Thucydides and Plato and to what purpose. Yet it is possible to observe what artistic provisions these writers make to accommodate, encourage, or direct interpretation on the part of their reader.

THUCYDIDES: OPEN–ENDED INTERPRETATION

In declaring the aims and methods of his work, Thucydides rejects as fundamentally flawed previous attempts to give an account of

---

[27] ἱερ[ολογ]εῖται μὲν οὖν καὶ ἀ[πὸ το]ῦ πρώτου [ἀεὶ] μέχρι οὗ [τελε]υταίου ῥήματος. ὡ[ς δηλοῖ] καὶ ἐν τῶι [εὐκ]ρινήτω[ι ἔπει· θ]ύρας γὰρ ἐπιθέ[σθαι κελ]εύσας τοῖ[ς ὠσὶ]ν αὐτ[οὺ]ς οὔτι νομο]θετεῖν φη[σιν τοῖς] πολλοῖς ... [τὴ]ν ἀκοὴν [ἀγνεύο]ντας. The supplement "but that he is addressing only" (Janko 2001: 21) fills a lacuna.

[28] Obbink 1997: 46. On Heraclitus, cf. DK 22 B17; Kahn 1979: 102–4.

human events (1.1–22). Those who have produced the flawed accounts consist of the poets and the prose writers (1.21), of whom the chief representatives are Homer and Herodotus.[29] Both the poets and prose writers reach their audiences mainly through oral performance.[30] Thucydides justifies the superiority of the account he is about to give by establishing an interrelated set of oppositions. The first item in the following list applies to his work, the second to that of his predecessors: written account versus oral performance, truth versus fiction, useful versus pleasing, critical reasoning versus memory.[31] Further, Thucydides objects not just to the flaws of the poets and prose writers, but also to the interaction between those predecessors and their audiences, and it is the audiences that are the root of the problem.

The audiences of the poets and prose writers, conceived of as people in general, are unwilling to undertake the painstaking process of critically seeking a true account of events; they believe what is convenient. This popular tendency, demonstrated in the Archaeology (1.2–19), in the account of the Athenian tyrant slayers and the Spartan kings (1.20.2–3), and elsewhere,[32] is described by Thucydides (1.20.1, 3):

> People unquestioningly accept the legends handed down by their
> forebears even when those legends relate to their own native

[29] Thucydides discusses Homer explicitly (1.3, 9–11). Thucydides does not mention Herodotus by name, but alludes to him when he corrects Herodotus' mistakes (1.20.3; cf. Herodotus 6.57, 9.53).

[30] Though some prose writers were probably being read privately by the late fifth century, Thucydides has in mind those who delivered their texts as lectures or, like Plato's Protagoras and Hippias, as epideictic speeches; cf. ἀκροάσει (1.21.1), ἀγώνισμα (1.22.4). See R. Thomas 2000: 257–69 on Herodotean performance, Thomas, this volume, on writing and epideictic speeches.

[31] See Edmunds 1993 and Allison 1997 on these oppositions and Thucydides' method. See Hunter, this volume, on the development of these oppositions in later stylistic tradition. On Thucydides' use of writing to achieve a new level of conceptual analysis, see Cole 1991: 104–12, Yunis 1998: 234–40. A sentence from the Funeral Oration joins these oppositions to the distinction between words and meaning (Thucydides 2.41.4): "We have no need of Homer as our praiser or of anyone who will give pleasure with his verses (epesi) but whose meaning (hyponoian) will be harmed by the truth of what happened" (trans. Rusten, adapted).

[32] E.g., 2.54 on reading oracles in accord with events.

history. . . . Most people expend very little effort on the search for truth and prefer to rely on ready-made answers.[33]

(trans. Blanco, adapted)

The poets and prose writers pander to their audiences' desire to be entertained: the poets exaggerate, the prose writers compose with a view to captivating their audience rather than pursuing the truth, and both end up admitting unbelievable, legendary material into their accounts (1.21.1). The interaction of uncritical audience and pandering author is precisely parallel to the unhealthy political interaction of irresponsible *dēmos* and pandering politician that Thucydides lays bare in his critique of Athens' post-Periclean democracy.[34]

In contrast to the interaction of uncritical audience and pandering author, Thucydides declares his preference for another kind of literary experience. Throughout the Archaeology he demonstrates his determination to undertake a painstaking search for the truth (especially 1.1.3, 1.20.3). Concluding his statement on method, he declares that he will not pander but seeks to be useful to a certain kind of reader (1.22.4):

> Those, however, who want a clear view of things as they were and, given human nature, as they will one day be again, more or less, may find this book a useful basis for judgment. My work was composed not as a competitive performance piece, to be heard and then forgotten, but as a work of permanent value.[35]

(trans. Blanco, adapted)

Rejecting both the epideictic speaker's pursuit of acclaim and the inclination of docile audiences to enjoy fleeting pleasure (recall Plato's representation of Ion, Hippias, Protagoras, and their audiences), the selfprofessed critical writer proclaims a didactic purpose and requires a critical reader if his new kind of account of human events is to be successful. As becomes evident in the course of the work, the didactic

---

[33] οἱ γὰρ ἄνθρωποι τὰς ἀκοὰς τῶν προγεγενημένων, καὶ ἢν ἐπιχώρια σφίσιν ἦι, ὁμοίως ἀβασανίστως παρ' ἀλλήλων δέχονται. . . . οὕτως ἀταλαίπωρος τοῖς πολλοῖς ἡ ζήτησις τῆς ἀληθείας, καὶ ἐπὶ τὰ ἑτοῖμα μᾶλλον τρέπονται.

[34] Yunis 1996: 87–116 on Thucydides' critique of Athenian democracy. Like poetry, politics in Athens was also a matter of live performance.

[35] ὅσοι δὲ βουλήσονται τῶν τε γενομένων τὸ σαφὲς σκοπεῖν καὶ τῶν μελλόντων ποτὲ αὖθις κατὰ τὸ ἀνθρώπινον τοιούτων καὶ παραπλησίων ἔσεσθαι, ὠφέλιμα κρίνειν αὐτὰ ἀρκούντως ἕξει. κτῆμά τε ἐς αἰεὶ μᾶλλον ἢ ἀγώνισμα ἐς τὸ παραχρῆμα ἀκούειν ξύγκειται.

payoff offered by Thucydides' text requires the reader to interpret the text critically.

How does Thucydides utilize the interpretive potential of written text to direct his reader's attention to the consideration of meaning? Clearly, Thucydides did not create a text designed to be interpreted allegorically or with linguistic stratagems in the way that fifth-century exegetes read Homer and Orpheus. Of the two constituent parts into which Thucydides conspicuously divides his work, the speeches and the narrative (cf. 1.22.1–2), I shall focus on the opportunity for critical reading provided by the speeches. That is not to imply that the speeches can be divorced from the narrative and retain their function or that the narrative and speeches considered together do not offer opportunities for critical reading. But considered on its own, Thucydides' narrative mostly presents a polished surface that claims to report events as they occurred.[36] The speeches, on the other hand, by calling attention to the absent author and his meaning, invite interpretation.

Each Thucydidean speech is conscientiously situated within the historical narrative. Ancient readers had no reason to expect, as some modern ones do, that the speeches would reproduce the words or arguments of the original speakers.[37] There was no background for such an expectation either within the canon of previous literature or anywhere else in Greek society. In the famous methodological statement on the speeches, Thucydides explained that he did not attempt to reproduce what the speakers actually said but composed speeches that in his view were the most effective statements of the position actually taken by each speaker (1.22.1).[38] Yet effectiveness depends on the particular audience

---

[36] The narrative is interrupted for Thucydides' comments on the plague, on the stasis in Corcyra, and occasional *obiter dicta* on political deliberation. Otherwise, Thucydides seldom mentions himself in the narrative and creates the impression of impersonal objectivity; cf. Barthes 1986a on the historian's objective narrative voice. On the interpretation of Thucydidean narrative, see Rood 1998.

[37] The ancient and modern expectations on this point are discussed by Finley 1985: 12–15.

[38] That is, both the words and the arguments of the speeches are Thucydidean; the only thing in Thucydides' text that can be attributed to the original speaker is his advocacy for or against the policy or action under debate. That is my understanding of this much disputed passage: see Yunis 1996: 61–3; Erbse 1989: 131–4. Garrity 1998 has proposed that in 1.22.1 Thucydides claims to reproduce the content of the speeches as accurately as possible but to present them in a form that in his view

being addressed, and every Thucydidean speech simultaneously addresses two different audiences. Are the speeches meant to be effective for the original audience being addressed by the speaker, as the formal commitment to the narrative suggests, or are they meant to be effective for Thucydides' audience, the person reading the text? Thucydides does not say, but he made the answer obvious: the speeches conspicuously depart from verisimilitude to the context that they represent. The aesthetic achievement of the speeches is so utterly distinct, the prose so powerfully concentrated and artistically constructed, the arguments are so unconventional that Thucydides is implicitly but loudly rupturing the formal proprieties of the narrative and asking the reader to consider that which he, the author who prominently announced his didactic purpose, has to say to the reader.[39]

A few examples must suffice. First, some speeches include a perspective that only the reader, and not the original audience, could possibly comprehend: Pericles' third speech, which conveys postwar reflections on the Athenian empire (2.60–4); Hermocrates' warning of the Athenian invasion and Athenagoras' rebuttal (6.33–40), which derive their effect from irony that only the reader can perceive; Alcibiades' speech to the Spartans (6.89–92), in which he responds to the Athenians for expelling him.[40] Second, there are the verbal and conceptual correspondences between speeches separated greatly in time and place, for instance, those that concern the balance of power among the warring states in the speeches on the eve of the war and those that concern retribution and justice extending from the Mytilene debate to the trial of the

---

would best suit each occasion. Not only is this interpretation of 1.22.1 unconvincing, it flies directly in the face of the speeches presented in the text. All the speeches have virtually the same formal features (see Schmid 1948: 167–81), which were clearly contrived by Thucydides for his reader rather than for the audiences represented in the text.

[39] The point was made most forcefully by Strasburger 1957, 1958, but was recognized also by de Ste. Croix 1972: 11–16. Since Homer and Herodotus also intersperse their narratives with direct mimetic speeches, the potential to exploit this duality indeed existed before Thucydides. But unlike Homer and Herodotus, Thucydides uses the speeches precisely to interrupt the narrative and to draw the reader's attention to the gap between words and meaning.

[40] Meyer 1899: 389–94 on Pericles' third speech; Allison 1997: 224–5 on Hermocrates' speech; Allison 1997: 184–5 on Alcibiades' speech.

Plataeans and the Melian dialogue. By means of these correspondences, different speakers repeat, reject, alter, and restate ideas and arguments uttered by other speakers in other parts of the history.[41] Third, speakers utter sentiments and advance arguments that go so far beyond the subject of the debate or so directly oppose Athens' claims to Panhellenic leadership that they could not have been uttered by the original speakers and are evidently aimed at the reader. Such are Diodotus' psychological argument against the effectiveness of the death penalty (3.45), Pericles' comparison of the Athenian empire to tyranny (2.63.2), and the Athenian statement in Melos that might makes right (5.105).[42]

The meanings expressed within the speeches but which extend beyond them can only be directed at the reader, and they draw his or her attention to a progressive, generalizing, but implicit dialogue composed by Thucydides on such topics as war, empire, deliberation, and the uses of political and military power. This dialogue constitutes the core of the historian's didactic purpose because it elucidates the patterns of human events – that is, events that both happened and will likely be repeated in the future (1.22.4) – rather than just the particular events that did happen, which are recorded in the narrative. It would not serve the present purpose to consider what Thucydides' latent dialogue has to say on any particular topic such as war, empire, and so forth. Such matters are a staple of Thucydidean scholarship; the genre is familiar.[43] But one aspect needs to be emphasized. As is the case for the interpretation of Homer and Orpheus, so, too, the interpretation of Thucydides does not have a formal point of departure, much less a formal conclusion or synthesis. In spite of being able to discuss, analyze, and contrast the views expressed by different Thucydidean speakers on the subject, for instance, of the justification of empire, the critical reader is hard pressed to state Thucydides' view. That is what one should expect from an intellectual endeavor that gives readers the freedom, or rather the burden, to interpret the text on their own.[44]

---

[41] de Romilly 1956: 194–239.   [42] Strasburger 1958.

[43] See Morrison 2000 for a recent exemplary case.

[44] "The historian's standpoint remains hidden and definitive interpretation is left to the reader. . . . Without the certainty attained through conclusive interpretation the reader is never released from the need to think creatively on his own" (Strasburger 1957: 763–4, 766).

Open-ended critical reading is especially suited to Thucydides. For him the core of historical practice and understanding is the discursive political scene, which by nature is open-ended and constantly changing.[45] The political scene is also the root and the preeminent embodiment of the Protagorean view that knowledge is determined by perspective.[46] Thucydides took the Protagorean view seriously, as is evident above all in his elaborate use of paired antilogical speeches, a Protagorean technique. By means of this technique, Thucydides presented arguments that put opposing views into the sharpest possible antithesis with no accommodation for synthesis.[47] Taken as a group, all the Thucydidean speeches function in a manner similar to a single antilogy, except with a broader, more complex range of perspectives. As a fixed written text, each speech crystallizes a political insight conditioned by one set of circumstances and one speaker's agenda. No single speech, not even any of those of Pericles, has ultimate authority; all compete in the reader's mind for interpretative potential. It is doubtful whether synthesis was possible or even desirable for a historian who both took seriously the Protagorean emphasis on individual perspective and made politics the key to human history. The "clear view" of the patterns of human events that Thucydides promises his critical reader (1.22.4) is not clear or transparent in any simple sense; it is nothing like a stable, unchanging, Platonic truth. It is, rather, a multifaceted glimpse into the multiplicity of events attained by the reader; therein, for Thucydides, lies its utility.[48]

PLATO: CRITICAL READING AND POETIC EXPERIENCE

Plato's view of poetic performance was discussed in connection with his account of the rhapsode Ion: insofar as the rhapsode's audience

[45] Strasburger 1954.

[46] DK 80 A20–1, B6a; Kerferd 1981: 83–110.

[47] Yunis 1998: 234–9 on the Protagorean background of this technique and Thucydides' use of it.

[48] Cf. Strasburger 1957: 765, and especially Allison 1997: 248, who articulates the extent of Thucydides' debt to Protagoras: "Although [Thucydides] shared Protagoras' reliance on perception as the beginning of *logos*, he successfully broke the Protagorean identity of *dokein* with *logoi*, 'what seems to each is "what is" ' (Plato, *Theaetetus* 170a). By inserting *dikaiōsis* and *axiōsis* between perception and the account [Thucydides 3.82.4], Thucydides allowed truth to surface as the conclusion in the process of representation (*dēlōsis*)."

undergo a poetic experience, they do not attend to the distinction between words and meaning and do not consciously consider what is the
meaning of that which is being said to them. Rhetoric, in Plato's view,
has a similar effect. Every rhetor tries to shape his message in such a
way that the audience will be unable to consider it in any light other
than that in which he presents it. If the audience were to become aware
of the form in which the message is cast, that awareness would diminish
its persuasive impact. Like the poet, the rhetor enchants the audience,
as Plato is fond of stating.[49] In both poetry and rhetoric, the critical
faculties of the audience, if they have any, are crippled; the audience
become spellbound, and they receive the discourse uncritically.[50]

Socratic discourse, on the other hand, forces the distinction between
words and meaning into the open. As part of the preliminary skirmish-
ing that typically leads into a Socratic elenchus, Socrates often claims
not to know, or at least declines to say, whether a statement uttered by
an interlocutor is true or false. At that point, as a means of advancing
the discussion, he frequently raises the question "What does he [i.e.,
the author of the statement] mean?"[51] For instance, Euthyphro says: "I
affirm that holiness is what the gods all love, and its opposite is what
the gods all hate, unholiness" (*Euthyphro* 9e, trans. Cooper, adapted).
Socrates is unwilling to grant that the statement is true but wants to
discover whether it is true or false. He says in response: "Are we to examine this position also, Euthyphro, to see if it is sound? . . . Must we not
look into what the speaker means?" In an ordinary, everyday sense, the
meaning of Euthyphro's statement is transparent; but Socrates is insisting that the statement is not transparent and requires interpretation.[52]
The interlocutor's statement may well seem to be true and therefore
worthy of belief, so long as it is understood in an everyday, uncritical
sense. As far as Socrates is concerned, therein lies danger. For Socrates,

---

[49] *Euthydemus* 290a; *Protagoras* 315a; *Menexenus* 235a–c. Cf. de Romilly 1975.

[50] *Ion* 535b; *Crito* 54d; *Symposium* 198b; *Phaedrus* 234d. The underlying similarity of
poetry and rhetoric is also the point of Gorgias' account of the poetic experience
quoted above (*Helen* 9); cf. Yunis 1996: 132–5.

[51] τί λέγει; E.g., *Gorgias* 489d; *Republic* 331e; 338c; *Apology* 21b; *Symposium* 200d,
206b; *Euthydemus* 287b, 301b; *Cratylus* 385a; *Laches* 195d.

[52] When Socrates and an interlocutor are speaking before a company of observers and
Socrates queries what a statement made by the interlocutor means, as often happens,
no one present has any trouble understanding the interlocutor's statement in the
everyday sense.

meaning is a question of what the statement entails, regardless of what the author of the statement intends;[53] and what the statement entails is only discovered by means of investigation with the elenchus. Once it is made evident what the statement entails, that is, what in Socrates' sense it means, it often becomes easy to recognize that the statement is false. In Euthyphro's case, when it has been ascertained to the mutual satisfaction of Socrates and Euthyphro that Euthyphro's statement about holiness entails a contradiction that was not apparent or even intended when the statement was initially uttered, the statement is clearly seen to be false and thus not worthy of belief (*Euthyphro* 10d–11b).[54]

Socrates makes the question of meaning, considered explicitly, into one of the most basic and common tools of his critical repertoire. Beyond the normal conversational setting of Socratic discourse, as in the conversation with Euthyphro, he asks the same question in other kinds of encounters. When Hippias completes his epideictic discourse on Homer, Socrates asks him what the discourse means (*Lesser Hippias* 363a–4c). When Protagoras completes his mythical discourse on the teachability of virtue, Socrates asks him whether he could state his point with more precision (*Protagoras* 328d–9c). When Socrates read Anaxagoras' book on mind and causality, he asked himself what the argument in the book meant and ultimately found it incoherent (*Phaedo* 97b–9c). When the god in Delphi says that no one is wiser than Socrates, Socrates queries that statement too, asking what the god means (*Apology* 21b). Plato's Socrates can be considered the critical reader par excellence: as a means of launching dialectic, he scrutinizes any utterance, discourse, or text that he encounters, without regard for the manner in which he encounters it, the person from whom it emanates, or the form that it has, and he asks "What does it mean?"

However, to depict Socrates as a critical reader overlooks the difference between reading a written text and responding to an utterance, which to Plato was a crucial difference. To assess poetic interpretation and written text as instructive media, Plato measures them both against Socratic dialectic, the ideal form of instructive discourse. He finds them both wanting for the same reason: the absence of the author of the text

---

[53] This position is made explicit by Critias at *Charmides* 164d–5b.

[54] This is just the first stage of Euthyphro's argument. His emended definition of holiness is then put to the test again, but it too fails.

makes it impossible to know what the author means and to subject that meaning to dialectical investigation.

In the *Protagoras*, Socrates responds to the sophist's attack on Simonides' ode to Scopas (previously discussed) by seeking to defend the poem's integrity. An initial misfire in which Prodicus' doctrine of synonyms is ridiculed (339e–41e) gives way to Socrates' own interpretation of the poem. Socrates refers ironically to an unknown Spartan tradition of philosophy, takes obvious and extravagant license with the poem's grammar and syntax, and attributes to the poet the Socratic maxim that no one does wrong willingly even though it is patently out of place (342a–7a). By demonstrating that the poem contains a perfectly coherent, thoroughly justified view of virtue, however foreign that may be to a natural reading of the poem, Socrates has conspicuously defeated the great sophist Protagoras at his own game.[55] But Socrates then reveals that the entire discussion of the poem, his own triumphant interpretation included, was just a game, which he now insists on breaking off in favor of serious pursuits, namely, arguing with the present company about what they understand virtue to be (*Protagoras* 347b–8a). Socrates likens interpretations of poetry to the bad entertainment hired by uncultured symposiasts who lack the ability to carry on serious conversation themselves. He says further (347e):

> No one can interrogate poets about what they say, and most often when they are introduced into the discussion some say the poet's meaning is one thing and some another, for the topic is one on which nobody can produce a conclusive argument.[56]   (trans. Guthrie)

This passage refers to the basic move underlying the interpretation of poetry: the use of the distinction between words and meaning to assign to the words of the poem a meaning that departs from the words themselves. The poetic interpreter attributes the newly discovered meaning to the poet, but Socrates challenges the casual manner in which that attribution is made: given the ease with which multiple, mutually exclusive poetic meanings can be generated, only the poet himself could affirm which of them, if any, he really intended. Of course, the poet is

---

[55] On Socrates' ironic interpretation of the poem, see Boder 1973: 119–20.

[56] οὓς οὔτε ἀνερέσθαι οἷόν τ᾽ ἐστὶν περὶ ὧν λέγουσιν, ἐπαγόμενοί τε αὐτοὺς οἱ πολλοὶ ἐν τοῖς λόγοις οἱ μὲν ταῦτά φασιν τὸν ποιητὴν νοεῖν, οἱ δ᾽ ἕτερα, περὶ πράγματος διαλεγόμενοι ὃ ἀδυνατοῦσι ἐξελέγξαι.

normally absent, as in the discussion in the *Protagoras*. But since poets, who in Plato's view produce their work under the influence of divine inspiration, are unable to explain their poetry (*Apology* 22a–c), even if the poet were present, that would not solve the inherent interpretative problem. The open-ended nature of the interpretative reading of poetry renders it, for Plato, useless as instructive discourse. The reader has neither a specific proposition to submit to the dialectical test nor a live human interlocutor to defend the coherence of the proposition.

Plato's criticism of written texts in the *Phaedrus* proceeds differently, but it includes the defect that plagues poetic interpretation in the *Protagoras*. Like the silence with which a painting greets its viewer, so (*Phaedrus* 275d):

> [written *logoi*] seem to talk to you as though they had some intelligent meaning, but if you ask them anything about what they say, from a desire to be instructed, they go on indicating just the same thing forever.[57]   (trans. Hackforth)

This statement presumes that the written text has a meaning distinct from the words of the text and that the reader seeks to determine what that meaning is. This is in accord with the Socratic impulse to ask of any discourse: what does it mean? Since the author is not present to explain what the meaning is, the questioning reader is left without an interlocutor. Socrates then deplores the uncontrolled, open-ended interpretation that will be foisted on a text as it circulates among readers who are not equipped to understand it. In the figural language of the *Phaedrus*, these readers will have no guidance from the text's "father," that is, the author, who is absent (*Phaedrus* 275e):

> Once a thing is put in writing, the composition, whatever it may be, drifts all over the place, getting into the hands not only of those who understand it, but equally of those who have no business with it; it doesn't know how to address the right people, and not to address the wrong. And when it is ill-treated and unfairly abused it always needs its father to come to its help, being unable to defend or help itself.[58]   (trans. Hackforth, adapted)

---

57 δόξαις μὲν ἂν ὥς τι φρονοῦντας αὐτοὺς λέγειν, ἐὰν δέ τι ἔρῃ τῶν λεγομένων βουλόμενος μαθεῖν, ἕν τι σημαίνει μόνον ταὐτὸν ἀεί.

58 ὅταν δὲ ἅπαξ γραφῇ, κυλινδεῖται μὲν πανταχοῦ πᾶς λόγος ὁμοίως παρὰ τοῖς ἐπαΐουσιν, ὡς δ' αὕτως παρ' οἷς οὐδὲν προσήκει, καὶ οὐκ ἐπίσταται λέγειν οἷς

As a writer who scorned the enchanting power of both poetry and rhetoric, who required a critical reader if he was to be instructive at all, but who also found the demands of dialectic to be scarcely reconcilable with written texts, Plato devised an ingenious compromise in his use of fictitious philosophical dialogues. I am not concerned with the genre of Socratic *logoi* as a whole, in which several writers exercised their talents, but solely with Plato's dialogues, which were unique in their combination of literary vividness and philosophical rigor.[59] Nor do I suggest that Plato considered that his texts could provide a philosophical education equivalent to one attained through live philosophical dialectic.[60] Nevertheless, the dialogues shape the reader's interpretative task in such a way that, unlike the fifth-century poetic exegetes and unlike Thucydides, critical reading can proceed without requiring the reader to interpret by seeking the absent author's meaning.

When the poetic interpreters seek the meaning of a poem, they consider what the author of the poem intends; this is necessarily the absent author whom Plato finds so troublesome. In Thucydides' case, the author conspicuously calls attention to himself as author and to the "clear view" of events that he promises the reader and makes available through critical reading. Plato, on the other hand, hides himself as author; he refrains from overtly signaling his presence or didactic purpose to the reader. He does not identify himself or his meaning with Socrates or

---

δεῖ γε καὶ μή. πλημμελούμενος δὲ καὶ οὐκ ἐν δίκηι λοιδορηθεὶς τοῦ πατρὸς ἀεὶ δεῖται βοηθοῦ · αὐτὸς γὰρ οὔτ᾽ἀμύνασθαι οὔτε βοηθῆσαι δυνατὸς αὐτῶι. See also Cohen, this volume: 79, on Demosthenes' insistence (21.224–5) that the written laws are helpless without human beings to enforce them.

[59] Kahn 1996: 1–35 on Plato's predecessors; Clay 2000 on "Plato's powers as a mimetic and dramatic poet" (p. 20).

[60] Szlezák 1999 shows the error of what he terms "hermeneutic esotericism," the view, which originated with Friedrich Schleiermacher, that Plato's written texts can be interpreted to reveal his deepest truths, otherwise vouchsafed to dialectic. Plato must have considered his texts, as he says in the *Phaedrus* (276d), a form of "amusement," but this is serious amusement, worthy of the philosopher, not the base amusement sought by ordinary people. Cf. also Dean-Jones, this volume: 119–20 with note 62, on written texts as advertisements for schools, where instruction was oral. The protreptic purpose of (some of) Plato's texts is discussed below.

with other figures in the dialogues. Thus, he does not mark his absence as author, but obscures it.[61]

In addition, Plato creates a text that disposes the reader to adopt a critical attitude that is focused on what is being portrayed in the text and that does not concern itself with the intention of an absent author. In order to follow the argument portrayed in the text, the reader is forced, as are Socrates' interlocutors, to employ the distinction between words and meaning. Yet the words to which the distinction is applied are not, according to the dramatic fiction, those of the author Plato but those of Socrates and the interlocutors; likewise, the meanings that emerge are not (explicitly) Plato's, but also those of Socrates and the interlocutors. It is true that no reader can actually be constrained from considering what Plato, the absent author, might mean. But it is not the case that the reader *must* consider what the author Plato means just to read critically, and certainly not in the sense that Thucydides' reader *is* required to consider what Thucydides means in order to read his text critically. Plato's meaning as author of any particular dialogue is in a fundamental sense irrelevant to the critical reading enacted in the text: the philosophical argument is made explicit in the text, and the critical project of understanding that argument is identical with reading the text.

The success of this endeavor depends on the supreme literary art with which Plato composed his dialogues; this art rivets the reader's attention on what transpires in the text and distracts attention from the status of the text as a text. The dramatic early and middle dialogues in particular convey the "effect of the real."[62] They engage the reader's emotions in the progress of the drama and give the reader a literary version of the poetic experience.[63] Yet the Platonic version of the poetic experience clearly differs from the merely enchanting experience offered by poetry or rhetoric. In order to experience the tension of a Platonic dialogue, the reader must follow the dialectic as it develops in the text, whereby the reader is compelled to think critically while reading. It is, in a manner

---

[61] On Plato's anonymity as author, see Edelstein 1962; Press 2000. On Plato's refusal to identify his meaning with Socrates, see Frede 1992. Cf. Lloyd, this volume: 135–36, on Euclid's anonymity and the attempt at impersonal, transparent demonstration.

[62] See note 5 on the "effect of the real"; Kahn 1996 on the protreptic, didactic aims of Plato's dramatic early and middle dialogues. The dialogues in question are those identified by Kahn, this volume: 160, as "exoteric or dramatic."

[63] Clay 2000 is a good account of Plato as literary poet.

of speaking, impossible to read a Platonic dialogue without reading critically.

Of course, written texts being what they are, it is always possible for Plato's reader to disengage from the critical poetic experience offered by his text and to read it as an interpreter freed from the author's devices. Philosophers and professional students of Plato have always done this, as is amply demonstrated by the history of Platonic interpretation, which knows few bounds.[64] Nothing in the current argument affects that body of work. As soon as the reader ponders what *Plato* means by any particular passage, the door to open-ended interpretation is thrown open and the reader assumes the burden of interpreting the absent author; for instance, when the dialogues are studied in conjunction with one another, the study of Plato's work cannot avoid interpretation of the absent author's intentions. Open-ended interpretation of Plato is in principle no different from open-ended interpretation of Homer, Orpheus, Thucydides or any other author; it is the province of experts, who in the guise of teachers, professors, scholars, priests, exegetes, and theorists have traditionally exercised interpretative authority over Western literature.[65] But there is also a crucial difference.

Thucydides encouraged his reader to turn away from the poetic experience in order to interpret the text critically, which makes Thucydidean reading an arduous process restricted to the few. Thucydides' critical reader is necessarily an expert devoted to the study of the text, as are the author of the Derveni commentary and critical readers of Homer, such as Protagoras, Metrodorus, and Stesimbrotus. Thucydides and Plato share the notion that an instructive written text requires the exercise of the reader's critical faculty, and in particular the distinction between words and meaning as a tool for deciding meaning. But Plato's attempt to portray critical reading vividly in the text makes the lessons of the text, or at least some of them, available to readers who shun the freedom and burden of the open-ended interpretation in which experts excel and dominate. These Platonic lessons are hardly dogmatic ones, as is evident from the aporetic dialogues; rather, the dialogues, not least the

---

[64] Tigerstedt 1977; Ausland 1997: 371–96; Tarrant 2000 on the history of Platonic interpretation.

[65] Raible 1983. The exoteric Plato emphasized in this paper is compatible with, though it is not the same as, the "historical esotericism" defended by Szlezák 1999. Every text, exoteric or esoteric, is always susceptible to interpretation.

aporetic ones, inform the reader both how dialectical argument is properly carried out and why it is so important to do so.[66] These are among Plato's most important lessons.

Unlike Thucydides, Plato gives his readers the option of dealing critically with the arguments in the text without contemplating the absent author. That option would be attractive not only to readers handicapped by the limits of their imagination, intelligence, schooling, and time, but also to those who, like Socrates, viewed the pursuit of the absent author as a fraudulent exercise or a waste of time. In this sense, as a literary artist Plato emulates the archaic poets Homer, Hesiod, and Solon, who addressed their lessons directly to their mass audience, rather than Thucydides, who obscured his lessons from the mass of readers as the price of making them available to the few.[67]

[66] Frede 1992.
[67] For criticism, I am grateful to André Laks, Steven Crowell, and Donald Morrison.

10

Reflecting on Writing and Culture

Theocritus and the Style of Cultural Change

Richard Hunter

The meeting and song exchange of Lycidas and Simichidas in Theocritus' seventh *Idyll*, the *Thalysia*, has a fair claim to be among not only the most discussed[1] but also the most powerful and strangely compelling scenes of all Greek poetry. Its hold over us lies in part not merely in the familiar attractiveness of the mysterious and riddling, but also in our pervasive sense of witnessing a dramatization of changing fashion, and one in which the present confronts, but perhaps fails to meet the challenge of, the past. In this chapter, I want to look anew at certain aspects of this encounter in the light of the central themes of this book in the hope of teasing out some strands of Hellenistic reflection upon poetic and cultural practice.

THINKING ABOUT STYLE

As the narrator, Simichidas, and his friends are walking from the town of Cos to a harvest festival in the countryside, they happen to fall in with Lycidas (but is it "chance"?), who is very obviously a goatherd (or is he?). Both Lycidas and Simichidas are poets, and they agree to an

---

[1] For recent bibliography, see Hunter 1999: 151, Köhnken and Kirstein 1995: 279–96. In what follows I have not always thought it worthwhile to signal my debts to and disagreements with the extensive modern discussion.

exchange of "bucolic song" as they travel together. Lycidas introduces his song as follows (*Idyll* 7.42–51):

> So, with a purpose, did I speak, and the goatherd answered, sweetly laughing, "I will give you my stick, because you are a young shoot all fashioned by Zeus for truth. So I abhor the builder who seeks to raise his house as high as the peak of Mt. Oromedon, and the cocks of the Muses who labor in vain, crowing against the Chian songster. But come, let us quickly begin bucolic song, Simichidas. And I – see, my friend, whether you like this little song which I recently worked out (*exeponasa*) on the mountainside."

As has often been remarked, the final verses of this passage look to an ideal of small-scale, careful workmanship (*ponos*, "labor"), which finds many echoes in Hellenistic and Roman poetry.[2] Theocritus' contemporary, Posidippus, for example, portrays his soul in an epigram as "previously laboring amongst books" but now tortured by desire.[3] That Lycidas' stylistic effort took place "on the mountain" sits in paradoxical juxtaposition to this ideal of modern craftsmanship. In composing "on the mountain," Lycidas is, of course, replaying the setting of Hesiod's meeting with the Muses in the opening of the *Theogony*, but Lycidas lays no claim to such inspiration. Indeed, he himself plays the role of the Muses in promising to give his staff to the young Simichidas, who has just declared himself to be a "clear voice of the Muses" (*Idyll* 7.37). That differing ideas about the sources of poetry are indeed relevant here is clear also from Lycidas' rejection of the "cocks of the Muses" who crow vainly against "the Chian songster" (i.e., Homer). These verses seem plainly to rework one of the most famous passages of Pindar's epinicians (*Olympian* 2.83–8):[4]

> I have many swift arrows under my arm in their quiver that speak to those who understand, but for the generality they need interpreters. Wise is he who knows many things by nature, whereas learners who are boisterous and long-winded are like a pair of crows that cry in vain against the divine bird of Zeus.   (trans. Race, adapted)

The ideal of knowledge derived from "natural gifts" (*physis*) is here set against the poverty of "learning," though the ancient commentators

---

[2]   Hunter 1999: 166. For ideas of *ponos* throughout the poem, see also Berger 1984: 17–20.

[3]   ἐν βύβλοις πεπονημένη (*Palatine Anthology* 12.98 = VI Gow – Page).

[4]   There is a useful discussion by Cozzoli 1996: 7–36.

on the Pindaric passage – with a fine eye for self-justification and advertisement – saw not just a hit at two of Pindar's "rivals," Simonides and Bacchylides, but also a statement of the need for poetic commentary, which would be one further way in which Pindar anticipated Hellenistic trends.[5] However we interpret these difficult Pindaric verses, the idea of "learning" takes us very close to imitation (*mimēsis*) as a model for poetic composition and to what we might, with an eye on later developments, be tempted to call "craftsmanship" (*technē*). Pindar's dichotomy between nature and learning – or at least one strong reading of that dichotomy – was at the heart of most ancient discussion of the sources of poetry; it was the almost unanimous view of ancient critics that the aspiring poet or orator needed in fact a mixture of natural gifts and studied craftsmanship: the requirements, as listed by Dionysius of Halicarnassus, are "natural gifts, careful study, laborious practice."[6]

If, like Pindar, Lycidas speaks "to those who understand," it would seem that Simichidas, the "professional" poet from the city with a repertoire of songs ready to hand (*Idyll* 7.92–5),[7] is not to be included in this privileged group, for when it is his turn to perform he adopts the fiction of "poetic inspiration" as though he has not understood the message of Lycidas' verses (*Idyll* 7.90-5):

> After him I spoke in my turn as follows: "Lycidas my friend, me too the Nymphs taught many other songs as I tended my herd (*boukoleonta*) on the mountain, excellent poems, which public report has perhaps carried even to the throne of Zeus. But this with which I shall do you honor is much the finest of them all: listen then, since you are dear to the Muses."

---

[5] *Scholia Pindarica* 1.98 Drachmann. It will be relevant to the ideas pursued in this essay that Dionysius of Halicarnassus similarly notes that the obscurity of Thucydides and Demosthenes "requires interpreters" (*Lysias* 4).

[6] φύσις δεξιά, μάθησις ἀκριβής, ἄσκησις ἐπίπονος (*On Imitation* frag. 2 Usener – Radermacher). For "art and nature" in the Hellenistic critics, see Brink 1971: 394–5 on Horace, *Ars poetica* 408–18; McKeown 1989: 399–400 on Ovid, *Amores* 1.15.13–14. Hutchinson 1988: 203 noted, in order to reject, the possibility that in *Idyll* 7.43–8, Lycidas may be referring to stylistic grandeur.

[7] Lycidas teases Simichidas with the behavior of a parasite (24–5). If we ask what Simichidas would give in return for entertainment, the answer must be not the jokes of a parasite, but poems. In some respects, Simichidas is a forerunner of Petronius' Eumolpus.

Simichidas sets himself up as a latter-day Hesiod whose poetic "initiation" by the Muses as he herded his lambs on Mt. Helicon is recorded in the opening of the *Theogony*. He is making a move very familiar in the poetry of the third century, however relevant Hesiod is for bucolic poetry in general and *Idyll* 7 in particular.[8] We may think particularly of Callimachus replaying Hesiodic experience in the *Aitia* or reconstructing the voice of Hipponax in the *Iambi*. The very fiction that Simichidas employs marks him, indeed, as a modern poet of a quite different kind from the model that he claims. Divine inspiration, whether from the Muses or the more appropriately bucolic nymphs, is now merely a "technical" gesture, a code shared between a poet and his audience. It is a code that Simichidas, like all modern professionals, can adopt or abandon at will in accordance with the generic demands of any particular song. When, however, Lycidas offers the first performance of a song that he has "recently crafted on the mountain," we have at least no prima facie reason to disbelieve him.

Before moving to the two songs themselves, it will be worth setting these ideas within a broader historical context. The most famous early statement of what we might call the ideal of "labor" (*ponos*) is the programmatic chapters of the first book of Thucydides' *History*. Here the "labor" of research (1.20.3, 22.3) is intimately linked to the pursuit of an account that is *saphēs*, both "true" and "clear" (1.1.3, 22.4), and *akribēs*, an "accurate and detailed" record of what was said and done (1.22.1–2). Those to whom Thucydides opposes himself are characterized not merely by intellectual sloppiness (1.20.3), but in particular by a reliance on "the mythical" in order to make their poems or *logoi* more attractive to listeners; here style and subject are equally at fault. Over these chapters there hovers a sense of another dichotomy, that between the written and the oral (especially 1.22.4). As a stylistic and intellectual ideal, "detailed accuracy" (*akribeia*) seems in fact to reflect an originary use for writing in the fields of record keeping, law codes, public decrees, and so forth, where the potential deceptiveness of oral traditions is most to be deprecated (1.20).[9] So, too, the fourth-century

---

[8] Partly, perhaps, as a result of *Idyll* 7, subsequent tradition made Hesiod a founding figure of pastoral; cf. Virgil, *Eclogue* 6.69–71.

[9] On these dichotomies in Thucydides' self-presentation, see Yunis, this volume: 198–201.

rhetorician Alcidamas, in his work *On the writers of written speeches or On sophists*, a defense of "improvised" speeches and an attack upon the use of carefully prepared texts, repeatedly associates such *akribeia* with written texts.[10]

Thucydides' broad dichotomy between himself and all others finds a familiar analogue in the stylistic and thematic distinction constructed between Aeschylus and Euripides in Aristophanes' *Frogs*. The facts are too well-known to need rehearsing here. Put broadly, the swollen, grand style of Aeschylus, which depends for its effects on irrational, emotional power (*ekplēxis*), is set beside the careful, clear, and accurate style of Euripides. There is no exact fit either with Thucydides' rhetoric or with any simple dichotomy of nature – art, but both the basic distinction between "grand" and "plain" and the link between stylistic and intellectual qualities (i.e., between the *how* and the *what*), which were to persist for centuries, are already there for all to see.[11] That the same or similar language is used to describe both what was said and the style in which it was said is crucial for the developments this chapter will trace, though a certain caution is needed. Thus, for later critics, Thucydides' style, particularly in the denser passages, was notoriously grand and "obscure" (*asaphēs*),[12] whatever intellectual virtues he might claim for his history. Nevertheless, the interplay of the stylistic and the intellectual will emerge as a fundamental leitmotif of what was ultimately a radical shift in Greek literary culture.

It must be stressed that these critical categories, whether applied to rhetoric or poetry, do not depend upon a distinction between the written and the oral, a distinction that, expressed in those terms, would be meaningless in the ancient world. Nevertheless, at least

---

[10] Cf. Alcidamas, *Sophists* 14, 16, 20, 25, 33–4. So, too, Alcidamas associates writing with "working out speeches in detail" (*kata mikron exergazesthai, Sophists* 16), a phrase that may remind us of Lycidas' *ekponein* (p. 214), and with the imitation of one's predecessors (*Sophists* 4), like Pindar's "crows," whose song comes from mere "learning" (p. 214). See Thomas, this volume: 186–7, on Alcidamas.

[11] Wehrli 1946; O'Sullivan 1992. Demetrius, *On Style* 36 notes that some people (with whom he does not agree) hold that there are only two types of style, the grand (*megaloprepēs*) and the plain (*ischnos*), because these two can never be combined.

[12] Dionysius of Halicarnassus, *Lysias* 3, *Demosthenes* 1, 10, *Thucydides* 24, etc. For Thucydides' sublimity, cf. Longinus, *On the Sublime* 14.1, 38.3.

two immediate qualifications to this assertion are necessary. First, it is clear that some of the stylistic distinctions between the grand and the plain do in fact correspond to observable distinctions in other cultures between oral and literate "literature."[13] Second, from Aristophanes to Longinus and beyond, the power of the grand style is intimately connected to its emotional effects upon an audience; the "transport" (*enthousiasmos*) of the poet or orator is transmitted in performance to the minds of the audience.[14] In an instructive passage of his essay on Demosthenes, Dionysius of Halicarnassus notes that the emotional thrill that he derives from *reading* a speech of Demosthenes makes him wonder what must have been the extraordinary emotional experience of the original audience who actually heard the great man speaking. What is crucial here is that Dionysius sees in the words of the speech their own stage directions, as it were.[15] Here we see how the performative, oral mode (even when it is of the imagination) has in fact very close links to notions of grandeur. Moreover, it is precisely this emotional and imaginative "transport" that explains and excuses the lack of "precision" and "accuracy" (*akribeia*) in the grand and the sublime.

One manifestation of this dichotomy that I have been sketching is the distinction, most familiar from an exposition in the third book of Aristotle's *Rhetoric* (3.12), between the "written style" (*lexis graphikē*) and the "performative style" (*lexis agōnistikē*). The "written style" is "most accurate" (*akribestatē*), whereas the "performative," marked by such techniques as lack of connectives (*asyndeton*) and repetition, is "most suited to delivery" (*hypokritikōtatē*). Two aspects of this chapter of the *Rhetoric* are of particular interest in the present context. In one passage, Aristotle seems to link the presence or absence of "precision" (*akribeia*) to the type of speech being delivered: a public political speech to a large audience is the wrong place for precision because it is not subject to very close inspection, whereas the courtroom, and particularly a case heard by only one judge, is the proper place: "where

---

[13] This is particularly so in the matter of redundancy and *copia*; cf. Ong 1982: 39–41. Cf. further Bing 1988: 46–7 on Callimachean aesthetics.

[14] So, too, Plato's portrayal of the Homeric rhapsode Ion; cf. Yunis, this volume: 190–2.

[15] Dionysius of Halicarnassus, *Demosthenes* 22, cf. also 53. Cf. Thomas, this volume, on the oral features of *epideixis* as preserved in written texts of epideictic speeches.

most hangs on delivery, there is there least precision" (1414a15–16).[16] Commentators have been puzzled by what seems to be a confusion between, or at least running together of, "precision" as a stylistic quality and precise reasoning or argumentation that will stand up to close examination.[17] In fact, however, such ambiguity is, as we have seen, a feature of the discourse of *akribeia* at least from the *Frogs* on; the *how* and the *what* travel together. Second, "written" and "performative" describe stylistic tendencies within drama and oratory rather than actual differences in the intended mode of reception; it is not that works that display the "written style" were only intended for reading.[18] Nevertheless, the possibility, indeed perhaps inevitability, of a parting of the ways between reading and performance is here at least foreshadowed.[19] This strikes with particular force when Aristotle introduces a class of poets whom he calls "the poets for reading" (*hoi anagnōstikoi, Rhetoric* 1413b12–17):

> But poets who write for reading are [also] much liked, for example, Chaeremon (for he is as precise [*akribēs*] as a professional speechwriter [*logographos*]) and, among the dithyrambic poets, Licymnius. On comparison, some written works seem thin when spoken, while some speeches of [successful] orators seem amateurish when examined in written form. The cause is that [their style] suits debate.
>
> (trans. Kennedy, adapted)

The *logographos* to whom the tragedian Chaeremon is compared must get the details right, but he has nothing whatsoever to do with how his writings are performed; that lies in the hands of others.

The style that is "most appropriate to delivery" is also likely to lack "precision" because the performance context excludes careful inspection by the mass audience. This stylistic analysis of oratory has obvious roots in the realities of Athenian democracy, but it finds a close analogue (and perhaps descendant) in the later criticism of poetry, where the popular audience is replaced by the individual reader or hearer.

---

[16] The speaker of Antiphon 3.2.1–2 (*Second Tetralogy*) apologizes to the jury for what might seem like excessive *akribeia*; cf. Dover 1968: 155. On this notion in general, cf. Kurz 1970.

[17] Cf. Cope 1877: 3.151–2 on Aristotle, *Rhetoric* 3.12.5, quoted with approval by Kennedy 1991: 256.

[18] Zwierlein 1966: 131. Demetrius, *On Style* 193 is particularly instructive here.

[19] Zwierlein 1966: 133.

Longinus notes that "strong and appropriate emotions and genuine sublimity are a specific palliative for multiple or daring metaphors, because their nature is to sweep and drive all these other things along with the surging tide (*parasyrein*) of their movement. Indeed, it might be truer to say that they *demand* the hazardous. They never allow the hearer leisure to count the metaphors, because he too shares the speaker's enthusiasm" (*On the Sublime* 32.4, trans. Russell). To the idea of "hazard" I will return, but it should be noted that we are here plainly in the realm of oral delivery – we have not in fact progressed far from the transport of both rhapsode and audience in Plato's *Ion* – and that the activity that is blocked off by "the transport of the sublime," namely, "leisured examination," is itself redolent of the Thucydidean ideal, the Aristophanic Euripides, Aristotle's account of "precision" (*akribeia*) in oratory, and the practices of Hellenistic scholarship.

The image of surging water (*parasyrein*) appears again in one of the most famous passages of *On the Sublime* (33.3–5):

> All human affairs are, in the nature of things, better known on their worse side; the memory of mistakes is ineffaceable, that of goodness is soon gone. I have myself cited not a few mistakes in Homer and other great writers, not because I take pleasure in their slips, but because I consider them not so much voluntary mistakes as oversights let fall at random through inattention and with the negligence of genius. I do, however, think that the greater good qualities, even if not consistently maintained, are always more likely to win the prize – if for no other reason, because of the greatness of spirit they reveal. Apollonius is an error-free poet in the *Argonautica*; Theocritus is very felicitous in the *Idylls* ... but would you rather be Homer or Apollonius? Is the Eratosthenes of that flawless little poem *Erigone* a greater poet than Archilochus, with his abundant, surging flood (*parasyrein*), that bursting forth of the divine spirit which is so hard to bring under the rule of law. Take lyric poetry: would you rather be Bacchylides or Pindar? Take tragedy: would you rather be Ion of Chios or Sophocles? Ion and Bacchylides are impeccable, uniformly beautiful writers in the polished manner; but it is Pindar and Sophocles who sometimes set the world on fire with their vehemence, for all that their flame often goes out without reason and they fall down dismally. Indeed, no one in his senses would reckon all Ion's works put together as the equivalent of the one play *Oedipus the King*.   (trans. Russell, adapted)

The influence of this "manifesto directed against what we may call the Callimachean ideal"[20] on modern attitudes to Hellenistic poetry would itself make for an entire book, but let us stay for the moment with ancient attitudes. As has often been remarked, stylistic metaphors are remarkably persistent over time throughout antiquity. Thus, for example, loud thundering is the hallmark of Homer's Zeus, Aristophanes' Aeschylus (*Frogs* 814), Callimachus' Zeus, and perhaps his inimitable Homer (frag. 1.20 Pfeiffer), and the unsurpassable "greatness" (*megethos*) of Longinus' Demosthenes (*On the Sublime* 34.4).[21] So, too, the same famous passages may remain central to critical discourses over centuries. Thus, the origin of the familiar image of the surging flood of language seems to be an Iliadic simile describing Ajax attacking the Trojans (*Iliad* 11.492–7):

> As when a river swollen in winter spate courses down to the plain
> from the mountains, sped by rain from Zeus, and sweeps into its
> current many dead trees, oaks and pines, and washes a mass of
> driftwood into the sea, so then glorious Ajax swept havoc over the
> plain, cutting down horses and men.   (trans. Hammond)

It is this passage that lies behind Aristophanes' description of Cratinus, like Archilochus another daring and unruly drunkard, at *Knights* 526–8,[22] Callimachus' "great Assyrian river, which sweeps along much filth of earth and much rubble" (*Hymn* 2.108–9),[23] and Horace's contrast

---

[20] Russell 1989: 308.   [21] Asper 1997: 196–8.

[22] Both Aristophanes himself and the ancient scholastic tradition fashion "the drunkard" Cratinus as a "grand" and daring poet who, unlike Aristophanes, paid insufficient attention to stylistic polish; cf. Cratinus *PCG* testimonia 2a (Cratinus like Aeschylus), 11, 17, 19. Cratinus *PCG* frag. 198 is also relevant. Note that in this same parabasis of *Knights*, Aristophanes represents himself as understanding what a tough job being a comic poet is and thus the need for a proper apprenticeship. This is not quite Cratinean "nature" versus Aristophanic "craftsmanship" (*technē* and *ponos*), but it is not far from it. Perhaps, Cratinus himself acknowledges the constructed dichotomy in the famous *PCG* frag. 342.

[23] The Homeric model is surprisingly often overlooked, but cf. Asper 1997: 116. Asper's whole discussion of "Wassermetaphorik" (pp. 109–34) rewards close study. Note that the Homeric *hapax* ἀφυσγετόν in the description of Ajax, which does not recur until Nicander and then Oppian, is glossed in the D-Scholia as συρφετόν, the word that Callimachus uses in the parallel passage.

of himself and Pindar, which will bring us back to Theocritus (*Odes* 4.2.1–12, 25–32):

> Anyone who strives to compete with Pindar,
> Iullus, trusts in pinions by Daedalean
> Expertise wax-joined and is doomed to name some
> Glassy-clear ocean.
> Like a mountain stream rushing down, which heavy
> Rain has swollen over its recognised banks,
> Pindar seethes and unconfined races on with
> Deep-thundering voice
> Winner of the crown of Apolline laurel
> Whether he rolls down in adventurous dithy-
> rambs his new-coined words and is borne along by
> Free-flowing rhythms, . . .
> Strong the air-stream lifting the Swan of Dirce
> Every time, Antonius, he soars aloft to
> Spacious cloudland. I, as a Matine bee in
>   Manner and method,
> Harvesting sweet thyme with intensive labour
> Round the woodland glades and the river-banks of
> Watered Tibur, small-scale I fabricate my
> Painstaking lyrics.   (trans. Lee)

Much in Horace's contrast between Pindar and himself requires little explanation in the light of the critical contrasts I have been tracing, but I note three points that are of particular relevance.

In the second stanza, Horace describes Pindar with a further adaptation of the simile from *Iliad* 11 in order, I would suggest, to make the point that Pindar's power in part derived from his own *aemulatio* of Homer.[24] Longinus notes that "imitation and emulation of great writers and poets of the past" is one path to sublimity (*On the Sublime* 13.2). Thus Herodotus, Stesichorus, Archilochus, and Plato, who, like the rain-fed river that is Pindar, "diverted to himself countless rills from the Homeric spring" and reached the heights by daring to compete with Homer. "It is a noble contest and prize of honour, and one well worth winning, in which to be defeated by one's elders is itself no disgrace"

---

[24] Sources for Horace are sometimes sought in Pindar's own verse, but no convincing passage has been adduced, though in principle the idea of a Pindaric model is perfectly sensible. The river "fed by rain" seems to go straight back to Homer, and I wonder whether *profundo | Pindarus ore* mimics the alliteration of the Homeric passage.

(*On the Sublime* 13.4, trans. Russell). This is the positive version of what in Horace is, quite literally (and, of course, ironically), a "fear of flying." It is at least suggestive that Horace's verb for how the rains cause rivers to swell, *alere* ("nourish"), is elsewhere used of intellectual nourishment of the relevant kind.[25] Be that as it may, much hangs on the identity and nature of the models you follow; this will become important when we return to Theocritus.

Second, if Pindar is an irresistible "life force," Horace, with his intricate and laborious efforts, is a "poet" (*carmina fingo*), and one who works (or does not) to order, as this poem demonstrates. So, too, is the Theocritean Simichidas, ever conscious of the need to measure himself against other poets, and one who even has a favorite from his own repertoire; we may compare Plato's rhapsode Ion, another competitive prize winner with a strongly developed sense of his status with regard to "professional rivals" (*Ion* 530c). This does not, of course, mean that "singers" like Pindar and Homer are not "poets," merely that within the dichotomy we have been tracing, an emphasis upon one's professional craft (*technē*) can go hand in hand with an alignment on the side of craftsmanship (*technē* also), as opposed to natural endowment and power. Seen in this light, Longinus' description of Apollonius as an "error-free poet" carries a loaded charge in both words. It is tempting to see here either a faded echo or a vigorous reconstruction of the gradual replacement in the fifth century of one kind of knowledge by a more professional and agonistic set of inquiries and experts.[26]

Finally, Horace sets the contrast of himself and Pindar within a poem that (in a narrow sense) is profoundly political; we should therefore ask about the link between politics and style. What is wrong with the emulation of Pindar is simply that it is too risky; one is almost certain to crash like Icarus, so it is better to keep your head low like the buzzing bee. Here, Horace gives life to the stylistic metaphor of falling,[27] itself very common in Longinus, and illustrates that critic's observation that "it may also be inevitable that low or mediocre abilities should maintain themselves generally at a correct and safe level, simply because they take no risks and do not aim at the heights, whereas greatness, just because

---

[25] Cf. *Ars poetica* 306–7 docebo . . . quid alat formetque poetam, Velleius 1.17.5 aluntur aemulatione ingenia.

[26] Lloyd 1987: Chapter 2.   [27] ἄπτωτος, ἀδιάπτωτος, πίπτειν, etc.

it is greatness, incurs danger" (*On the Sublime* 33.2, trans. Russell). It is "risk taking" that unites great writers to the sociopolitical context in which they live. As the correspondent of Dionysius of Halicarnassus puts it: "It is not possible to achieve great success in anything without taking and facing the kind of risks that inevitably involve failure."[28] In fact, Longinus is one of our witnesses to a cultural narrative, which flourished in the first century C.E.,[29] according to which political quiescence, that is, an absence of democracy, is responsible for the dearth of literary grandeur (*On the Sublime* 44.2–5). In such a narrative, freedom of expression and greatness of thought go hand in hand with political freedom. Risk taking (and its avoidance) is yet another phenomenon shared by subject and style. Unsurprisingly, then, a written "private" poetry (note how Horace represents his voice drowned out by the throngs cheering Augustus) is associated with a concentration of power. When power lies with the one or the few, you have to watch what you write, for it will indeed be open to "close inspection"; one mistake, one nodding off, may be one too many. From our perspective, of course, this is radically misleading in the case of, say, Pindar, who wrote for the commissions of powerful men, but it is easy enough to understand how distinctions within classical power structures are flattened out by a critical narrative that looks back over centuries and is fundamentally concerned with the present, not the past. As it happens, Longinus rejects this "common explanation" for the decline in literary grandeur in favor of a more moralizing, "philosophical" one. But if some of the stylistic differences I have been tracing, and their import, may be found on show in *Idyll* 7, then Simichidas' self-presentation as a poet who may hope for (or even claims) royal patronage – this surely is the implication of verse 93, "[my songs] which report has perhaps carried even to the throne of Zeus" – suggests perhaps that this cultural narrative has relevance in the Hellenistic world also.[30] Nor would this be surprising. To some extent, the first century C.E. modeled itself upon the Hellenistic experience, both in its (partly self-constructed) "anxiety of

---

[28] Dionysius of Halicarnassus, *Letter to Cn. Pompeius* 2.15. For these ideas, and Horace's "theoretical" reservations, cf. Brink 1971: 363 on Horace, *Ars Poetica* 352.

[29] This remains true whatever date we assign to Longinus (on which, cf. Heath 1999). For a summary of these narratives, cf. G. Williams 1978: Chapter 1.

[30] On the representation of poetic patronage in Hellenistic poetry, see Hunter forthcoming.

influence" and in its adoption, or forcible rejection, of "Callimachean" ideals.[31]

FROM SONGS TO POEMS?

The undoubted differences between the two songs of Lycidas and Simichidas are perhaps easier to sense than to describe;[32] descriptions such as "high" versus "low" and "lyrical" versus "comic" are not inaccurate, but simply not very helpful, and the first task must be to try to be more precise about the qualities of these two poems.

Lycidas' song falls roughly into four verse paragraphs (52–60, 61–70, 71–82, 83–9) defined by repetition (52/61) and framing (61/69–70, 83/89).[33] Connections between the sections and between individual sentences are unelaborated – normally a simple connective (de, kai) suffices – and such noncomplex structures are very familiar in both classical lyric and its Hellenistic imitations.[34] The most marked features of the verbal style of this song, however, are a tendency to amplification and repetition (a "fault" for which "Euripides" criticizes "Aeschylus" in Frogs 1152–76), features that work strongly against ancient critical notions of "precision" (akribeia) and "clarity" (saphēneia).[35] Poeticisms are not rare,[36] and the history of reception shows how "unclear" (asaphēs) is the extraordinary expression "you labored through the spring of the year" (85).[37] Lycidas' use of epithets in particular marks a "poetic" style: for example, "hot love burns" (56), "to the box sweet-smelling with soft flowers" with a mannered chiastic arrangement (81), and "wet

---

[31] Relevant here is Velleius' analysis of decline in terms of cyclical epochs at 1.16–17; his parallel for what has happened to Rome is (unsurprisingly) postclassical Athens.

[32] The bibliography is large, I have found particular profit in Krevans 1983; Segal 1981: 135–48; Kühn 1958; Ott 1969: 157–9; Lawall 1967: 87–101; Walsh 1985: 11–16.

[33] Cf. Weingarth 1967: 127.

[34] "Lykidas's song unfolds in the discursive manner familiar to us from Pindaric odes (and, indeed, for choral lyric in general)" (Dover 1971: 155 on Idyll 7.52–89).

[35] So, too, hyperbaton: 80–1 (σιμαὶ . . . μέλισσαι), 82 (γλυκὺ . . . νέκταρ). Repetition: 52–3/61–2, 57/59 (contributing to grandeur and pathos), 84. Amplification is produced by lists: 57–8, 63–4, 68, 76–7, 88. On the rising tricolon of verse 68, a kind familiar in high poetry, see Hunter 1999: 278 on Idyll 13.45. It is tempting also to associate the repeated connective τε with Demetrius, On Style 54, where such repetition is said to be capable of lending grandeur even to insignificant things; Demetrius' example is a list of Boeotian towns at Iliad 2.497.

[36] E.g., κακαῖσιν ἀτασθαλίαισιν (79).   [37] ἔτος ὥριον ἐξεπόνασας.

waves" (53–4), which not only has good parallels in high poetry[38] but might serve as an illustration of Aristotle's dictum that "in poetry it is appropriate to speak of white milk, but in prose it is less appropriate" (*Rhetoric* 1406a12). As marks of "poetic" style, perhaps we ought to add internal rhymes (62, 80) and matched synonyms (55–6, 74).[39] The opening image, in which cosmic signs in some sense imitate the human characters, as Orion "sets his feet upon the Ocean" while Ageanax heads for Mytilene (52–4), is a trope taken from the highest forms of poetry.[40]

At one level, the structure of Simichidas' song is rather looser: the sense units are short,[41] and the direction changes rapidly, though never so as to create obscurity. Gilbert Lawall helpfully refers to Simichidas' "jocular, offhand manner as if he were extemporizing,"[42] though we know that this poem is Simichidas' prize composition (91–5). Simichidas' level of diction is certainly "plain," verging indeed on what ancient stylistic theory would call "humble" or "lowly" (*tapeinon*). Virtually his whole lexicon is derived from "ordinary words" (*kuria onomata*), the language appropriate to a style that aims at "precision" (*akribeia*) and "clarity" (*saphēneia*), as first and most properly exemplified in Euripides[43] and one also appropriate to the low physicality of some of his subject matter. Simple epithets are sparsely used, largely in the more elevated prayer mode of 103–4 and 115–16. Repetition and variation take place within the plainest of ranges (99, 102). We may even wish to associate the harsh, mimetic alliteration of 109–10 with Demetrius' observation that such "harshness of sound" (*kakophōnia*) may be conducive to "envisionment" (*enargeia*), which is a particular feature of the plain style (*On Style* 219). Most striking of all, perhaps, is Simichidas' careful use of connecting and antithetical particles, which suggests an elaboration quite at odds with the loose "extemporizing"

---

[38] See Hunter 1999: 168 on this passage.

[39] Cf. Aristotle, *Rhetoric* 1405a1 on the usefulness of synonyms to poets.

[40] To some extent, the verses function as what Philip Hardie, in his study of "general correspondences between events in the natural *cosmos* and events in the human, historical world" in epic, calls a "cosmic overture" (Hardie 1986: 63).

[41] Note the programmatically concise opening (96). For short *kōla* as a mark of the plain style, cf. Demetrius, *On Style* 204. On the structure of Simichidas' song, cf. Weingarth 1967: 151–2.

[42] Lawall 1967: 95.

[43] Aristotle, *Poetics* 1458a19; *Rhetoric* 1404b24–5; Demetrius, *On Style* 190, 203.

structure. He begins with a neat *men/de* opposition – every move in this poem is very much planned – but particularly remarkable is the (scarcely translatable) triple sequence of such connectives at 106–14:

> [1] **And if** (*kei men*) you do this, dear Pan, may the Arcadian lads not whip you with squills about the flanks and shoulders, whenever meat is scarce. **But if** (*ei de*) you decide otherwise, [2] **both** (*men*) may you be bitten and with your nails scratch your whole body and sleep in nettles, **and** (*de*) may you [3] **both** (*men*) be on the mountains of the Edonians in midwinter, turned towards the river Hebrus, near the north star, **and** (*de*) in summer may you herd among the furthest Ethiopians, beneath the rock of the Blemyes, from which the Nile can no longer be seen. [44]

In discussing the characteristics of elevated style, Demetrius notes: "Connective particles such as *men* and *de* should not answer each other too exactly (*akribōs*). Exactitude is petty" (*On Style* 53, trans. Innes). Later in the same treatise, Demetrius observes: "Asyndeton and lack of all connection leads to a complete lack of clarity (*asaphēs*). . . . This disconnected style is perhaps more suited to the immediacy of debate, and is in fact called the dramatic style (*hypokritikē*), because the lack of connectives stimulates dramatic delivery, whereas the written style is easier to read and because its parts are fitted together and, as it were, secured in place by connectives" (*On Style* 192–3, trans. Innes, adapted). Longinus too sees such careful patterning as inimical to sublimity (*On the Sublime* 22.1–2). Thus, Simichidas' style tells a clear story: here is modern poetry for a modern, literate audience.

The analysis of verbal style may be supplemented by other approaches. In an important discussion, Nita Krevans contrasted Lycidas' use of high, archaic poetry (Sappho, Stesichorus, etc.) with Simichidas' recourse to classics of the lower iambic mode, such as Archilochus and

---

[44] κεἰ μὲν ταῦτ᾽ ἔρδοις, ὦ Πὰν φίλε, μήτι τυ παῖδες Ἀρκαδικοὶ σκίλλαισιν ὑπὸ πλευράς τε καὶ ὤμως τανίκα μαστίζοιεν, ὅτε κρέα τυτθὰ παρείη· εἰ δ᾽ ἄλλως νεύσαις, κατὰ μὲν χρόα πάντ᾽ ὀνύχεσσι δακνόμενος κνάσαιο καὶ ἐν κνίδαισι καθεύδοις· εἴης δ᾽ Ἠδωνῶν μὲν ἐν ὤρεσι χείματι μέσσῳ Ἕβρον πὰρ ποταμὸν τετραμμένος ἐγγύθεν Ἄρκτῳ, ἐν δὲ θέρει πυμάτοισι παρ᾽ Αἰθιόπεσσι νομεύοις πέτρᾳ ὕπο Βλεμύων, ὅθεν οὐκέτι Νεῖλος ὁρατός.

Hipponax, and with the obvious links in Simichidas' poem to fashionable third-century poetic forms, such as the curse poem and nearly contemporary poets such as Asclepiades.[45] Through a study of these echoes and the use of geography in the poem to evoke literary tradition, Krevans concluded that "Theocritus establishes two interwoven patterns of opposition ... the contrast between poetry which arises from divine or natural inspiration and poetry which evolves from earlier poetry.... Second, there is the contrast between the archaic authors, with their half-mythical world, and the immediate predecessors and contemporaries of Theocritus."[46] It is certainly the iambic mode that is evoked by Simichidas' liberal use of (to us at least) obscure proper names, the sense that the poem is full of in-jokes,[47] the joking prayer to Pan, and the persistent detached irony that is so remote from the true pathos that is productive of elevation (Longinus, *On the Sublime* 8.4). This last quality could be extended to much Hellenistic poetry and is in good measure responsible for its lukewarm modern reception.

In recreating the iambic mode, as in his adoption of the Hesiodic fiction, Simichidas is again entirely modern. Poems such as Callimachus' *Iambus* 13 and Herodas 8 show that the modern imitation of archaic iambus was felt to be a particularly exemplary case of reconstructive poetic archaeology; whatever popular poetic traditions continued unbroken, imitation of archaic iambus, particularly choliambic poetry, was a notable example of artful and artificial "resurrection," and quite literally in fact in the case of Callimachus' Hipponax. The very lowness of such poetry – its claim to a "popular voice" – made it a paradoxically perfect vehicle for the exploitation of the new possibilities of written poetry and new types of audience. Thus, for example, whereas Lycidas speaks in a prophetic, incantatory, semimystical manner that hints at a magical control of the world (the halcyons, etc.) and recalls the original link between poet and seer, Simichidas includes the description of a distant, but allegedly contemporary, rustic magical rite, with which he

---

[45] Cf. Weingarth 1967: 164–5; Seiler 1997: 133–6. Lycidas' song may, of course, also contain echoes of (e.g.) Philitas and other near-contemporary poets.

[46] Krevans 1983: 212.

[47] We may see here one version of the technique for establishing a sense of community between poet and different audiences that Scodel 1996 has studied for Alcaeus, and Schmitz 1999 for the much-changed reception context of Callimachus.

himself has nothing to do and about which he has learned, so we are to understand, from a book.

It must be stressed that there can be no suggestion that the stylistic contrast between the songs of Lycidas and Simichidas is a simple "grand–plain" contrast, or even "oral–written." Both poems, like both characters, are of course Theocritean products that reflect Theocritean poetics.[48] Moreover, the stylistic level of Lycidas' song seems more "smooth" (*glaphyron*) or "decorated" than grand, and it would in any case be more than surprising if the Theocritean contrast formed a perfect fit with any of the dichotomies of rhetorical teaching, let alone with Longinus' treatise. Nevertheless, there does seem to be a sense in which, within the parameters of Theocritean poetics, the difference between the songs is not merely an exemplification of two different elements within contemporary poetry, but also maps or constructs an evolution in poetic style that has intimate links to wider cultural practice. The next step will be to see whether anything similar is observable when we move from style to subject.

A CATALOGUED WORLD

Simichidas' interest in cult and geography that is (to us at least) obscure clearly belongs to his "modernity"; neither a connection of Pan with the Thessalian plain of Homole, nor the Arcadian squill rite, nor the "rock of the Blemyes," nor the spring of Hyetis are otherwise attested. It is not, however, these erudite fireworks, important though they are, to which I wish to draw attention here. If the world of Simichidas' in-jokes remains (perhaps deliberately) closed to us, he makes very sure that we understand his geographical and cultic allusions. The cause of the

---

[48] Whether Theocritus thought primarily in terms of a written reception or reception through recitation/performance for *Idyll* 7 may be thought relevant to this discussion. Unfortunately, however, we must rely in this matter on general assessments of the Hellenistic context rather than indications specific to Theocritus. For what it is worth, my sense is that Theocritus' poems are more open to both modes of transmission and reception than is the work of Callimachus and Apollonius, and it is tempting to associate this difference with the fact that there is no evidence that Theocritus worked as a "scholar." We may compare the palpable difference between Theocritus and "the Alexandrians" in terms of philological engagement with the text of Homer within the poetry itself.

Arcadian rite is explained (108), the location of the "rock of the Blemyes" specified (114), and the relevance of Oikous spelled out (116). Here is "precision" (*akribeia*) and (perhaps paradoxically) "clarity" (*saphēneia*) of *what* is said, as well as of *how* it is said. In his scholastic version of the iambic mode, Simichidas offers no "mythic narrative" as such, just a world marked out by cult sites and practices. Lycidas, however, finds personal, exemplary comfort in the bucolic and aipolic heroes of his own world – Daphnis and Komatas – and what is important, as it had traditionally been in the poetic representation of myth, is how their stories, their *pathē*, act as paradigms for his own experience.[49]

Lycidas' telling – or rather the telling which he puts in Tityrus' mouth – of the stories of Daphnis and Komatas is highly allusive, that is, it seems to assume an audience, whether that be just Lycidas himself or some wider group, to which those stories are known and significant. I hope that the similarity of this last sentence to some familiar "definitions" of myth is apparent. Thus, Richard Buxton posits myth "as a narrative about the deeds of gods and heroes . . . handed on as a tradition . . . and of collective significance to a particular social group or groups."[50] How "traditional" the stories of Daphnis and Komatas were is, of course, unclear, and it is hardly worth asking how Lycidas "changes" the narratives to suit his own position. What is important is that the allusive narrative mode, seen most famously in the song of Daphnis in *Idyll* 1, suggests "tradition,"[51] as it also constructs for itself an interpretive community. Here, literary allusiveness, intertextuality if you like, and mythic allusiveness function in similar ways.[52] The different gods who question Daphnis in *Idyll* 1 embody different levels of knowledge and curiosity, thus dramatizing the text's construction of its audience, but this device also foregrounds the allusiveness that implies familiarity while conjuring up the generic world of myth and constructing a community to whom that myth is significant, who need constantly to (re-)interpret it. A search for "the facts," the "precise"

---

[49] Macleod 1983: 168–9.
[50] Buxton 1994: 15, cf. Hunter 1999: 67. For discussion of such definitions, cf. Bremmer 1986.
[51] Cf. Hunter 1999: 63. For the importance of tradition in the definition of "the mythic," see Burkert 1979b: 17–8.
[52] Bing 1988: 74–5 offers a different, but perhaps complementary, account of literary allusiveness.

details of "what happened," would be misguided. Finally, we may note that Lycidas wishes to listen to songs that preserve the fame of great heroes; for him, poetry is both a traditional form and a preserver of tradition.

It would be tempting to set this contrast between Lycidas' high allusiveness and Simichidas' plain specificity within that broad movement that we have come to know, and seek to deconstruct, as the shift from myth to mythology. But let me return first to what Simichidas actually says. The pursuit of novelty, another "vice" that Longinus saw as endemic in his own day (*On the Sublime* 5.1), is obviously connected to the self-conscious craftsmanship (*technē*) of the professional, but it leaves, as I noted earlier, a world marked out by (often arcane) cult and ritual names rather than by narratives of personal or collective significance.[53] Many modern readers of Callimachus' *Hymns* might feel at home within Simichidas' "written" religious world, in which the scholarly gloss is the standard discursive mode, but this "precision" of names, which there is no reason not to connect with the prevalence of systematic written history, has a place in the wider evolution of mythic narrative. The modern study of fiction has taught us that detailed names and places are the "effects of the real" that create the fictional illusion[54] – an irony that Thucydides would presumably not have appreciated. Such *akribeia* goes hand in hand with the telling of stories as coherent, self-contained wholes in which temporal and spatial sequence are of primary importance, and here the link between *saphēs* as "true" and *saphēs* as "clear" comes into its own. If we leap forward from Thucydides to Theocritus, the narrative that most demands attention in this context is Simaitha's first-person narration of her affair with Delphis in *Idyll* 2. This self-conscious tale is replete with "effects of the real" – the names of Simaitha's circle, her clothes, places in the town.[55] We are here clearly dealing with some kind of "realistic fiction," and I would speculate that development toward this new kind of literature is intimately connected to the differing styles of mythic narrative in

---

[53] This is to be connected with the phenomenon whereby so much Hellenistic mythic narrative is presented as aetiological of ritual practice; Henrichs 1999 is fundamental here.

[54] Cf. Barthes 1986b; Yunis, this volume: 191 note 5.

[55] Note the variation on the "where do I begin?" motif (*Idyll* 2.64–5), familiar from the *Odyssey* onward; particularly helpful on this narrative is Andrews 1996.

Hellenistic poetry.[56] With hindsight, we can see that the vast sea of Greek myth was fertile ground for the development of fictionalizing instincts: Walter Burkert once noted that what is distinctive and "utterly confusing for non-specialists and often for specialists" about Greek myth is its extraordinarily profuse detail of names, genealogies, and interrelationships with, in other words (though Burkert certainly did not say this), "effects of the real" waiting to happen.[57] If we are forced to name a crucial moment in this process, the classicist may think of Aristophanes' Euripides, whose prologizing gods told "the whole story" (*Frogs* 946–7), that is, organized disparate strands (and disparate names) into a connected narrative; such "narrative exactness" (*akribologia*) shows the way to later mythography.[58] Of course, "graphy" – writing – has a place at the heart of these developments.[59]

As for Lycidas' stories of Daphnis and Komatas, it is tempting to suggest that the allusive mode of telling, related forms of which are familiar enough from the choral lyric of the archaic and classical periods, is a direct response to developments in "systematic mythography" and to what I have called the "fictionalizing" impulses that go with that systematization. Quite different poetic responses to these same developments in historiography and mythography are in fact on show in Callimachus' *Aitia* and Lycophron's *Alexandra*. In the *Idylls*, Theocritus recreates or invents an oral style of "traditional tale" beyond systematization (and certainly beyond Simichidas) and only preserved in the folk memories of shepherds and goatherds. This would, in fact, be the manifestation in the field of myth of the aetiology of bucolic poetry as a mode of popular song that is written into the surviving poems, particularly *Idyll* 1.[60] The Theocritean corpus makes clear that various thematic and stylistic developments that are usually treated separately are in fact interlinked in ways that shed light on the gradual, often imperceptible, changes in Greek culture that came with the

[56] There is no evidence that what we call *Idylls* 1 and 2 were ever juxtaposed in ancient editions, and a lot of evidence is against this; cf. Gutzwiller 1996. Virgil seems to have brought them together in *Eclogue* 8 on the formal grounds of the shared refrain. Nevertheless, critics have made the obvious connections between *Idyll* 1 and Lycidas' song and *Idyll* 2 (the song of Simaitha) and Simichidas' song. This is indeed a helpful heuristic device for thinking about narrative technique, but we must not assume an authorized juxtaposition within a poetry book.

[57] Burkert 1979b: 30.   [58] Cf. Demetrius, *On Style* 209.

[59] Rösler 1980b.   [60] Hunter 1999: 61–2.

ever deepening assimilation of literacy. *Idyll* 7 emerges as a remarkable dramatization of such change.

RETROSPECT

I have so far ignored one text that seems at the heart of this whole subject, namely, Plato's *Phaedrus*. The relation of this dialogue to bucolic literature has attracted previous critical attention,[61] but there may yet be more to be said in the context of this chapter.

Like Simichidas, Phaedrus has studied "books" (in his case the written speech of Lysias), but he seeks to conceal the fact, pretending instead to rely on an imperfect memory of a once-heard speech (227a–8e); the speech itself is one that Lysias had "written at leisure, over a long period of time" (228a). Thus, Phaedrus' intensive study of Lysias' speech should be viewed as a kind of second-level "labor" (*ponos*), imitative of the "labor" of the original author, which itself recalls the Thucydidean ideal and looks forward to Horace's demand for unremitting toil in writing. Be that as it may, the fact that it is Lysias who is the object of imitation is suggestive for the reception of the *Phaedrus* in *Idyll* 7. When Phaedrus has delivered the Lysianic speech, he asks Socrates: "How does the speech seem to you, Socrates? Doesn't it seem to you to be extraordinarily well done, especially in its language?" (234c, trans. Rowe). This seems to be the observation that Socrates picks up a few lines later: "Should you and I also praise the speech on the grounds that its creator has said what he should, and not just because he has said things clearly [*saphē*] and in a well-rounded fashion and each and all of his words are precisely [*akribōs*] turned?" (234e). For later ages, Lysias was indeed the model of pure, ordinary diction (*saphēneia*), "precise language" (*akribeia*), "envisionment" (*enargeia*), and an artful artlessness that avoided all suspicion of poetic tropes and made his speeches appear uncontrived and "natural."[62] The *Phaedrus* has clearly played its

---

[61] Hunter 1997, 1999: 14 (with bibliography), 145–6.

[62] Cf. Dionysius of Halicarnassus, *Lysias* passim, especially 8, 13. The negative side to this is Alcidamas' observation that *logographoi* aim to write speeches that appear improvised and "shun *akribeia*," thus showing (in Alcidamas' view) the superiority of real improvisation (frag. 1.13 Avezzù). This, too, is suggestive for Simichidas. Lysias' "plainness" is an important element in Socrates' feigned response of astonishment (*ekplēxis*) to Phaedrus' performance (234d); this is just how one should *not* react to Lysias.

part in this characterization, but the scholastic reception of Lysias may also throw light on one reception of the *Phaedrus*. Having summarized Lysias' stylistic virtues, Dionysius of Halicarnassus then characterizes him negatively (*Lysias* 13):

> There is nothing sublime or imposing about the style of Lysias. It certainly does not excite us or move us to wonder, nor does it portray pungency, intensity or fear; nor again does it have the power to grip the attention, and to keep it in rapt suspense; nor is it full of energy and feeling, or able to match its moral persuasiveness with an equal power to portray emotion. . . . It is a conservative style rather than an adventurous one. (trans. Usher, adapted)

Horace, too, opted for safety before risk.[63] Let me stress again that this is not a matter of Simichidas being merely a "poetic Lysias" – too much of his song lies in the realm of the "vulgar" (*to phortikon*) for that – but the stylistic analogue between the two (which reinforces the similarity of Phaedrus and Simichidas, both naive enthusiasts who encounter an ironic wisdom beyond their understanding) is indeed suggestive within the overall relation between the *Phaedrus* and *Idyll* 7.

We do not need the ancient critics to help us ascertain that Socrates' formal speeches in the *Phaedrus*, particularly the second one, are characterized by poeticism and sublimity, but it is a help that they do.[64] At one level, Socrates is the completely "natural," untrained orator, though his opening invocation to the Muses (237a) reveals by its playful etymologizing that "inspiration" has little to do with what he will proceed to say; the effect is perhaps not unlike the "mixed signals" that introduce Lycidas' song. Be that as it may, I intend no disrespect to Plato when I say that he has anticipated Theocritus in dramatizing a cultural difference, in which writing plays a central part, and which both manifests itself in and is represented by perceived stylistic difference. There is, of course, another narrative one could tell.

---

[63] Longinus also implies that Lysias belongs with the "flawless" writers – those who do not take risks (*On the Sublime* 32.8, 35.2).

[64] Dionysius of Halicarnassus, *Demosthenes* 7.

Bibliography

ABBREVIATIONS

CEG   *Carmina epigraphica graeca*, P. A. Hansen, ed. (Berlin, 1983, 1989).

DK   *Die Fragmente der Vorsokratiker*, 6th ed., H. Diels and W. Kranz, eds. (Berlin, 1960).

FGrH   *Die Fragmente der griechischen Historiker*, F. Jacoby, ed. (Berlin, Leiden, 1923–58).

ICret   *Inscriptiones creticae, opera et consilio Friderici Halbherr collectae*, M. Guarducci, ed. (Rome, 1935–40).

IG I³   *Inscriptiones graecae* I³ = *Inscriptiones atticae Euclidis anno anteriores*, 3rd ed., D. Lewis et al., eds. (Berlin, 1981–98).

LIMC   *Lexicon iconographicum mythologiae classicae*, H. C. Ackermann, J.-R. Gisler, et al., eds. (Zurich, 1981–99).

ML   *A Selection of Greek Historical Inscriptions to the End of the Fifth Century B.C.*, R. Meiggs and D. Lewis, eds. (Oxford, 1969).

OCD   *Oxford Classical Dictionary*, 3rd ed., S. Hornblower and A. Spawforth, eds. (Oxford, 1996).

PCG   *Poetae comici graeci*, R. Kassel and C. Austin, eds. (Berlin, 1983–).

PMG   *Poetae melici graeci*, D. L. Page, ed. (Oxford, 1962).

RE   *Realencyclopädie der classischen Altertumswissenschaft*, A. Pauly, G. Wissowa, and W. Kroll, eds. (Stuttgart, 1893–1972).

SEG   *Supplementum epigraphicum graecum* (Amsterdam, 1923–).

TrGF   *Tragicorum graecorum fragmenta*, B. Snell et al., eds. (Göttingen, 1971–).

Alexander, L. (1990) "The Living Voice: Scepticism Towards the Written Word in Early Christianity and in Graeco-Roman Texts." In D. J. Clines et al., eds., *The Bible in*

Bibliography

Three Dimensions. Journal for the Study of the Old Testament, suppl. series 87. Sheffield. 221–47.

Allen, D. S. (2000) *The World of Prometheus: The Politics of Punishing in Democratic Athens.* Princeton.

Allison, J. W. (1997) *Word and Concept in Thucydides.* Atlanta.

Anderson, Ø. (1987) "Mündlichkeit und Schriftlichkeit im frühen Griechentum." *Antike und Abendland* 23: 29–44.

Andrews, N. E. (1996) "Narrative and Allusion in Theocritus, *Idyll* 2." In M. A. Harder, R. F. Regtuit, and G. C. Wakker, eds., *Theocritus.* Groningen. 21–53.

Anonymous. (1982) "Der orphische Papyrus von Derveni." *Zeitschrift für Papyrologie und Epigraphik* 47: 1–12 following page 300.

Asper, M. (1997) *Onomata Allotria: Zur Genese, Struktur und Funktion poetologischer Metaphern bei Kallimachos.* Stuttgart.

Assmann, A., J. Assmann, and C. Hardmeier, eds. (1983) *Schrift und Gedächtnis. Beiträge zur Archäologie der literarischen Kommunikation.* Munich.

Ausland, H. W. (1997) "On Reading Plato Mimetically." *American Journal of Philology* 118: 371–416.

Baker, J. H. (1990) *An Introduction to English Legal History.* 3rd ed. Oxford.

Barrett, W. S. (1964) *Euripides: Hippolytos.* Oxford.

Barthes, R. (1976) *S/Z.* Paris.

    (1986a) "The Discourse of History." In R. Barthes, *The Rustle of Language.* Trans. R. Howard. New York. 127–40.

    (1986b) "The Reality Effect." In R. Barthes, *The Rustle of Language.* Trans. R. Howard. New York. 141–48.

Baumgarten, R. (1998) *Heiliges Wort und Heilige Schrift bei den Griechen: Hieroi Logoi und verwandte Erscheinungen.* ScriptOralia 110. Tübingen.

Beazley, J. D. (1948) "Hymn to Hermes." *American Journal of Archaeology* 52: 336–40.

Benveniste, E. (1969) *Le vocabulaire des institutions indo-européennes.* 2 vols. Paris.

Berger, H. (1984) "The Origins of Bucolic Representation: Disenchantment and Revision in Theocritus' Seventh *Idyll.*" *Classical Antiquity* 3: 1–39.

Betegh, G. (forthcoming) *The Derveni Papyrus: Cosmology, Theology, and Interpretation.* Cambridge.

Bierl, A. (2001) *Der Chor in der Alten Komödie. Ritual und Performativität.* Beiträge zur Altertumskunde 126. Munich/Leipzig.

Bing, P. (1988) *The Well-Read Muse: Present and Past in Callimachus and the Hellenistic Poets.* Göttingen.

Blanck, H. (1992) *Das Buch in der Antike.* Munich.

    (1997) "Un nuovo frammento del 'Catalogo' della biblioteca di Tauromenion." *Parola del Passato* 52: 241–55.

Boardman, J., J. Dörig, W. Fuchs, and M. Hirmer. (1984) *Die griechische Kunst.* 3rd ed. Munich.

Boder, W. (1973) *Die sokratische Ironie in den platonischen Frühdialogen.* Amsterdam.

Bottéro, J. (1992) *Mesopotamia: Writing, Reasoning, and the Gods.* Chicago.

Bourdieu, P. (1990) "Reading, Readers, the Literate, Literature." In P. Bourdieu, *In Other Words: Essays Towards a Reflexive Sociology.* Trans. M. Adamson. Stanford. 94–105.

Bibliography

Bowman, A. K., and G. Woolf, eds. (1994) *Literacy and Power in the Ancient World*. Cambridge.

Bowra, C. M. (1953) "The Proem of Parmenides." In C. M. Bowra, *Problems in Greek Poetry*. Oxford. 38–53.

Boylan, P. (1922) *Thoth, the Hermes of Egypt: A Study of Some Aspects of Theological Thought in Ancient Egypt*. London.

Bremmer, J. (1986) "What is a Greek Myth?" In J. Bremmer, ed., *Interpretations of Greek Mythology*. Totowa. 1–9.

——— (1991) "Orpheus: From Guru to Gay." In P. Borgeaud, ed., *Orphisme et Orphée en l'honneur de Jean Rudhardt*. Recherches et rencontres 3. Geneva. 13–30.

Brink, C. O. (1971) *Horace on Poetry: The Ars Poetica*. Cambridge.

Brooks, E. B., and A. T. Brooks. (1998) *The Original Analects*. New York.

Burkert, W. (1979a) *Structure and History in Greek Mythology and Ritual*. Sather Classical Lectures 47. Berkeley.

——— (1979b) "Mythisches Denken. Versuch einer Definition an Hand des griechischen Befundes." In H. Poser, ed., *Philosophie und Mythos*. Berlin. 16–39.

——— (1985) *Greek Religion*. Trans. J. Raffan. Cambridge, Mass.

——— (1986) "Der Autor von Derveni: Stesimbrotos Περὶ τελετῶν?" *Zeitschrift für Papyrologie und Epigraphik* 62: 1–5.

——— (1987) "Offerings in Perspective: Surrender, Distribution, Exchange." In T. Linders and G. Nordquist, eds., *Gifts to the Gods: Proceedings of the Uppsala Symposium 1985*. Acta Universitatis Upsaliensis, Boreas 15. Uppsala. 43–50.

——— (1990) "Herodot als Historiker fremder Religionen." In G. Nenci, ed., *Hérodote et les peuples non-grecs*. Entretiens Hardt 35. Vandœuvres/Geneva. 1–39.

——— (1992) *The Orientalizing Revolution: Near Eastern Influence on Greek Culture in the Early Archaic Age*. Cambridge, Mass.

——— (1999) *Da Omero ai magi. La tradizione orientale nella cultura greca*. Venice.

Burns, A. (1981) "Athenian Literacy in the Fifth Century B.C." *Journal of the History of Ideas* 43: 371–87.

Burnyeat, M. (1997) "Postscript on Silent Reading." *Classical Quarterly* 47: 74–76.

Buxton, R. (1994) *Imaginary Greece*. Cambridge.

Calame, C. (1995) *The Craft of Poetic Speech in Ancient Greece*. Trans. J. Orion. Ithaca.

Calhoun, G. M. (1919) "Oral and Written Pleading in Athenian Courts." *Transactions of the American Philological Association* 50: 177–93.

Camassa, G. (1988) "Aux origines de la codification écrite en Grèce." In M. Detienne, ed., *Les savoirs de l'écriture en Grèce ancienne*. Cahiers de Philologie 14. Lille. 130–55.

Cambiano, G. (2001) "Istituzioni e forme dell' attività scientifica in età ellenistica e romana." In G. E. R. Lloyd, ed., *Storia della scienza*. Vol. 1, part 4, *La scienza greca*. Rome.

Cambiano, G., L. Canfora, and D. Lanza, eds. (1992) *Lo spazio letterario della Grecia antica*. 3 vols. Rome.

Canfora, L. (1988) "Discours écrit / discours réel chez Démosthène." In M. Detienne, ed., *Les savoirs de l'écriture en Grèce ancienne*. Cahiers de Philologie 14. Lille. 211–20.

Carratelli, P., ed. (1996) *The Greek World: Art and Civilization in Magna Graecia and Sicily*. Trans. A. Ellis et al. New York.

Bibliography

Chadwick, J. (1970) *The Decipherment of Linear B*. 2nd ed. Cambridge.

(1989) *Linear B and Related Scripts*. Berkeley.

Clanchy, M. T. (1985) "Literacy, Law, and the Power of the State." In *Culture et idéologie dans la genèse de l'état moderne. Actes de la table ronde organisée par le Centre national de la recherche scientifique et l'École française de Rome*. Rome. 25–34.

(1993) *From Memory to Written Record: England 1066–1307*. 2nd ed. Oxford.

Clay, D. (2000) *Platonic Questions: Dialogues with the Silent Philosopher*. University Park.

Cohen, D. (1995) *Law, Violence, and Community in Classical Athens*. Cambridge.

Cohen, E. E. (1973) *Ancient Athenian Maritime Courts*. Princeton.

(1992) *Athenian Economy and Society: A Banking Perspective*. Princeton.

Cohn-Haft, L. (1956) *The Public Physicians of Ancient Greece*. Northhampton.

Cole, T. (1991) *The Origins of Rhetoric in Ancient Greece*. Baltimore.

Cope, E. M. (1877) *The Rhetoric of Aristotle with a Commentary*. 3 vols. Edited by J. E. Sandys. Cambridge.

Coxon, A. H. (1986) *The Fragments of Parmenides*. Assen.

Cozzoli, A.-T. (1996) "Aspetti intertestuali nelle polemiche letterarie degli antichi: da Pindaro a Persio." *Quaderni Urbinati di Cultura Classica* 54: 7–36.

Craik, E. M. (1998) *Hippocrates: Places in Man*. Oxford.

Csikszentmihalyi, M., and M. Nylan. (forthcoming) "Constructing Lineages and Inventing Traditions in the *Shiji*."

Cullen, C. (1996) *Astronomy and Mathematics in Ancient China: the Zhou Bi Suan Jing*. Cambridge.

Dareste, R., B. Haussoullier, and T. Reinach. (1891–1904) *Recueil des inscriptions juridiques grecques*. 2 vols. Paris.

Davies, J. K. (1977–78) "Athenian Citizenship: The Descent Group and the Alternatives." *Classical Journal* 73: 105–21.

Davison, J. A. (1968) "Literature and Literacy in Ancient Greece." In J. A. Davison, *From Archilochus to Pindar: Papers on Greek Literature of the Archaic Period*. London. 86–128. Originally published in *Phoenix* 16 (1962): 141–56, 219–33.

Day, J. W. (1989) "Rituals in Stone: Early Greek Grave Epigrams and Monuments." *Journal of Hellenic Studies* 109: 16–28.

(2000) "Epigram and Reader: Generic Force as (Re-)Activation of Ritual." In M. Depew and D. Obbink, eds., *Matrices of Genre: Authors, Canons, and Society*. Cambridge, Mass. 37–57.

Demand, N. (1996) "Medicine and Rhetoric: The Attic Orators." In R. Wittern and P. Pellegrin, eds., *Hippokratische Medizin und antike Philosophie*. Hildesheim. 91–99.

Demont, P. (1993) "Die *Epideixis* über die *Techne* im V. und IV. Jahrhundert." In W. Kullmann and J. Althoff, eds., *Vermittlung und Tradierung von Wissen in der griechischen Kultur*. Tübingen. 181–209.

Derderian, K. (2001) *Leaving Words to Remember: Greek Mourning and the Advent of Literacy*. Mnemosyne Suppl. 209. Leiden.

de Romilly, J. (1956) *Histoire et raison chez Thucydide*. Paris.

(1975) *Magic and Rhetoric in Ancient Greece*. Cambridge, Mass.

de Ste. Croix, G. E. M. (1972) *The Origins of the Peloponnesian War*. London.

Bibliography

Detienne, M., ed. (1988) *Les savoirs de l'écriture en Grèce ancienne*. Cahiers de Philologie 14. Lille.

——— (1989) *L'écriture d'Orphée*. Paris.

Dillon, M. P. J. (1994) "The Didactic Nature of the Epidaurian *Iamata*." *Zeitschrift für Papyrologie und Epigraphik* 101: 239–60.

Dodds, E. R. (1951) *The Greeks and the Irrational*. Berkeley.

Dover, K. J. (1968) *Lysias and the Corpus Lysiacum*. Berkeley.

——— (1971) *Theocritus: Select Poems*. London.

——— (1997) *The Evolution of Greek Prose Style*. Oxford.

Dow, S. (1953–57) "The Law Codes of Athens." *Proceedings of the Massachusetts Historical Society* 71: 3–36.

——— (1960) "The Athenian Calendar of Sacrifices: The Chronology of Nikomakhos' Second Term." *Historia* 9: 270–93.

——— (1961) "The Walls Inscribed with Nikomakhos' Law Code." *Hesperia* 30: 58–73.

——— (1963) "The Athenian Anagrapheis." *Harvard Studies in Classical Philology* 67: 37–54.

——— (1968) "Six Athenian Sacrificial Calendars." *Bulletin de correspondance hellénique* 92: 170–86.

Ducatillon, J. (1969) "Collection Hippocratique. *Du Régime*, III. Les deux publics." *Revue des études grecques* 82: 33–42.

Dunbar, N. (1995) *Aristophanes: Birds*. Oxford.

Easterling, P. E. (1988) "Tragedy and Ritual." *Metis* 3: 87–109.

Edelstein, L. (1962) "Platonic Anonymity." *American Journal of Philology* 83: 1–22.

Eden, K. (1987) "Hermeneutics and the Ancient Rhetorical Tradition." *Rhetorica* 5: 59–86.

——— (1997) *Hermeneutics and the Rhetorical Tradition: Chapters in the Ancient Legacy and Its Humanist Reception*. New Haven.

Eder, W. (1986) "The Political Significance of the Codification of Law in Archaic Societies: An Unconventional Hypothesis." In K. A. Raaflaub, ed., *Social Struggles in Archaic Rome: New Perspectives on the Conflict of the Orders*. Berkeley. 262–300.

Edmunds, L. (1993) "Thucydides in the Act of Writing." In R. Pretagostini, ed., *Tradizione e innovazione nella cultura greca da Omero all' età ellenistica*. Rome. 831–52.

Edmunds, L., and R. W. Wallace, eds. (1997) *Poet, Public, and Performance in Ancient Greece*. Baltimore.

Edwards, M. J. (1991) "Notes on the Derveni Commentator." *Zeitschrift für Papyrologie und Epigraphik* 86: 203–11.

Edwards, M. W. (1997) "Homeric Style and 'Oral Poetics'." In I. Morris and B. Powell, eds., *A New Companion to Homer*. Leiden. 261–83.

Edwards, R. B. (1979) *Kadmos the Phoenician: A Study in Greek Legends and the Mycenaean Age*. Amsterdam.

Erbse, H. (1989) *Thukydides-Interpretationen*. Berlin.

Faraone, C. A. (1996) "Taking the 'Nestor's Cup Inscription' Seriously: Conditional Curses and Erotic Magic in the Earliest Inscribed Hexameters." *Classical Antiquity* 15: 77–112.

——— (2000) "Handbooks and Anthologies: The Collection of Greek and Egyptian Incantations in Late Hellenistic Egypt." *Archiv für Religionsgeschichte* 2: 195–214.

Bibliography

Faraone, C. A., and D. Obbink, eds. (1991) *Magika Hiera: Ancient Greek Magic and Religion*. New York.

Fell, M. (1997) "Konkordanz zu den frühen griechischen Gesetzestexten." *Zeitschrift für Papyrologie und Epigraphik* 118: 183–96.

Ferrari, F. (1989) "P. Berol. inv. 13270: i canti de Elefantina." *Studi classici e orientali* 31: 181–228.

Finley, M. I. (1965) "Myth, Memory, and History." *History and Theory* 4: 281–302.

(1975) *The Use and Abuse of History*. London.

(1985) *Ancient History: Evidence and Models*. London.

Finnegan, R. H. (1977) *Oral Poetry: Its Nature, Significance, and Social Context*. Cambridge.

(1988) *Literacy and Orality: Studies in the Technology of Communication*. Oxford.

Flashar, H. (1958) *Der Dialog Ion als Zeugnis platonischer Philosophie*. Berlin.

Foley, J. M. (1985) *Oral-Formulaic Theory and Research: An Introduction and Annotated Bibliography*. New York.

(1997) "Oral Tradition and Its Implications." In I. Morris and B. Powell, eds., *A New Companion to Homer*. Leiden. 146–73.

Fontenrose, J. (1978) *The Delphic Oracle: Its Responses and Operations*. Berkeley.

Ford, A. (1993) "L'inventeur de la poésie lyrique: Archiloque le colon." *Métis* 8: 59–73.

(1997) "The Inland Ship: Problems in the Performance and Reception of Early Greek Epic." In E. Bakker and A. Kahane, eds., *Written Voices, Spoken Signs: Tradition, Performance, and the Epic Text*. Cambridge, Mass. 83–109.

(1999) "Performing Interpretation: Early Allegorical Exegesis of Homer." In M. Beissinger, J. Tylus, and S. Wofford, eds., *Epic Traditions in the Contemporary World: The Poetics of Community*. Berkeley. 33–53.

(2002) *The Origins of Criticism: Literary Culture and Poetic Theory in Classical Greece*. Princeton.

Frede, M. (1992) "Plato's Arguments and the Dialogue Form." In J. C. Klagge and N. D. Smith, eds., *Oxford Studies in Ancient Philosophy*. Suppl. vol., *Methods of Interpreting Plato and His Dialogues*. Oxford. 201–19.

Frier, B. (1985) *The Rise of the Roman Jurists: Studies in Cicero's Pro Caecina*. Princeton.

Furley, W. D., and J. M. Bremer. (2001) *Greek Hymns: Selected Cult Songs from the Archaic to the Hellenistic Period*. Studien und Texte zu Antike und Christentum 9–10. Tübingen.

Gagarin, M. (1981) *Drakon and Early Athenian Homicide Law*. New Haven.

(1986) *Early Greek Law*. Berkeley.

(1992) "The Poetry of Justice: Hesiod and the Origins of Greek Law." *Ramus* 21: 61–78.

(1999) "The Orality of Greek Oratory." In E. A. Mackay, ed., *Signs of Orality: The Oral Tradition and Its Influence in the Greek and Roman World*. Leiden. 163–80.

(2001) "The Gortyn Code and Greek Legal Procedure." In E. Cantarella and G. Thür, eds., *Symposion 1997. Akten der Gesellschaft für griechischen und hellenistischen Rechtsgeschichte*. Vol. 13. Cologne. 41–52.

Gager, J. G. (1992) *Curse Tablets and Binding Spells from the Ancient World*. New York.

Gantz, T. (1993) *Early Greek Myth: A Guide to the Literary and Artistic Sources*. Baltimore.

Bibliography

Garrity, T. F. (1998) "Thucydides 1.22.1: Content and Form in the Speeches." *American Journal of Philology* 119: 361–84.

Gentili, B. (1988) *Poetry and Its Public in Ancient Greece: From Homer to the Fifth Century.* Trans. A. T. Cole. Baltimore.

Goldhill, S. (1986) *Reading Greek Tragedy.* Cambridge.

Goldhill, S., and R. Osborne, eds. (1999) *Performance Culture and Athenian Democracy.* Cambridge.

Goody, J. (1977) *The Domestication of the Savage Mind.* Cambridge.

(1986) *The Logic of Writing and the Organization of Society.* Cambridge.

(1987) *The Interface Between the Written and the Oral.* Cambridge.

(2000) *The Power of the Written Tradition.* Washington.

Goody, J., and I. Watt. (1963) "The Consequences of Literacy." *Comparative Studies in Society and History* 5: 304–45. Reprinted in J. Goody, ed., *Literacy in Traditional Societies.* Cambridge, 1968. 27–68.

Graham, A. C. (1981) *Chuang-tzu: the Seven Inner Chapters.* London.

(1989) *Disputers of the Tao.* La Salle.

Graf, F. (1985) *Nordionische Kulte. Religionsgeschichtliche und epigraphische Untersuchungen zu den Kulten von Chios, Erythrai, Klazomenai, und Phokaia.* Bibliotheca Helvetica Romana 21. Rome.

(1986) "Orpheus: A Poet Among Men." In J. Bremmer, ed., *Interpretations of Greek Mythology.* Totowa. 80–106.

(1997) *Magic in the Ancient World.* Cambridge, Mass.

Grensemann, H. (1975) *Knidische Medizin. Teil I.* Berlin.

Gribble, D. (1998) "Narrator Interventions in Thucydides." *Journal of Hellenic Studies* 118: 41–67.

Gutzwiller, K. J. (1996) "The Evidence for Theocritean Poetry Books." In M. A. Harder, R. F. Regtuit, and G. C. Wakker, eds., *Theocritus.* Groningen. 119–48.

Hahn, R. (2001) *Anaximander and the Architects: The Contributions of Egyptian and Greek Architectural Technologies to the Origins of Greek Philosophy.* Albany.

Hall, E. (1995) "Lawcourt Dramas: The Power of Performance in Greek Forensic Oratory." *Bulletin of the Institute of Classical Studies* 40 (new series vol. 2): 39–58.

(1996) "Is There a *Polis* in Aristotle's *Poetics*?" In M. S. Silk, ed., *Tragedy and the Tragic.* Oxford. 295–309.

Hamilton, R. (2000) *Treasure Map: A Guide to the Delian Inventories.* Ann Arbor.

Hanson, A. E. (1997) "Fragmentation and the Greek Medical Writers." In G. W. Most, ed., *Collecting Fragments – Fragmente Sammeln.* Göttingen. 289–311.

Hardie, P. (1986) *Virgil's Aeneid: Cosmos and Imperium.* Oxford.

Harris, D. (1995) *The Treasures of the Parthenon and Erechtheion.* Oxford.

Harris, W. V. (1989) *Ancient Literacy.* Cambridge, Mass.

Harrison, T. (2000) *Divinity and History: The Religion of Herodotus.* Oxford.

Harvey, F. D. (1966) "Literacy in the Athenian Democracy." *Revue des études grecques* 79: 585–635.

Havelock, E. A. (1963) *Preface to Plato.* Cambridge, Mass.

(1978) "The Alphabetization of Homer." In E. A. Havelock and J. P. Hershbell, eds., *Communication Arts in the Ancient World.* New York. 3–21.

(1982) *The Literate Revolution in Greece and Its Cultural Consequences.* Princeton.

(1983) "The Linguistic Task of the pre-Socratics." In K. Robb, ed., *Language and Thought in Early Greek Philosophy*. La Salle. 7–82.

(1986) *The Muse Learns To Write: Reflections on Orality and Literacy from Antiquity to the Present*. New Haven.

Healey, R. F. (1984) "A Gennetic Sacrifice List in the Athenian State Calendar." In K. J. Rigsby, ed., *Studies Presented to Sterling Dow on His Eightieth Birthday*. Greek, Roman and Byzantine Monographs 11. Durham. 135–41.

Heath, M. (1999) "Longinus, *On Sublimity*." *Proceedings of the Cambridge Philological Society* 45: 43–75.

Henrichs, A. (1990) "Between Country and City: Cultic Dimensions of Dionysos in Athens and Attica." In M. Griffith and D. J. Mastronarde, eds., *Cabinet of the Muses. Essays on Classical and Comparative Literature in Honor of Thomas G. Rosenmeyer*. Atlanta. 257–77.

(1995) "Why Should I Dance? Choral Self-Referentiality in Greek Tragedy." *Arion* 3: 56–111.

(1996a) *Warum soll ich denn tanzen? Dionysisches im Chor der griechischen Tragödie*. Lectio Teubneriana 4. Leipzig.

(1996b) "Epiphany." In S. Hornblower and A. Spawforth, eds., *Oxford Classical Dictionary*. 3rd ed. Oxford. 546.

(1998) "Dromena und Legomena: Zum rituellen Selbstverständnis der Griechen." In F. Graf, ed., *Ansichten griechischer Rituale. Geburtstags-Symposium für Walter Burkert*. Stuttgart/Leipzig. 33–71.

(1999) "Demythologizing the Past, Mythicizing the Present: Myth, History, and the Supernatural at the Dawn of the Hellenistic Period." In R. Buxton, ed., *From Myth to Reason?* Oxford. 223–48.

(2000) "Drama and *Dromena*: Bloodshed, Violence, and Sacrificial Metaphor in Euripides." *Harvard Studies in Classical Philology* 100: 173–88.

(2002) "*Hieroi Logoi and Hierai Bibloi*: The (Un)written Margins of the Sacred in Ancient Greece." *Harvard Studies in Classical Philology* 101.

Henry, M. (1986) "The Derveni Commentator as Literary Critic." *Transactions of the American Philological Association* 116: 149–64.

Herington, C. J. (1985) *Poetry Into Drama: Early Tragedy and the Greek Poetic Tradition*. Berkeley.

Hesk, J. (2000) *Deception and Democracy in Classical Athens*. Cambridge.

Hirsch, E. D. (1976) *The Aims of Interpretation*. Chicago.

Hölkeskamp, K.-J. (1992) "Written Law in Archaic Greece." *Proceedings of the Cambridge Philological Society* 38: 87–117.

(1995) "Arbitrators, Lawgivers, and the 'Codification of Law' in Archaic Greece: Problems and Perspectives." *Métis* 7: 49–81.

(1999) *Schiedsrichter, Gesetzgeber und Gesetzgebung im archaischen Griechenland*. Historia Einzelschriften 131. Stuttgart.

Hornblower, S. (1991) *A Commentary on Thucydides*. Vol. 1, *Books I–III*. Oxford.

(2000) "The Old Oligarch (Pseudo-Xenophon's *Athenaion Politeia*) and Thucydides: A Fourth-Century Date for the Old Oligarch?" In P. Flensted-Jensen, T. H. Nielsen, and L. Rubinstein, eds., *Polis and Politics: Studies in Ancient Greek History*. Copenhagen. 363–84.

Bibliography

Hose, M. (1998) "Fragment und Kontext. Zwei Methoden der Interpretation in der griechischen Literatur." In J. Holzhausen, ed., ψυχή – *Seele – anima. Festschrift für Karin Alt zum 7. Mai 1998.* Stuttgart. 89–112.

Hsu, E. (forthcoming) *Canggongzhuan.*

Hudson-Williams, H. L. (1949) "Isocrates and Recitations." *Classical Quarterly* 43: 65–69.

Humphreys, S. (1985) "Social Relations on Stage: Witnesses in Classical Athens." *History and Anthropology* 1: 313–69.

Hunter, R. (1997) "Longus and Plato." In M. Picone and B. Zimmermann, eds., *Der antike Roman und seine mittelalterliche Rezeption.* Basel. 15–28.

(1999) *Theocritus: A Selection.* Cambridge.

(forthcoming) *Theocritus, Encomium of Ptolemy.* Berkeley.

Hutchinson, G. (1988) *Hellenistic Poetry.* Oxford.

Immerwahr, H. R. (1964) "Book Rolls on Attic Vases." In Charles Henderson, Jr., ed., *Classical, Mediaeval, and Renaissance Studies in Honor of Berthold Louis Ullman.* Vol. 1. Rome. 17–48.

(1990) *Attic Script: A Survey.* Oxford.

Inwood, B. (1992) *The Poem of Empedocles: A Text and Translation with an Introduction.* Toronto.

Irigoin, J. (1952) *Histoire du texte du Pindare.* Paris.

Isserlin, B. S. J. (1982) "The Earliest Alphabetic Writing." In J. Boardman et al., eds., *Cambridge Ancient History.* 2nd ed. Vol. 3, part 1. Cambridge. 794–818.

Jackson, R. (1988) *Doctors and Diseases in the Roman Empire.* Norman.

Jacob, C. (1998) "Vers une histoire comparée de bibliothèques. Questions préliminaires entre Grèce et Chine anciennes." *Quaderni di Storia* 48: 87–122.

Jacoby, F. (1947) "The First Athenian Prose Writer." *Mnemosyne* 13: 13–64.

Jacques, J.-M. (1998) *Ménandre: Le Bouclier.* Paris.

Jaeger, W. (1912) *Studien zur Entstehungsgeschichte der Metaphysik des Aristoteles.* Berlin.

(1944) *Paideia: The Ideals of Greek Culture.* Trans. G. Highet. Oxford.

Jahandarie, K. (1999) *Spoken and Written Discourse: A Multi-Disciplinary Perspective.* Stamford.

Jameson, M. H., D. R. Jordan, and R. D. Kotansky, eds. (1993) *A Lex Sacra from Selinous.* Greek, Roman and Byzantine Studies Suppl. 11. Durham.

Janko, R. (1990) "The *Iliad* and its Editors: Dictation and Redaction." *Classical Antiquity* 9: 326–34.

(1997) "The Physicist as Hierophant: Aristophanes, Socrates, and the Authorship of the Derveni Papyrus." *Zeitschrift für Papyrologie und Epigraphik* 118: 61–94.

(2001) "The Derveni Papyrus (Diagoras of Melos, *Apopyrgizontes Logoi?*): A New Translation." *Classical Philology* 96: 1–32.

Jeffery, L. H. (1982) "Greek Alphabetic Writing." In J. Boardman et al., eds., *Cambridge Ancient History.* 2nd ed. Vol. 3, part 1. Cambridge. 819–33.

(1990) *The Local Scripts of Archaic Greece.* Rev. ed. with supplement by A. W. Johnston. Oxford. First edition, 1961.

Johne, R. (1991) "Zur Entstehung einer 'Buchkultur' in der zweiten Hälfte des 5. Jahrhunderts v. u. Z." *Philologus* 135: 45–54.

Bibliography

Johnson, W. A. (2000) "Towards a Sociology of Reading in Classical Antiquity." *American Journal of Philology* 121: 593–627.

Jolowicz, H. F., and B. Nicholas. (1972) *Historical Introduction to the Study of Roman Law.* 3rd ed. Cambridge.

Jordan, D. R. (2000) "New Greek Curse Tablets (1985–2000)." *Greek, Roman and Byzantine Studies* 41: 5–46.

Josipovici, G. (1999) *On Trust: Art and the Temptations of Suspicion.* New Haven.

Jouanna, J. (1974) *Hippocrate: Pour une archéologie de l'école de Cnide.* Paris.

(1975) *Hippocrate. La nature de l'homme.* Berlin.

(1984) "Rhétorique et médecine dans la Collection Hippocratique." *Revue des études grecques* 97: 26–44.

(1988) *Hippocrate. Des Vents, de l'Art.* Paris.

(1999) *Hippocrates.* Trans. M. B. DeBevoise. Baltimore.

Kahn, C. H. (1960) *Anaximander and the Origins of Greek Cosmology.* New York.

(1963) "Plato's Funeral Oration: The Motive of the *Menexenus.*" *Classical Philology* 58: 220–34.

(1979) *The Art and Thought of Heraclitus.* Cambridge.

(1983) "Philosophy and the Written Word." In K. Robb, ed., *Language and Thought in Early Greek Philosophy.* LaSalle. 110–24.

(1996) *Plato and the Socratic Dialogue: The Philosophical Use of a Literary Form.* Cambridge.

(2001) *Pythagoras and the Pythagoreans.* Indianapolis.

Kelly, D. (1996) "Oral Xenophon." In I. Worthington, ed., *Voice Into Text: Orality and Literacy in Ancient Greece.* Leiden. 149–63.

Kennedy, G. A., trans. (1991) *Aristotle: A Theory of Civic Discourse.* New York.

Kerferd, G. B. (1981) *The Sophistic Movement.* Cambridge.

King, H. (1998) *Hippocrates' Woman: Reading the Female Body in Ancient Greece.* London.

Kirchner, J. (1948) *Imagines inscriptionum Atticarum: ein Bilderatlas epigraphischer Denkmäler Attikas.* 2nd ed. Berlin.

Kirk, G. S., J. E. Raven, and M. Schofield. (1983) *The Presocratic Philosophers.* 2nd ed. Cambridge.

Knoblock, J. (1988–94) *Xunzi: A Translation and Study of the Complete Works.* 3 vols. Stanford.

Knox, B. M. W. (1985) "Books and Readers in the Greek World: From the Beginnings to Alexandria." In P. E. Easterling and B. M. W. Knox, eds., *The Cambridge History of Classical Literature.* Vol. 1, *Greek Literature.* Cambridge. 1–16.

Koerner, R. (1993) *Inschriftliche Gesetzestexte der frühen griechischen Polis.* Cologne.

Köhnken, A., and R. Kirstein. (1995) "Theokrit 1950–1994 (1996)." *Lustrum* 37: 203–307.

Kollesch, J. (1992) "Zur Mündlichkeit hippokratischer Schriften." In J. A. López Férez, ed., *Tratados hipocráticos (Estudios acerca de su contenido, forma e influencia).* Madrid. 335–42.

Kotansky, R. (1991) "Incantations and Prayers for Salvation on Inscribed Greek Amulets." In C. A. Faraone and D. Obbink, eds., *Magika Hiera: Ancient Greek Magic and Religion.* New York. 106–37.

Bibliography

Krevans, N. (1983) "Geography and the Literary Tradition in Theocritus 7." *Transactions of the American Philological Association* 113: 201–20.

Krummen, E. (1998) "Ritual und Katastrophe: Rituelle Handlung und Bildersprache bei Sophokles und Euripides." In F. Graf, ed., *Ansichten griechischer Rituale. Geburtstags-Symposium für Walter Burkert.* Stuttgart/Leipzig. 296–325.

Kudlien, F. (1967) *Der Beginn des medizinischen Denkens bei den Griechen.* Zurich.

Kühn, J.-H. (1958) "Die Thalysien Theokrits (id. 7)." *Hermes* 86: 40–79.

Kurz, D. (1970) AKPIBEIA. *Das Ideal der Exaktheit bei den Griechen bis Aristoteles.* Göppingen.

Laks, A. (2001) "Ecriture, prose, et les débuts de la philosophie grecque." *Methodos* 1: 131–51.

Laks, A., and G. W. Most, eds. (1997) *Studies on the Derveni Papyrus.* Oxford.

Langdon, M. K. (1976) *A Sanctuary of Zeus on Mount Hymettos.* Hesperia Suppl. 16. Princeton.

Lawall, G. (1967) *Theocritus' Coan Pastorals.* Washington, D. C.

Leduc, C. (1976) *La constitution d'Athènes attribué à Xenophon.* Paris.

Lesher, J. H. (1992) *Xenophanes of Colophon.* Toronto.

Lévy-Bruhl, L. (1923) *Primitive Mentality.* Trans. L. A. Clare. London.

(1926) *How Natives Think.* Trans. L. A. Clare. London.

Lewis, M. E. (1999) *Writing and Authority in Early China.* Albany.

Linforth, I. (1941) *The Arts of Orpheus.* Berkeley. Reprint, New York: 1973.

Lissarague, F. (1987) *Un flot d'images: une esthétique du banquet grec.* Paris.

Lloyd, G. E. R. (1979) *Magic, Reason, and Experience.* Cambridge.

(1987) *The Revolutions of Wisdom: Studies in the Claims and Practice of Greek Science.* Berkeley.

(1990) *Demystifying Mentalities.* Cambridge.

(1996) *Adversaries and Authorities.* Cambridge.

Lloyd, G. E. R., and N. Sivin. (forthcoming) *The Way and the Word.*

Lloyd-Jones, H. (1998) "Ritual and Tragedy." In F. Graf, ed., *Ansichten griechischer Rituale. Geburtstags-Symposium für Walter Burkert.* Stuttgart/Leipzig. 271–95.

Lonie, I. M. (1983) "Literacy and the Development of Hippocratic Medicine." In F. Lasserre and P. Mudry, eds., *Formes de pensée dans la collection hippocratique.* Geneva. 145–61.

Lord, A. B. (1960) *The Singer of Tales.* Cambridge, Mass.

(2000) *The Singer of Tales.* 2nd ed. Edited by S. Mitchell and G. Nagy. Cambridge, Mass.

MacDowell, D. (1990) "The Meaning of *alazôn*." In E. M. Craik, ed., *"Owls to Athens": Essays on Classical Subjects Presented to Sir Kenneth Dover.* Oxford. 287–92.

Mackay, E. A., ed. (1999) *Signs of Orality: The Oral Tradition and Its Influence in the Greek and Roman World.* Leiden.

Macleod, C. (1983) *Collected Essays.* Oxford.

Maffi, A. (1988) "Écriture et pratique juridique dans la Grèce classique." In M. Detienne, ed., *Les savoirs de l'écriture en Grèce ancienne.* Cahiers de Philologie 14. Lille. 188–210.

Majno, G. (1975) *The Healing Hand: Man and Wound in the Ancient World.* Cambridge, Mass.

Bibliography

Manetti, G. (1993) *Theories of the Sign in Classical Antiquity*. Trans. C. Richardson. Bloomington.

Mann, J. (forthcoming) *A Translation and Commentary of Peri Technes*.

Mansfeld, J. (1990) *Studies in the Historiography of Greek Philosophy*. Assen.

Martin, A., and O. Primavesi. (1999) *L'Empédocle de Strasbourg (P. Strasb. gr. Inv. 1665–1666)*. Berlin.

McKeown, J. C. (1989) *Ovid: Amores*. Vol. 2, *A Commentary on Book One*. Leeds.

Meier, C. (1993) *The Political Art of Greek Tragedy*. Trans. A. Webber. Cambridge.

Meyer, E. (1899) *Forschungen zur alten Geschichte*. Vol. 2. Halle.

Miller. G. L. (1990) "Literacy and the Hippocratic Art: Reading, Writing and Epistemology in Ancient Greek Medicine." *Journal of the History of Medicine and Allied Sciences* 45: 11–40.

Morgan, K. (2000) *Myth and Philosophy from the Presocratics to Plato*. Cambridge.

Morgan, T. J. (1999) "Literate Education in Classical Athens." *Classical Quarterly* 49: 46–61.

Morrison, J. V. (2000) "Historical Lessons in the Melian Episode." *Transactions of the American Philological Association* 130: 119–48.

Most, G. W. (1984) "Rhetorik und Hermeneutik: Zur Konstitution der Neuzeitlichkeit." *Antike und Abendland* 30: 62–79.

(1994) "Simonides' Ode to Scopas in Contexts." In I. J. F. de Jong and J. P. Sullivan, eds., *Modern Critical Theory and Classical Literature*, Mnemosyne Suppl. 130. Leiden. 127–52.

(1997) "The Fire Next Time: Cosmology, Allegoresis, and Salvation in the Derveni Papyrus." *Journal of Hellenic Studies* 117: 117–35.

(1999) "The Poetics of Early Greek Philosophy." In A. A. Long, ed., *The Cambridge Companion to Early Greek Philosophy*. Cambridge. 332–62.

Mueller, I. (1981) *Philosophy of Mathematics and Deductive Structure in Euclid's Elements*. Cambridge, Mass.

Nagy, G. (1996) *Poetry as Performance: Homer and Beyond*. Cambridge.

Nails, D. (1995) *Agora, Academy, and the Conduct of Philosophy*. Dordrecht.

Nestle, W. (1942) *Vom Mythos zum Logos*. 2nd ed. Stuttgart.

Netz, R. (1999) *The Shaping of Deduction in Greek Mathematics*. Cambridge.

Nilsson, M. P. (1905) "ΚΑΤΑΠΛΟΙ." *Rheinisches Museum* 60: 161–89.

Nutton, V. (1995) "The Medical Meeting Place." In Ph. J. van der Eijk, H. F. J. Horstmanshoff, and P. H. Schrijvers, eds., *Ancient Medicine in its Socio-Cultural Context*. Amsterdam. 3–25.

Nylan, M. (1994) "The *Chin wen/Ku wen* Controversy in Han times." *T'oung Pao* 80: 83–143.

Obbink, D. (1997) "Cosmology as Initiation vs. the Critique of Orphic Mysteries." In A. Laks and G. W. Most, eds., *Studies on the Derveni Papyrus*. Oxford. 39–54.

Ober, J. (1989) *Mass and Elite in Democratic Athens: Rhetoric, Ideology and the Power of the People*. Princeton.

(1998) *Political Dissent in Democratic Athens: Intellectual Critics of Popular Rule*. Princeton.

O'Donnell, J. J. (1998) *Avatars of the Word: From Papyrus to Cyberspace*. Cambridge, Mass.

Bibliography

Olson, D. R. (1994) *The World on Paper: The Conceptual and Cognitive Implications of Writing and Reading.* Cambridge.

Olson, D. R., and N. Torrance, eds. (1991) *Literacy and Orality.* Cambridge.

Ong, W. J. (1967) *The Presence of the Word: Some Prolegomena for Cultural and Religious History.* New Haven.

(1971) *Rhetoric, Romance, and Technology: Studies in the Interaction of Expression and Culture.* Ithaca.

(1977) *Interfaces of the Word: Studies in the Evolution of Consciousness and Culture.* Ithaca.

(1982) *Orality and Literacy: The Technologizing of the Word.* London.

Osborne, M. (1981–82) *Naturalization in Athens.* 2 vols. Brussels.

Osborne, R. (1997) "Law and Laws: How Do We Join Up the Dots." In L. Mitchell and P. Rhodes, eds., *The Development of the Polis.* London. 74–82.

Ostwald, M. (1969) *Nomos and the Beginnings of Athenian Democracy.* Oxford.

(1973) "Was There a Concept *agraphos nomos* in Classical Greece?" In E. N. Lee, A. P. D. Mourelatos, and R. M. Rorty, eds., *Exegesis and Argument: Studies in Greek Philosophy Presented to Gregory Vlastos.* Phronesis Suppl. 1. 70–104.

(1986) *From Popular Sovereignty to the Sovereignty of Law: Law, Society, and Politics in Fifth-Century Athens.* Berkeley.

O'Sullivan, N. (1992) *Alcidamas, Aristophanes, and the Beginnings of Greek Stylistic Theory.* Stuttgart.

(1996) "Written and Spoken in the First Sophistic." In I. Worthington, ed., *Voice Into Text: Orality and Literacy in Ancient Greece.* Leiden. 115–27.

Ott, U. (1969) *Die Kunst des Gegensatzes in Theokrits Hirtengedichten.* Hildesheim.

Palaima, T. G. (1987) "Comments on Mycenaean Literacy." In J. T. Killen, J. L. Melena, and J.-P. Olivier, eds., *Studies in Mycenaean and Classical Greek Presented to John Chadwick. Minos.* Vols. 20–22. Salamanca. 499–510.

Palmer, L. R. (1950) "The Indo-European Origins of Greek Justice." *Transactions of the Philological Society* 49: 149–68.

Parke, H. W. (1967a) *Greek Oracles.* London.

(1967b) *The Oracles of Zeus: Dodona, Olympia, Ammon.* Cambridge, Mass.

(1985) *The Oracles of Apollo in Asia Minor.* London.

Parker, R. (1987) "Festivals of the Attic Demes." In T. Linders and G. Nordquist, eds., *Gifts to the Gods: Proceedings of the Uppsala Symposium 1985.* Acta Universitatis Upsaliensis, Boreas 15. Uppsala. 137–47.

(1996) *Athenian Religion: A History.* Oxford.

(1998) "Pleasing Thighs: Reciprocity in Greek Religion." In C. Gill, N. Postlethwaite, and R. Seaford, eds., *Reciprocity in Ancient Greece.* Oxford. 105–25.

Parry, M. (1971) *The Making of Homeric Verse: The Collected Papers of Millman Parry.* Edited by A. Parry. Oxford.

Patterson, C. (1980) *Pericles' Citizenship Law of 451–50.* New York.

Peek, W. (1955) *Griechische Vers-Inschriften.* Vol. 1, *Grab-Epigramme.* Berlin.

Perlman, P. (2001) "Gortyn. The First Seven Hundred Years (Part II): Written Law and Gortynian Society in the Sixth Century B.C." In *Acts of the Copenhagen Polis Centre.* Vol. 6. Copenhagen.

Bibliography

Petersen, J. O. (1995) "Which Books did the First Emperor of Ch'in Burn? On the Meaning of *Pai Chia* in Early Chinese Sources." *Monumenta Serica: Journal of Oriental Studies* 43: 1–52.

Pfeiffer, R. (1968) *History of Classical Scholarship from the Beginnings to the End of the Hellenistic Period.* Oxford.

Pickard-Cambridge, A. W. (1988) *The Dramatic Festivals of Athens.* 2nd ed. Oxford.

Pleket, H. W. (1983) "Arts en maatschapij in het oude Griekenland. De sociale status van de arts." *Tijdschrift voor Geschiedenis.* 325–47.

Pöhlmann, E. (1989) "Der Schreiber als Lehrer in der klassischen Zeit." In J. G. Prinz von Hohenzollern and M. Liedtke, eds., *Schreiber, Magister, Lehrer.* Schriftenreihe Ichenhausen, Band 8. Bad Heilbrunn. 73–82.

(1990) "Zur Überlieferung griechischer Literatur vom 8. bis zum 4. Jh." In W. Kullmann and M. Reichel, eds., *Der Übergang von der Mündlichkeit zur Literatur bei den Griechen.* Tübingen. 11–30.

Poland, F. (1909) *Geschichte des griechischen Vereinswesens.* Leipzig.

Pollitt, J. J. (1974) *The Ancient View of Greek Art.* New Haven.

Pollock, F., and F. W. Maitland. (1898) *The History of English Law Before the Time of Edward I.* 2nd ed. Cambridge.

Porta, F. R. (1999) "Greek Ritual Utterances and the Liturgical Style." Ph. D. diss., Harvard University.

Powell, B. B. (1988) "The Dipylon Oinochoe Inscription and the Spread of Literacy in 8th Century Athens." *Kadmos* 27: 65–86.

(1989) "Why Was the Greek Alphabet Invented? The Epigraphical Evidence." *Classical Antiquity* 8: 321–50.

(1991) *Homer and the Origin of the Greek Alphabet.* Cambridge.

Press, G. A., ed. (2000) *Who Speaks for Plato? Studies in Platonic Anonymity.* Lanham.

Price, S. (1999) "A Rhetorical Shift in the Hippocratic *Nature of Man.*" Paper presented at Society of Ancient Medicine, Dallas.

Queen, S. A. (1996) *From Chronicle to Canon: The Hermeneutics of the Spring and Autumn, according to Tung Chung-shu.* Cambridge.

Radermacher, L. (1951) *Artium Scriptores (Reste der voraristotelischen Rhetorik).* Vienna.

Raible, W. (1983) "Vom Text und seinen vielen Vätern oder: Hermeneutik als Korrelat der Schriftkultur." In A. Assman, J. Assman, and C. Hardmeier, eds., *Schrift und Gedächtnis. Beiträge zur Archäologie der literarischen Kommunikation.* Munich. 20–23.

Reynolds, L. D., and N. G. Wilson. (1991) *Scribes and Scholars: A Guide to the Transmission of Greek and Latin Literature.* 3rd ed. Oxford.

Richardson, N. J. (1975) "Homeric Professors in the Age of the Sophists." *Proceedings of the Cambridge Philological Society* 21: 65–81.

(1992) "Aristotle's Reading of Homer and Its Background." In R. Lamberton and J. J. Keaney, eds., *Homer's Ancient Readers: The Hermeneutics of Greek Epic's Earliest Exegetes.* Princeton. 30–40.

Riedweg, C. (1998) "Initiation – Tod – Unterwelt. Beobachtungen zur Kommunikationssituation und narrativen Technik der orphisch-bakchischen Goldblättchen."

Bibliography

In F. Graf, ed., *Ansichten griechischer Rituale. Geburtstags-Symposium für Walter Burkert*. Stuttgart/Leipzig. 359–98.

Robb, K. (1994) *Literacy and Paideia in Ancient Greece*. Oxford.

Rood, T. (1998) *Thucydides: Narrative and Explanation*. Oxford.

Rosivach, V. J. (1994) *The System of Public Sacrifice in Fourth-Century Athens*. American Classical Studies 34. Atlanta.

Rösler, W. (1980a) *Dichter und Gruppe: Eine Untersuchung zu den Bedingingen und zur historischen Funktionen früher griechischer Lyrik am Beispiel Alkaios*. Munich.

(1980b) "Die Entdeckung der Fiktionalität in der Antike." *Poetica* 12: 283–319.

Roth, C. P. (1976) "The Kings and the Muses in Hesiod's *Theogony*." *Transactions of the American Philological Association* 106: 331–38.

Ruschenbusch, E. (1966) *Solonos Nomoi*. Historia Einzelschriften 9. Wiesbaden.

Russell, D. A. (1989) "Greek Criticism of the Empire." In G. A. Kennedy, ed., *The Cambridge History of Literary Criticism*. Vol. 1, *Classical Criticism*. Cambridge. 297–329.

Rutherford, R. (1995) *The Art of Plato*. London.

Ruzé, F. (1988) "Aux débuts de l'écriture politique: le pouvoir de l'écrit dans la cité." In M. Detienne, ed., *Les savoirs de l'écriture en Grèce ancienne*. Cahiers de Philologie 14. Lille. 82–94.

(2001) "La loi et le chant." In J.-P. Brun and P. Jockey, eds., *Techniques et sociétés en Méditerranée (Hommage à Marie-Claire Amouretti)*. Paris. 709–17.

Schenkeveld, D. M. (1992) "Prose Usages of ἀκούειν." *Classical Quarterly* 42: 129–41.

Schibli, H. S. (1990) *Pherekydes of Syros*. Oxford.

Schloemann, J. (2000) "Freie Rede. Rhetorik im demokratischen Athen zwischen Schriftlichkeit und Improvisation." Ph.D. diss., Humboldt University, Berlin.

Schmid, W. (1948) *Geschichte der griechischen Literatur*. Part I, vol. 5.2.2. Munich.

Schmitz, T. A. (1999) " 'I Hate All Common Things': The Reader's Role in Callimachus' *Aetia* Prologue." *Harvard Studies in Classical Philology* 99: 151–78.

Schulz, F. (1946) *History of Roman Legal Science*. Oxford.

Scodel, R. (1996) "Self-Correction, Spontaneity, and Orality in Archaic Poetry" In I. Worthington, ed., *Voice Into Text: Orality and Literacy in Ancient Greece*. Leiden. 59–79.

Scribner, S., and M. Cole. (1981) *The Psychology of Literacy*. Cambridge, Mass.

Seaford, R. (1989) "Homeric and Tragic Sacrifice." *Transactions of the American Philological Association* 119: 87–95.

Sedgwick, W. B. (1948) "The Frogs and the Audience." *Classica et Mediaevalia* 9: 1–9.

Segal, C. (1981) *Poetry and Myth in Ancient Pastoral*. Princeton.

(1982) "Tragédie, oralité, écriture." *Poétique* 50: 131–54.

Seiler, M. A. (1997) ΠΟΙΗΣΙΣ ΠΟΙΗΣΕΩΣ. Stuttgart.

Shapiro, A. (1990) "Oracle-Mongers in Peisistratid Athens." *Kernos* 3: 335–45.

Shapiro, H. A. (1989) *Art and Cult under the Tyrants in Athens*. Mainz.

Sickinger, J. P. (1999) *Public Records and Archives in Classical Athens*. Chapel Hill.

Simon, E. (1983) *Festivals of Athens: An Archaeological Commentary*. Madison.

Sivin, N. (1995a) "Text and Experience in Classical Chinese Medicine." In D. Bates, ed., *Knowledge and the Scholarly Medical Traditions*. Cambridge. 177–204.

Bibliography

(1995b) *Medicine, Philosophy, and Religion in Ancient China: Researches and Reflections*. Aldershot.

Skoyles, J. R. (1990) "The Origin of Classical Greek Culture: The Transparent Chain Theory of Literacy/Society Interaction." *Journal of Social and Biological Structures* 13: 321–53.

Small, J. P. (1997) *Wax Tablets of the Mind: Cognitive Studies of Memory and Literacy in Classical Antiquity*. London.

Smith, K. (Forthcoming) "Sima Tan and the Invention of Daoism, 'Legalism,' et cetera." *Journal of Asian Studies*.

Sokoloswki, F. (1955) *Lois sacrées de l'Asie Mineure*. Paris.

(1962) *Lois sacrées des cités grecques*. Suppl. Paris.

(1969) *Lois sacrées des cités grecques*. Paris.

Solmsen, F. (1968) "The Tablets of Zeus." In F. Solmsen, *Kleine Schriften*. Vol. 1. Hildesheim. 137–40. Originally published in *Classical Quarterly* 58 (1944): 27–30.

Sourvinou-Inwood, C. (1997) "Tragedy and Religion: Constructs and Readings." In C. Pelling, ed., *Greek Tragedy and the Historian*. Oxford. 161–86.

(2000) "What is *Polis* Religion?" and "Further Aspects of *Polis* Religion." In R. Buxton, ed., *Oxford Readings in Greek Religion*. Oxford. 13–37, 38–55.

Steiner, D. T. (1994) *The Tyrant's Writ: Myths and Images of Writing in Ancient Greece*. Princeton.

Steiner, G. (1989) *Real Presences: Is There Anything In What We Say?* London.

Stewart, A. (1990) *Greek Sculpture: An Exploration*. 2 vols. New Haven.

Strasburger, H. (1954) "Die Entdeckung der politischen Geschichte durch Thukydides." *Saeculum* 5: 395–428.

(1957) "Einleitung zu Thukydides." In *Thukydides. Der Peloponnesische Krieg*. Trans. A. Horneffer. Bremen. Reprinted in and cited from H. Strasburger, *Studien zur alten Geschichte*. Vol. 2. Hildesheim, 1982. 709–76.

(1958) "Thukydides und die politische Selbstdarstellung der Athener." *Hermes* 86: 17–40.

Stratton, J. (1980) "Writing and the Concept of Law in Ancient Greece." *Visible Language* 14: 99–121.

Street, B. V. (1984) *Literacy in Theory and Practice*. Cambridge.

ed. (1993) *Cross-Cultural Approaches to Literacy*. Cambridge.

(1995) *Social Literacies: Critical Approaches to Literacy in Development, Ethnography and Education*. London.

Stroud, R. (1979) *The Axones and Kyrbeis of Drakon and Solon*. University of California Publications, Classical Studies 19. Berkeley.

Svenbro, J. (1993) *Phrasikleia: An Anthropology of Reading in Ancient Greece*. Trans. J. Lloyd. Ithaca.

Szegedy-Maszak, A. (1978) "Legends of the Greek Lawgivers." *Greek, Roman and Byzantine Studies* 19: 199–209.

Szlezák, T. A. (1999) *Reading Plato*. Trans. G. Zanker. London.

Talamanca, M. (1979) "Dikazein e krinein nelle testimonanze greche piu antiche." In A. Biscardi, ed., *Symposion 1974: Vorträge zur griechischen und hellenistischen Rechtsgeschichte*. Cologne. 103–35.

Bibliography

Tarrant, H. (2000) *Plato's First Interpreters*. Ithaca.

Thomas, K. (1986) "The Meaning of Literacy in Early Modern England." In G. Baumann, ed., *The Written Word*. Oxford. 97–131.

Thomas, R. (1989) *Oral Tradition and Written Record in Classical Athens*. Cambridge.

(1992) *Literacy and Orality in Ancient Greece*. Cambridge.

(1994) "Literacy and the City-State in Archaic and Classical Greece." In A. K. Bowman and G. Woolf, eds., *Literacy and Power in the Ancient World*. Cambridge. 33–50.

(1996) "Written in Stone? Liberty, Equality, Orality, and the Codification of Law." In L. Foxhall and A. D. E. Lewis, eds., *Greek Law in its Political Setting: Justifications not Justice*. Oxford. 9–31. Originally published in *Bulletin of the Institute of Classical Studies* 40 (1995): 59–74.

(2000) *Herodotus in Context: Ethnography, Science and the Art of Persuasion*. Cambridge.

Tigerstedt, E. N. (1977) *Interpreting Plato*. Uppsala.

Todd, S. (1996) "Lysias against Nikomachos: The Fate of the Expert in Athenian Law." In L. Foxhall and A. D. E. Lewis, eds., *Greek Law in its Political Setting: Justifications not Justice*. Oxford. 101–31.

Trencsényi-Waldapfel, I. (1966) *Untersuchungen zur Religionsgeschichte*. Amsterdam.

Tsantsanoglou, K. (1997) "The First Columns of the Derveni Papyrus and their Religious Significance." In A. Laks and G. W. Most, eds., *Studies on the Derveni Papyrus*. Oxford. 93–128.

Turner, E. G. (1952) *Athenian Books in the Fifth and Fourth Centuries B.C.* London.

(1965) "Athenians Learn to Write: Plato, *Protagoras* 326d." *Bulletin of the Institute of Classical Studies* 12: 67–69.

Usener, K. (1990) "'Schreiben' im Corpus Hippocraticum." In W. Kullman and M. Reichel, eds., *Der Übergang von der Mündlichkeit zur Literatur bei den Griechen*. Tübingen. 291–99.

Usener, S. (1994) *Isokrates, Platon und ihr Publikum. Hörer und Leser von Literatur im 4. Jahrhundert v. Chr.* Tübingen.

van Effenterre, H., and F. Ruzé. (1995) *Nomima: recueil d'inscriptions politiques et juridiques de l'archaïsme grec*. 2 vols. Rome.

van Straten, F. T. (1981) "Gifts for the Gods." In H. S. Versnel, ed., *Faith, Hope and Worship: Aspects of Religious Mentality in the Ancient World*. Leiden. 65–151.

(1987) "Greek Sacrificial Representations: Livestock Prices and Religious Mentality." In T. Linders and G. Nordquist, eds., *Gifts to the Gods: Proceedings of the Uppsala Symposium 1985*. Acta Universitatis Upsaliensis, Boreas 15. Uppsala. 159–70.

(1995) *Hierà Kalá. Images of Animal Sacrifice in Archaic and Classical Greece*. Religions in the Graeco-Roman World 127. Leiden.

(2000) "Votives and Votaries in Greek Sanctuaries." In R. Buxton, ed., *Oxford Readings in Greek Religion*. Oxford. 191–223.

Verdenius, W. J. (1981) "Gorgias' Doctrine of Deception." In G. B. Kerferd, ed., *The Sophists and Their Legacy*. Hermes Einzelschriften 44. Wiesbaden. 116–28.

von Fritz, K. (1953) "Der gemeinsame Ursprung der Geschichtsschreibung und der exakten Wissenschaften bei den Griechen." *Philosophia Naturalis* 2: 201–376.

Bibliography

von Reden, S., and S. Goldhill. (1999) "Plato and the Performance of Dialogue" In S. Goldhill and R. Osborne, eds., *Performance Culture and Athenian Democracy*. Cambridge. 257–89.

von Staden, H. (1989) *Herophilus: the Art of Medicine in Early Alexandria*. Cambridge.

von Ungern-Sternberg, J., and H. Reinau, eds. (1988) *Vergangenheit in mündlicher Überlieferung*. Stuttgart.

Wallace, R. (1995) "Speech, Song, and Text, Public and Private. Evolutions in Communications Media and Fora in Fourth-Century Athens." In W. Eder, ed., *Die athenische Demokratie im 4. Jahrhundert v. Chr.* Stuttgart. 199–217.

(1998) "Sophists in Athens." In D. Boedeker and K. Raaflaub, eds., *Democracy, Empire, and the Arts in Fifth-Century Athens*. Cambridge, Mass. 203–22.

Walsh, G. B. (1985) "Seeing and Feeling: Representation in Two Poems of Theocritus." *Classical Philology* 80: 1–19.

Watkins, C. (1994) "Observations on the 'Nestor's Cup' Inscription." In C. Watkins, *Selected Writings*. Vol. 2. Innsbruck. 544–59.

Watson, J., ed. (2001) *Speaking Volumes: Orality and Literacy in the Greek and Roman World*. Leiden.

Webster, T. B. L. (1973) *Athenian Culture and Society*. Berkeley.

Wehrli, F. (1946) "Der erhabene und der schlichte Stil in der poetisch-rhetorischen Theorie der Antike." In *Phyllobolia für Peter von der Mühll*. Basel. 9–34.

Weingarth, G. (1967) "Zu Theokrits 7. Idyll." Ph.D. diss., Freiburg im Breslau.

West, M. L. (1983) *The Orphic Poems*. Oxford.

Westbrook, R. (1989) "Cuneiform Law Codes and the Origins of Legislation." *Zeitschrift für Assyriologie und vorderasiatische Archäologie* 79: 201–22.

Wetzel, M. S., D. M. Eisenberg, and T. J. Kaptchuk. (1998) "Courses Involving Complementary and Alternative Medicine at U.S. Medical Schools." *Journal of the American Medical Association* 280: 784–87.

Whitehead, D. (1986) *The Demes of Attica 508/7-ca. 250 B.C.: A Political and Social Study*. Princeton.

Whitley, J. (1997) "Cretan Laws and Cretan Literacy." *American Journal of Archaeology* 101: 635–61.

Wickkiser, B. (Forthcoming) *The Appeal of Asklepios and the Politics of Healing in the Greco-Roman World*.

Wilamowitz-Moellendorff, U. von. (1900) *Textgeschichte der griechischen Lyriker*. Berlin. (1907) *Einleitung in die Griechische Tragödie*. Berlin.

Williams, G. (1978) *Change and Decline: Roman Literature in the Early Empire*. Berkeley.

Williams, R. (1976) *Keywords: A Vocabulary of Culture and Society*. Rev. ed. Oxford.

Winiarczyk, M. (1990) "Methodisches zum antiken Atheismus." *Rheinisches Museum* 133: 1–15.

Wise, J. (1998) *Dionysus Writes: The Invention of Theatre in Ancient Greece*. Ithaca.

Woodard, R. D. (1997) *Greek Writing from Knossos to Homer: A Linguistic Interpretation of the Origin of the Greek Alphabet and the Continuity of Ancient Greek Literacy*. New York.

Woodbury, L. (1976) "Aristophanes' *Frogs* and Athenian Literacy: Ran. 52–3, 1114." *Transactions of the American Philological Association* 106: 349–57.

(1983) Review of Havelock 1982. *Echos du monde classique* 3: 329–52.

Bibliography

(1986) "The Judgement of Dionysus: Books, Taste and Teaching in the *Frogs*." In M. J. Cropp, E. Fantham, and S. E. Scully, eds., *Greek Tragedy and Its Legacy: Essays Presented to D. J. Conacher*. Calgary. 241–57.

Wormald, P. (1999) *The Making of English Law: King Alfred to the Twelfth Century*. Oxford.

Worthington, I., ed. (1996) *Voice Into Text: Orality and Literacy in Ancient Greece*. Leiden.

Yunis, H. (1988) *A New Creed: Fundamental Religious Beliefs in the Athenian Polis and Euripidean Drama*. Hypomnemata 91. Göttingen.

(1996) *Taming Democracy: Models of Political Rhetoric in Classical Athens*. Ithaca.

(1998) "The Constraints of Democracy and the Rise of the Art of Rhetoric." In D. Boedeker and K. A. Raaflaub, eds., *Democracy, Empire, and the Arts in Fifth-Century Athens*. Cambridge, Mass. 223–40.

Zwierlein, O. (1966) *Die Rezitationsdramen Senecas, mit einem kritisch-exegetischen Anhang*. Meisenheim am Glan.

Index

Index

Index

Index

Index

Index

Index

Index